Literacy Instruction in Multicultural Settings

Literacy Instruction in Multicultural Settings

Kathryn H. Au

Kamehameha Schools

Harcourt Brace College Publishers

Fort Worth   Philadelphia   San Diego
New York   Orlando   Austin   San Antonio
Toronto   Montreal   London   Sydney   Tokyo

Editor-in-chief	Ted Buchholz
Acquisitions editor	Jo-Anne Weaver
Developmental editor	Tracy Napper
Project editor	Steve Norder
Production manager	Jane Tyndall Ponceti
Senior book designer	John Ritland

Literary and illustration credits are on p. 201.

Library of Congress Catalog Card Number: 92-073482

ISBN: 0-03-076847-0

Address for Editorial Correspondence
Harcourt Brace College Publishers, 301 Commerce Street, Suite 3700,
Fort Worth, TX 76102.

Address for Orders
Harcourt Brace & Company, 6277 Sea Harbor Drive, Orlando, FL 32887.
1-800-782-4479, or 1-800-433-0001 (in Florida)

Printed in the United States of America

5 6 7 8 9 0 1   090   9 8 7 6 5

in memory of
Ah Lun Hew Zane

Preface

Literacy Instruction in Multicultural Settings was written to acquaint pre-service teachers with issues they will face in teaching reading and writing to students of diverse cultural and linguistic backgrounds. It is intended to serve as a supplementary textbook in an introductory or other reading/ language arts methods course; it will be especially useful if the course emphasizes a social constructivist, process, or whole language approach.

The overall theme of the book is that the reading and writing of students of diverse backgrounds can be dramatically improved if teachers make changes to typical school instructional situations. Familiar patterns of instruction are contrasted with new ones, and numerous classroom examples enable preservice teachers to visualize the new patterns and situations.

Each chapter gives both research background and practical advice on topics central to the literacy instruction of students of diverse backgrounds. The first five chapters provide an overviews of such broad topics as the nature of literacy, constructivist approaches to instruction, and classroom management. The next six chapters deal with specific topics. Two chapters each are devoted to cultural differences and to language differences, and two more focus on multiethnic literature and the process approach to writing in multicultural classrooms. Each chapter begins with a statement of major purposes, includes activities and suggested readings, and ends with a summary. Key points in the text are boxed for emphasis.

Considerable information about the literacy instruction of students of diverse backgrounds is currently available, but much of it is to be found only in journal articles and in books not written specifically for teachers. This book seeks to make this information accessible to preservice teachers in as clear, interesting, and readable a fashion as possible. Information about the instruction of students of African American, Asian American, Hispanic American, and Native American backgrounds is included. This information spans the curriculum from kindergarten through high school, with an emphasis on elementary classrooms.

Throughout the process of writing this book, I received the help of many colleagues. Alice Kawakami of the Pacific Region Educational Laboratory read the first drafts of each chapter, spent many hours helping me organize the flow of ideas in the book as a whole, and encouraged me to give the book a social conscience. Linda Vavrus of the University of Nebraska, Lincoln, wrote precise, detailed critiques of each chapter and offered a multitude of valuable suggestions. Ronald Gallimore and Claude Goldenberg, both of the University of California, Los Angeles, gave the book a thorough, critical reading, taking into account a wide range of theoretical issues and research findings on many complex and controversial topics. Jacqueline Comas of the University of Florida, Gainesville; J. David Cooper of Ball State University; Susan McMahon of the University of Wisconsin, Madison; Ileana Seda of the Pennsylvania State University; and Rose-Marie Weber of the State University of New York at Albany made helpful comments on all chapters and called my attention to specific issues that might be of interest to an audience of preservice teachers. I am deeply grateful for the thoughts shared by all of these reviewers and for the time taken from their already busy schedules.

I also wish to acknowledge the help of my editors at Harcourt Brace Jovanovich College Publishers, who were always quick to respond to my concerns. Jo-Anne Weaver provided much needed doses of enthusiasm, and Tracy Napper showed care and insight in her attention to issues large and small.

Finally, I wish to express my appreciation to the students, teachers, and staff of the Kamehameha Elementary Education Program (KEEP), whose talents and accomplishments have been a source of inspiration to me for over twenty years. A special word of thanks is due to the KEEP students, teachers, and staff at Waianae Elementary School, who have taught me so much about the importance of a sense of community.

Table of Contents

chapter 1

The Schooling of Students of Diverse Backgrounds: An Overview

—————————— CHAPTER PURPOSES ——————————

1. Discuss students of diverse backgrounds and the importance of addressing their educational needs;
2. Explain the concepts of culture and the American mainstream;
3. Outline two theories used to explain schools' poor record with students of diverse backgrounds;
4. Define culturally responsive instruction and show why it is beneficial;
5. Present a framework for empowering students of diverse backgrounds.

This book focuses on concepts and instructional practices that teachers can use to improve the school literacy learning of students of diverse backgrounds. The theme that runs through all chapters is the need for schools to break out of familiar old instructional patterns and to begin putting new patterns in place. Many of the ideas in this first chapter are applicable to instruction in general; later chapters focus on literacy instruction in particular.

Students of Diverse Backgrounds

In this book, the term **students of diverse backgrounds** will be used to refer to students who may be distinguished by their ethnicity, social class, and/or language. **Ethnicity** is determined by the national origin of one's ancestors. Members of an ethnic group also feel a sense of peoplehood, reflecting shared history, values, and behaviors (Gollnick and Chinn, 1990). Many students of diverse backgrounds are from groups labeled African American, Asian American, Hispanic American, and Native American, although these are not the terms students and their families typically use to describe their ethnicity. Rather, individuals are likely to speak of their ethnicity in more specific terms, such as Haitian, Vietnamese, Puerto Rican, or Navajo.

Class or socioeconomic status is also a factor with students of diverse backgrounds. Among the indicators of class are parents' occupations and family income. Students from diverse backgrounds are generally from families in the working class or from families living in poverty, while students from mainstream backgrounds are usually from middle-class families. The concept of the mainstream will be discussed in detail later in this chapter.

Language is another important factor. Often, the first language of students from diverse backgrounds is either a nonmainstream variety of English or a language other than English. For example, many Native Hawaiian students speak a variety of English known as Hawaiian Creole English, and many Hispanic American students speak Spanish as their first language. Many students of diverse backgrounds are bilingual, or able to speak two languages, their home language and English. Students' speaking of a home language other than English is not in itself a barrier to success in school, especially if teachers allow students to use strengths in their home language as the basis for learning to read and write in English (Snow, 1990).

> Students of diverse backgrounds are distinguished by their ethnicity, social class, and/or language.

Inequality in Literacy Achievement

Students' ethnicity, social class, and language do not automatically determine their eventual level of academic achievement. However, it is true that schools are usually less successful in raising the achievement levels of students who are of non-European backgrounds, whose families live in poverty, and who speak a first language other than standard American English (for example, Pallas, Natriello, and McDill, 1989). The reasons for schools' relative lack of success with these students will be discussed throughout this book.

Extensive evidence supports the need for schools to improve the literacy instruction of students of diverse backgrounds. The National Assessment of Educational Progress (NAEP), for example, examines the achievement of African American and Hispanic American students in comparison to their European American peers. Hispanic and African American students at all three grade levels tested (third, seventh, and eleventh grade) do not read and write as well as their European American classmates (Applebee, Langer, and Mullis, 1988). On the whole, African American, Hispanic American, and disadvantaged urban eleventh graders read only slightly better than seventh graders in the nation as a whole.

It is certainly not the case that all African American and Hispanic American students are poor readers — some of the best readers and writers at all age levels are African American and Hispanic American students. Also, some of the weakest readers and writers at all age levels are European American students. But neither of these considerations

changes the fact that, on the whole, there are substantial differences between the performance of European American students and African and
Hispanic American students. These differences in reading achievement
are evident by fourth grade, and the gap remains even for students who
attend college. Similar differences between the achievement of African
and Hispanic American students, and European American students, are
observed in the area of writing.

Population Trends

Clearly, there is a need for schools to improve the literacy instruction of
students of diverse backgrounds. This need is becoming even more urgent
given the population trends in the United States. In 1982 nearly three of
four American young people (ages 0 to 17) were European American (Pallas, Natriello, and McDill, 1989), but by 2020 only one of two young people
will be European American. In 1982 only one of 10 young people was
Hispanic, while it is estimated that this figure will change to one of four
in 2020. Over this same period, the number of children living in poverty
is expected to increase by 37 percent, from 14.7 million to 20 million.
Schools will need to serve 5.4 million more children living in poverty in
2020 than they served in 1984.

As Pallas et al. suggest, these population trends make it clear that the
schooling of students of diverse backgrounds cannot be seen as an issue
to be addressed through special remedial programs that target just a small
number of students in each school. Instead, we will need to make major
changes in the approaches we use in the regular classroom and throughout
the school system as a whole.

Focusing on Needs

There is an urgent need for teachers to understand how to improve the
school literacy learning of students of diverse backgrounds. To address
this need, this book will discuss new patterns of instruction that appear
beneficial to the school literacy learning of students of diverse backgrounds,
as well as familiar old patterns of instruction that appear detrimental.

In general, the new patterns of instruction to be highlighted are also
likely to be beneficial to students of mainstream backgrounds. For example, chapter 5 discusses the value of having students of diverse backgrounds work in collaborative groups with their peers. Certainly, having
the opportunity to work collaboratively with peers can be a valuable experience for students of mainstream backgrounds as well.

Nevertheless, because the focus of this book is on the educational
needs of students of diverse backgrounds, there will not be a repeated
emphasis on the value of new patterns of instruction for students of main-

stream backgrounds. All students deserve the best educational experiences that schools have to offer, but, in general, students of diverse backgrounds are offered lower-quality educational experiences than students of mainstream backgrounds (for example, Allington, 1991). For this reason, the need for improving the literacy instruction in classrooms with many students of diverse backgrounds is often more urgent than the need for improving instruction in classrooms with many students of mainstream backgrounds.

Culture and the American Mainstream

To understand why schools are generally more successful with mainstream students than with students of diverse backgrounds, let us look at the concept of culture and the concept of the mainstream.

Culture may be defined as a system of values, beliefs, and standards which guides people's thoughts, feelings, and behavior (Hernandez, 1990). While this system forms an integrated whole, it is by no means static. Culture involves a dynamic process which people use to make sense of their lives and the behavior of other people (Spindler and Spindler, 1990).

> Culture is
>   Learned;
>   Shared;
>   An adaptation;
>   Continually changing.

The complex and dynamic nature of culture is highlighted in the following characteristics (Gollnick and Chinn, 1990). First, culture is learned. That is, people are not born knowing their culture but are initiated into it through the actions of family members and others. People actively seek to construct an understanding of the different cultures in which they participate. Even so, no individual ever learns everything there is to know about a particular culture, and each individual's understanding of a culture is somewhat different from that of every other individual (Wolcott, 1991). Second, culture is shared. Members of a cultural group have a common understanding of the system, of ways of thinking and ways of behaving. Third, culture is an adaptation. A culture may adapt to its natural environment or to particular political and economic conditions. Fourth, culture is continually changing. Changes may be as minor as a new hairstyle or as dramatic as a long-term trend such as the replacement of industrial workers by robots.

A culture has physical aspects, such as buildings, clothing, and works of art, and mental or behavioral aspects, such as beliefs about raising children or standards for politeness. The physical aspects of culture can be called **visible culture**, while the mental and behavioral aspects of culture can be called **invisible culture** (Philips, 1983). This book will be concerned with invisible culture, especially values and standards for behavior, because differences in invisible culture appear to cause great difficulty in many classrooms with students of diverse backgrounds (see chapters 6 and 7).

In the United States, as in other complex societies, there is a dominant or **mainstream** culture, and subordinate cultures or subcultures. The dominant or mainstream culture is the culture of the group or groups that hold power and largely control the society. The subordinate cultures are the cultures of the groups that have less power and control fewer resources.

In the popular view, the mainstream in American society is supposed to include only European American Protestants. However, as George and Louise Spindler (1990) suggest, there are many other people who think of themselves as being characteristically "American" in terms of their behaviors and values, and who would see themselves as part of the mainstream, too. This group would include many European American Catholics and Jews, and a certain number of African, Asian, Hispanic, and Native Americans. The Spindlers write:

> Taken from this view, the mainstream includes anyone who acts like a member of the mainstream, dominant American population and has the income to support this lifestyle.   (p. 22)

The Spindlers extend our understanding of the mainstream by listing the core values mainstream Americans appear to hold. The five major values of the mainstream are:

Freedom of speech and other personal forms of freedom;

Rights of the individual;

Equal opportunity;

Achievement through hard work;

Social mobility.

Although the word *democracy* was seldom used, those surveyed by the Spindlers believed that these five values could serve as a working definition of democracy.

As the Spindlers suggest, it is possible to be a mainstream American without being a European American Protestant. In a similar vein, Trueba (1990) suggests that mainstream Americans are those who:

Are fluent in English;

Have internalized core American values (such as those identified by the Spindlers);

Participate meaningfully in American institutions (social, political, and economic);

Accept mainstream affiliation as part of their personal identity.

Trueba's definition is consistent with the view of culture adopted in this book. Two points are important in this regard. The first point is that, given the opportunity, people from many different ethnic groups can participate in the mainstream American culture. Participating in the mainstream culture is a matter of learning that culture, not of being born into it. One problem is that students from diverse backgrounds often lack opportunities to learn to participate in the mainstream culture. For example, Williams (1990) describes a situation in which African American students from lower-class families were isolated in a neighborhood stripped of the economic resources and models of behavior formerly provided by middle class families:

> All the different social classes spent their days in each other's presence. Often poor children had a lower-middle class neighbor, who helped to socialize them, and every street had residents who were trying to "uplift" the neighborhood. Children respected residents and were embarrassed if caught by them engaging in inappropriate behavior. People were proud of where they lived, both the professional and the poor.   (pp. 151-52).

Open housing laws enacted in the 1960s and 1970s led the more well-to-do African Americans in this neighborhood to move to other neighborhoods. As a result of this migration, the neighborhood lost its middle-class residents, along with their businesses. The neighborhood began to decline, and as it did, so did the systems that supported students' socialization to mainstream ways.

The second point in regard to culture is that individuals may participate both in the mainstream culture and in a particular ethnic culture, without necessarily having to choose one or the other. These individuals may be bicultural (knowledgeable of mainstream culture as well as their home culture) and also bilingual. Citing the case of Chicanos in the professions, Trueba (1990) writes:

> The very elastic nature of ethnic affiliation functions as a solution to culture conflicts. Professional Chicanos can be competitive, successful, independent, yet humble, respectful of family and community, and generous. A monolithic, monocultural ethnic affiliation to either Chicano or mainstream culture is not necessary.   (p. 126)

> Individuals may participate both in the mainstream culture and in a particular ethnic culture.

Trueba's point may be applied to students as well. Students can learn to be bicultural, knowledgeable of their own ethnic culture and of the mainstream culture. Teachers can act as cultural mediators (Banks, 1988), helping students of diverse backgrounds to develop the proficiency in literacy and other academic areas, as well as the interpersonal skills required to enjoy success in school and other mainstream settings.

Examples of Cultural Differences

Some people believe that differences between cultures are trivial and that all people are basically the same. The error in this thinking is highlighted by the Spindlers and many other anthropologists who have documented profound differences in the values and ways of life of many cultural groups within the United States. To illustrate these differences, consider some findings reported by the Spindlers (1990) from their long-term study with the Menominee in north central Wisconsin. The Menominee are a Native American people whose traditional Algonkian culture has been in place, although not unchanged, for hundreds of years.

The nature of the deep differences in values between mainstream culture and Menominee culture can be illustrated by considering two of the ten contrasts identified by the Spindlers: (1) material power versus spiritual power; and (2) individualism versus autonomy. From the mainstream American point of view, power is often seen in terms of wealth and material possessions. From the traditional Menominee point of view, the only real power is spiritual power, gained by fasting and observing the proper rituals, while in the right frame of mind.

For the mainstream American, the individual is the central unit of social action. However, the individual is often expected to conform to the expectations of others and to participate in hierarchical systems of authority (for example, parent over child, teacher over student, supervisor over employee). The mainstream concept of individualism overlaps somewhat with the Menominee concept of autonomy, but the two are significantly different. The Spindlers write:

> Traditional Menominee persons are so autonomous that there can be no concept of "chief," a concept which was a construct of Euro-American cultural perceptions anyway. Within the traditional framework, the only way that a group can be brought together in decision-making is through unanimous and unpressured consent. We saw many instances of this during our field work. It took us a long time to understand that no one could represent another person and that no one had authority over another person — not even parents over children.   (1990, p. 74)

The Spindlers' comparison of mainstream American culture and traditional Menominee culture shows the profound nature of possible cultural differences among groups within the United States.

Having the willingness and ability to understand cultural differences may help a teacher know how to make instruction more effective. For example, a teacher working with a group of Menominee students might show respect for traditional values by not issuing orders or expecting all students to do the same thing at the same time. Instead, the teacher might acknowledge students' autonomy by discussing their goals for literacy learning in individual or small group meetings, and working with students on a plan to move toward their goals. Use of a process approach to writing (to be discussed in chapter 10), in which students select the topics they want to write about, would be another way of acknowledging students' autonomy.

Culture and cultural differences will be discussed at many points in this book, for the purpose of looking at educational practices and their effects upon groups of students from different cultural backgrounds. Sometimes teachers reject information about cultural differences because they equate generalizing with stereotyping (Haberman, 1990), which is the process of attributing certain characteristics to all members of a particular group, without exception. Social scientists make generalizations in an attempt to describe broad patterns, but do not claim to account for every case. In this book you will be reading about generalizations about cultural groups established through social science research.

Knowledge and awareness of cultural differences can give teachers new insights about their students and about literacy instruction. When teachers take the time to get to know their students' backgrounds and special qualities as individuals, they avoid stereotyping and find that generalizations apply in many, but not necessarily all, cases.

Why Have Schools Failed?

Why have American schools been so much less successful in educating students from diverse backgrounds compared to students from mainstream backgrounds? Two major theories have been advanced for schools' failure to help students of diverse backgrounds achieve high levels of academic success. These are the theory of cultural discontinuity and the theory of structural inequality.

Theory of Cultural Discontinuity

The theory of **cultural discontinuity** centers on a possible mismatch between the culture of the school and the culture of the home, which results in misunderstandings between teachers and students in the classroom. "Cultural difference" and "communication process" are other labels applied to this theory (Erickson, 1987; Jacob and Jordan, 1987). Cultural discontinuity may be seen in many aspects of classroom activity, including the way teachers interact with students and the way students are asked to complete their assignments.

As discussed in detail in chapters 2, 6, and 7, mismatches between the invisible culture of the home and the invisible culture of the school often work against the school literacy learning of many students from diverse backgrounds. For example, many Native Hawaiian families follow practices of sibling caretaking (Gallimore, Boggs, and Jordan, 1974). This means that older siblings, under the general supervision of parents and other adults in the family, are highly involved in the raising of their younger brothers and sisters. Children raised in a system of sibling caretaking adopt the pattern of orienting to other children and learning from them.

In the classroom, teachers often follow the traditional pattern of having students complete assignments individually, without helping one another. If students need help, they are expected to turn to the teacher, not to another student. Students who seek help from others are judged to be cheating. In classrooms with young Native Hawaiian children, this pattern can result in conflicts between the teacher and students. The teacher may see students' efforts to help one another as disruptive and disobedient, or even dishonest. Students in turn may think it unfair and unreasonable for the teacher not to let them help one another. Fortunately, this mismatch can be overcome if teachers build opportunities for children to work together into many classroom activities. For example, first grade teachers might have students choose a partner or form groups of three to read a book together. Gradually, teachers can teach the children to distinguish times when they are to work alone and seek help only from the teacher, and times when they may seek help from peers.

As this example suggests, mismatches between the culture of the home and the culture of the school can be overcome when teachers break out of a familiar old pattern of instruction, such as an overreliance on individual assignments, and put a new pattern in place, such as the use of partner reading. New patterns contribute to the creation of composite classroom cultures which reflect aspects of both the home and school cultures. These composite cultures result when teachers and students have the opportunity to adapt to one another's preferred values and styles of interaction and to develop shared understandings about how classroom activities can be structured to promote school learning. Composite classroom cultures will be discussed further in chapter 5.

The culture of the classroom can be seen as a dynamic system of values, beliefs, and standards, developed through understandings which the teacher and the students have come to share. Too often, the learning environments of classrooms have been insensitive to students' own culture and language (Erickson, 1987). For example, even a decade ago, it was common for schools to forbid students to speak Spanish or other non-English languages, even at recess. However, if the classroom culture is a composite one, reflecting the values of the home as well as the school, the classroom environment will be comfortable for students and teacher alike. For example, students may be allowed to assist one another with school tasks by providing explanations in their home language. Such a classroom environment may be labeled culturally responsive, or compatible with the values of students' own culture and also aimed at improving students' academic learning. The concept of culturally responsive instruction is further discussed later in this chapter.

Another way of thinking about this same idea is to recognize that, in going from the home and community into the school, students of diverse backgrounds must move from one world to another (Phelan, Davidson, and Cao, 1991). Students are better able to manage the boundary crossings between worlds if teachers introduce new patterns of instruction that enable students to participate actively and constructively. For example, Phelan et al. describe the case of Donna, a Mexican American high school student who maintained a C average but found it hazardous to cross the boundaries between the world of school and the world of family and peers. Donna did well in classrooms where teachers communicated a sense of caring about her as an individual, and where instruction was built upon standards and behaviors valued in the world of her family and peers, such as putting the group above the self, empathizing with others, and being a good mediator. In these classes teachers used approaches based on discussion, the sharing of ideas, and cooperative learning, which conveyed a sense of respect and caring for students. These teachers saw Donna as a model student. In contrast, Donna did poorly in classes where instruction was teacher-centered, interaction among students was discouraged, and a passive style of learning was expected. Teachers in these classes hardly knew Donna at all.

Theory of Structural Inequality

The theory of **structural inequality** looks beyond mismatches between the culture of the home and the culture of the school to the larger historical, political, economic, and social forces which have shaped relationships among ethnic groups in the United States. In this theory, conditions of schooling are seen as a reflection of these larger forces. This theory may also be labeled the secondary discontinuity or perceived labor market theory (Gollnick and Chinn, 1990; Jacob and Jordan, 1987). Grouping, tracking, and testing are three pervasive examples of familiar patterns that persist and affect the learning opportunities of students of diverse backgrounds.

In the theory of structural inequality, some groups are seen as subordinate or oppressed and some groups are seen as dominant. The terms *minority group* and *majority group* do not simply refer to relative numbers of people but are often used as synonyms for *subordinate group* and *dominant group*. Members of ethnic minority groups are also referred to as "people of color." Describing groups as subordinate or dominant emphasizes the idea that inequality in educational outcomes is rooted in the power relationships among groups (for example, McLaren, 1989; Ogbu, 1987).

From this point of view, schools function primarily to maintain the status quo, not to provide all students with a high-quality education. The familiar old patterns of instruction that prevent students of diverse backgrounds from achieving high levels of literacy, such as assessment that devalues their home languages and instruction that violates the values of students' own cultures, result from the power dominant groups have to impose their values and standards upon subordinate groups. The process of domination is carried out through widely accepted school practices that are part of the school's hidden curriculum or invisible culture. For example, in many elementary school classrooms a disproportionate number of students from diverse backgrounds end up in the bottom reading group, while students from mainstream backgrounds are in the higher groups (Oakes, 1985). In high school, students from diverse backgrounds tend to be tracked into vocational programs, while students from mainstream backgrounds tend to enter college preparatory programs.

Most educators do not intend to discriminate against students, but discrimination results when old patterns are perpetuated. In addition to the dangers of tracking, there are dangers associated with familiar patterns of testing. For example, teachers often administer tests which highlight the language abilities of mainstream children but devalue the language abilities of African American children (Labov, 1972). Or teachers may unconsciously select for success only those children who are from higher-status, mainstream backgrounds similar to their own (Spindler and Spindler, 1990).

Taken together, these two theories help to explain why teachers need to be alert to the dangers of falling into familiar patterns which prevent students of diverse backgrounds from achieving high levels of literacy. The theory of structural inequality shows us how these patterns have come about. The theory of cultural discontinuity helps us to understand how these patterns work at the classroom level to hinder communication among teachers and students. Both theories are useful in guiding our thinking about how the schooling of students of diverse backgrounds can be improved (Trueba, 1991).

Individualism versus Egalitarianism

When thinking about the lack of school success experienced by students of diverse backgrounds, many people experience a direct conflict between two mainstream American core values: individualism and egalitarianism. **Individualism** is the belief that individuals control their own destiny and will advance in society on the basis of their own efforts (Gollnick and Chinn, 1990). **Egalitarianism** is the belief that all individuals should have the same opportunities for social, political, and economic success, as well as for educational success.

Due to the value attached to individualism, it is popular for Americans to attribute inequality of educational outcomes to the failings of students and their families. Students of diverse backgrounds are blamed for not trying hard enough in school, and their families are faulted for failing to provide them with the assistance needed to achieve success.

The flaw in this explanation is that individualism assumes a level playing field. In fact, children from mainstream families enter the game of schooling with significant advantages. These advantages are conferred through school practices that conform to the values and standards of the dominant culture, as suggested by the theory of structural inequality. School practices tend to fit better with the experiences and expectations of students from mainstream backgrounds than with those of students from diverse backgrounds (Snow, 1990). Students from diverse backgrounds enter the game with many disadvantages, because school practices often do not recognize the values and standards of their own culture, as discussed further in chapters 6 and 7.

Cultural Identity and Resistance to Schooling

Cultural identity and resistance to school are additional concepts used to explain schools' failure to help students of diverse backgrounds succeed in school. Throughout this book attention will be called to the importance of schools recognizing and building upon the **cultural identity** of students of diverse backgrounds, as a way of improving opportunities for literacy learning. Cultural identity may be defined as one's sense of belonging to, or being connected with, a particular culture or subculture. Cultural identity is not a simple matter, because every American participates in a number of different cultural groups or subcultures, based on factors such as class, ethnicity, gender, exceptionality (whether a handicap or a talent), religion, language, and age (Gollnick and Chinn, 1990).

As mentioned earlier, the term "students of diverse backgrounds" refers to students whose cultural identity is especially influenced by the factors of ethnicity, class, and language. Teachers need to have an understanding of the cultural identities of students of diverse backgrounds in order to develop effective means of fostering students' literacy learning. Yet teachers must also be careful to avoid stereotyping or jumping to conclusions about students on the basis of ethnicity, class, or language. To avoid stereotyping students, it is important to remember that cultural identity is a matter of choice and so differs from ethnic identity. Not all students of a particular ethnicity will feel a strong affiliation with their ethnic culture. Students of the same ethnicity may have different perspectives because they come from middle-class backgrounds, rather than working-class backgrounds. However, cultural identity is not always related to class. For example, middle-class students may come from families that identify with the culture of a predominantly poor or working-class group. A student's home language does not necessarily determine cultural identity either, since a student may identify with a group without speaking the native language of that group.

The approaches teachers use to work with students of diverse backgrounds should allow students to retain and feel pride in their own ethnic and cultural identity. It is not enough just to include content from other cultures in the curriculum, a point to be discussed further in chapter 11. Part of the teacher's role is to act as a cultural mediator by helping students to feel comfortable with their own identities within the school context. Too often, students of diverse backgrounds find themselves in the position of having to choose between school success and their cultural identity. Fordham (1991), for example, describes how high schools may pressure African American students to "act white" and give up their own cultural identity as the price for being academically successful.

Fordham and Ogbu (1986) suggest that, because schools fail to recognize and respect their abilities, students of diverse backgrounds may adopt patterns of resistance to the authority of teachers and schools, which they perceive as part of the dominant culture. Due to the persistence of familiar school practices, students fail to develop the academic skills and motivation needed to do well in school. In the face of failure, students' resistance to school becomes a means of maintaining self-esteem and affirming their cultural identity. Many students eventually drop out of school, narrowing their life opportunities and consigning themselves to remain at the lowest level of society (McLaren, 1989). In some urban areas, the dropout rate for African American and Hispanic American students may exceed 60 percent (Pallas, Natriello, and McDill, 1989).

Culturally Responsive Instruction

The problem of bridging the gap between the school and the world outside is an urgent one. Earlier, it was suggested that one way of addressing this problem was through the use of **culturally responsive instruction**, or instruction consistent with the values of students' own cultures and aimed at improving academic learning. Other terms for this same concept are "culturally compatible" and "culturally congruent" instruction. For example, earlier in this chapter it was shown how Native Hawaiian students, raised in families that practive sibling caretaking, might feel more comfortable learning from peers than from an adult teacher. Another example is that a teacher working with Native American students might find individual or small group meetings an effective teaching format, since private (as opposed to public) discussions show respect for the traditional value of autonomy. Other examples of culturally responsive instruction will be discussed in chapters 6 and 7.

As Ogbu and Fordham point out, students of diverse backgrounds often feel they must choose between being successful in school and being true to their own cultural identities. But if teachers use culturally responsive forms of instruction, they help students to be academically successful while still taking pride in their own cultural identity.

A question that frequently arises deals with the use of culturally responsive instruction in classrooms where students are of many different ethnic groups. In this chapter examples of culturally responsive instruction for Native Hawaiian and Native American students were given. In these examples, the application of the idea seemed quite straightforward. However, a common situation in urban schools is to find classrooms where students come from a dozen different ethnic groups and speak a half dozen different languages. How can instruction be responsive to many different cultures at once? The answer is that the use of culturally responsive instruction does not simply involve a matching of instruction to cultural features. Rather, it is also a matter of adjusting and adapting instruction to meet the needs of all students. The use of culturally responsive instruction requires a departure from familiar patterns of instruction and a willingness to experiment with new patterns. As each adjustment is made, the teacher weighs its effectiveness and decides if further adjustments are needed. Are all students participating comfortably? Are there some for whom special measures must be taken?

Consider the example of the classroom with Native Hawaiian students. In public school classrooms with many Native Hawaiian students, there are also students from other ethnic groups, including African Americans, European Americans, Filipino Americans, Japanese Americans, and Samoan Americans. When a teacher begins to use peer work groups, he or she usually finds that most of the students turn readily to their peers for help. However, there are generally a few students who refuse to accept assistance from their peers and keep coming to the teacher with questions. The teacher answers these questions at first, and then gradually begins referring the students' questions to other children in their peer work group. The teacher helps students learn to offer help and to seek help from one another, and makes clear the value of these skills of working with other students. Gradually, all students are able to teach and learn in peer work groups.

In short, the teacher seeks instructional approaches that work with the majority of students in the class and supports all students in becoming successful within these approaches. Special steps are taken to make sure that all students have access to learning through these approaches, and students are never excluded from participation because of their cultural backgrounds. These points are discussed further in chapter 5, which deals with classroom organization and the community of learners.

Another question that frequently arises with respect to culturally responsive instruction has to do with the content of instruction. In classrooms with many students of diverse backgrounds, does the use of culturally responsive instruction mean that there should be an emphasis on culturally relevant topics? For example, with Native Hawaiian students would there be an emphasis on Hawaiian legends, rather than on American tall tales or European folktales? The study of culturally relevant topics and works of literature can be rewarding and reaffirming to students, and an avenue to learning the principles and concepts in many academic areas, as discussed in chapter 11. For example, in this case the teacher might use Hawaiian legends to teach students about some of the characteristics of folktales. Also, when unfamiliar topics are introduced, the teacher takes steps to link the topic to students' background knowledge and experiences, as discussed in chapter 7. In brief, certain changes in the content of the curriculum, which reinforce students' cultural identities and give them an appreciation for other cultures, appear to be beneficial to students of diverse backgrounds.

Nevertheless, the position taken here is that the overall goals for instruction and standards for achievement should remain largely the same for students of diverse backgrounds as they are for students of mainstream backgrounds. Without a command of the same academic skills and content as mainstream students, students of diverse backgrounds will continue to be marginalized, remaining outside the mainstream, and problems of inequality will persist (Fordham, 1991). Having a command of the same academic skills and content will enable students of diverse backgrounds to compete successfully in mainstream settings, if they wish. Thus, there should be considerable overlap in the content of curricula designed for students of diverse backgrounds and the content of curricula designed for students of mainstream backgrounds. At the same time, a vigorous effort should be made to broaden the literacy curriculum to give all students more experience with multiethnic literature and diverse points of view.

Framework for Empowering Students of Diverse Backgrounds

This chapter closes by presenting a framework that pulls together many of the ideas presented so far and also previews other ideas to be discussed in future chapters. This theoretical framework for empowering students of diverse backgrounds was developed by Jim Cummins (1986). Peter McLaren (1989) describes **empowerment** as:

> Not only helping students to understand and engage with the world around them, but also enabling them to exercise the kind of courage needed to change the social order where necessary. (p. 182)

In other words, students who are empowered have the ability to analyze social and political situations in a critical manner and to take positive action to remedy the situation for themselves and others. Cummins' framework seems to take into account factors considered important in both theories of cultural discontinuity and structural inequality. This framework is shown in figure 1.1.

The societal context is shown at the top of the figure, to remind us of the social, political, economic, and historical trends that form the context for schooling, as highlighted in the theory of structural inequality. Within the societal context there is a dominant or mainstream group and a dominated or subordinate group. As mentioned earlier, students of diverse backgrounds may also be referred to as subordinate group students.

The next level of the figure depicts the school context and what Cummins terms "educator role definitions." Cummins believes that educators must break away from familiar beliefs and adjust their actions in

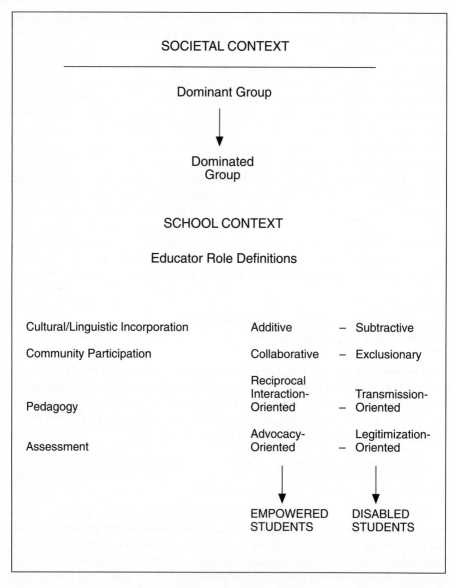

Figure 1.1   Empowerment of Minority Students: A Theoretical Framework

each of four areas if they are to help students of diverse backgrounds succeed in school.

The first area, cultural/linguistic incorporation, has to do with the degree to which students' language and culture are made a part of the school program. Cummins suggests that students of diverse backgrounds will achieve at higher academic levels when schools recognize and build upon strengths in students' home language and reinforce students' cultural identity. Typically, schools take a subtractive approach and try to replace students' home language and culture with the mainstream language and culture. The new pattern involves an additive approach, in which students retain their home language and culture, and their existing skills and knowledge serve as the foundation for learning standard American English, reading and other academic skills. Chapter 9 shows how students who speak Spanish as a first language can use their skills in Spanish to improve their reading of English.

The second area, community participation, deals with the extent to which communities become empowered through their interactions with the school. In a collaborative situation, there is a partnership between the school and the community, while in an exclusionary situation, the community has little or no say or involvement in the running of the school. Cummins suggests that students of diverse backgrounds will be more successful in school when their communities are aware of barriers to their success, work to overcome these barriers, and provide students with the support to reinforce academic learning. An important part of community participation has to do with teachers welcoming parents' participation in their children's schooling, as discussed in chapter 9.

The third area in Cummins' framework is pedagogy or instruction. Here Cummins contrasts the familiar pattern of transmission-oriented instruction with the new pattern of reciprocal interaction-oriented instruction. These two patterns will be referred to as the **transmission** and **constructivist** models of instruction, and they will be discussed at length in chapter 3. Cummins hypothesizes that schooling will be more beneficial for students of diverse backgrounds when teachers use constructivist rather than transmission models of instruction. He believes constructivist approaches will be more effective because they involve a genuine dialogue between student and teacher (both oral and written), they emphasize reasoning and other higher-level thinking skills, and they encourage students to set their own goals and to collaborate with other students.

The fourth area in the framework is assessment. Cummins contrasts the familiar pattern of legitimization-oriented assessment with the new pattern of advocacy-oriented assessment. He describes legitimization-oriented assessment as assessment that locates the cause of a student's academic difficulties within the student. Legitimization-oriented assessment usually involves the use of traditional psychological tests that purport to measure various areas of cognitive and linguistic functioning. The use of these tests results in students being given labels such as "learning disabled" or "language impaired" (for further discussion of language assessment, refer to chapter 8). As a result of receiving these labels, students are typically placed in special programs or classes, essentially a process of segregation that prevents their receiving the high-quality educational experiences available to mainstream students (Shepard, 1991). Many studies have demonstrated that labels assigned through testing are essentially arbitrary (Shepard,

Smith, and Vojir, 1983; Cummins, 1984; Taylor, 1991) and change depending on the availability of services within a school system (Mehan, Hertweck, and Meihls, 1986).

In contrast, with advocacy-oriented assessment, educators recognize that problems of schooling can be remedied by locating the problem in the social and educational context, rather than by locating the problem in the student. An example of this approach can be seen in the questions for assessing instructional situations presented in chapter 8. Educators with an advocacy-oriented attitude toward assessment are aware of the weaknesses in typical psychological assessment (such as those identified by Figueroa [1990]), avoid the arbitrary labeling of students, and seek to boost the learning of students of diverse backgrounds largely by strengthening the instruction they receive in the regular classroom.

In short, Cummins' framework shows how some of the different factors discussed in this chapter, at a broad societal level and at the level of the school and classroom, fit together. He identifies four areas in which educators' attitudes play an important part in either empowering or disabling students of diverse backgrounds. Cummins argues that educators must move away from traditional attitudes and adopt new ones that will serve to counteract the power relations and negative patterns in the wider society, as outlined in the theory of structural inequality. Cummins' notion of an additive stance is consistent with the theory of cultural discontinuity and the idea of culturally responsive instruction. His notion of community involvement speaks to bridging the gap between the home and school. As suggested in this chapter, Cummins views the culture of the school and classroom as subject to change, and his framework defines four critical areas for change. You will learn more about each of the areas in Cummins' framework in later chapters.

Summary

Students of diverse backgrounds are distinguished by their ethnicity, class, and language. Typically, schools are less successful in promoting the literacy achievement of these students than the literacy achievement of students of mainstream backgrounds. Culture may be defined as a system of values and standards for behavior, with dynamic properties that allow for change. Mainstream American culture is open to participation by individuals of diverse backgrounds who may become bicultural. Schools' failure to meet the academic needs of students of diverse backgrounds has been explained by two major theories: the theory of cultural discontinuity and the theory of structural inequality. One solution to schools' difficulties may be found in the use of culturally responsive instruction, instruction compatible with the values of students' own cultures and aimed at helping them achieve at high levels. Finally, Cummins' framework for empowering students of diverse backgrounds suggests the importance of changes in educators' attitudes about students' culture and language, community participation, instruction, and assessment.

Application Activities

1. Discuss your own cultural background and identity. How do you think your cultural identity might affect your teaching of students from diverse backgrounds?

2. Have you had any experiences that made you aware of cultural differences? How do you think a knowledge of cultural differences might help you as a teacher?

3. Why do you think schools are generally successful with students from mainstream backgrounds, but generally unsuccessful with students from diverse cultural backgrounds? Try to put ideas from this chapter together with your own ideas and experiences.

Suggested Readings

Banks, J.A. (1988). *Multiethnic Education: Theory and Practice*, 2d ed. Boston: Allyn and Bacon.

Gollnick, D.M., and P.C. Chinn (1990). *Multicultural Education in a Pluralistic Society*, 3d ed. Columbus, OH: Merrill.

Trueba, H. (1990). "Mainstream and Minority Cultures: A Chicano Perspective." In G. Spindler and L. Spindler, *The American Cultural Dialogue and Its Transmission*. London: Falmer Press, pp. 122-43.

chapter 2

An Expanded
Definition of Literacy

1. Define the term *literacy* as it is used in this text;
2. Explain the importance of the social context in discussions of literacy;
3. Show how literacy practices may vary from community to community;
4. Suggest ways in which school literacy can be redefined to improve the learning of students of diverse backgrounds.

A Definition of Literacy

> Literacy is defined as: The ability and the willingness to use reading and writing to construct meaning from printed text, in ways which meet the requirements of a particular social context.

Consider the various parts of this definition and their relationship to instruction in multicultural settings.

Willingness to Use Literacy

First, the definition addresses one's willingness, as well as one's ability, to use literacy. This feature is important, because students of diverse backgrounds may have the ability to use literacy but be unwilling to do so. This situation is illustrated in the following example. A teacher asks her third grade students to complete a textbook exercise that requires them to write a friendly letter. On this exercise, students show little ability to compose letters. A few days later, the teacher announces that she has arranged for everyone in the class to have a pen pal. Now, with a real audience for their writing, the students show a great deal of letter-writing ability. The teacher sees that students have a sense of the information their pen pals will find interesting, and that they know how to write a greeting and a closing for their letters.

As a comparison of these two letter-writing activities reveals, students' literacy ability might appear very different depending on the nature of the literacy activity. The textbook exercise shows the old familiar pattern of teaching literacy as a set of skills in isolation, apart from useful communication. Having students write to pen pals is an example of a new, more beneficial pattern based on teaching literacy in a meaningful context, with an authentic purpose for communication. While instruction centered on meaningful, rewarding activities is beneficial to all students, it may be critical to the success of students of diverse backgrounds. The reasons for this situation are addressed in work by D'Amato (1988), to be discussed in chapters 3 and 7.

Much depends on the teacher's ability to provide opportunities for literacy learning that students find meaningful and interesting. Students' willingness is an important factor in their demonstrating existing literacy skills and learning new ones. Literacy is not just a matter of skill or cognitive strategies, it is also a matter of will or feelings and emotions (Winograd and Paris, 1988).

Reading and Writing

Second, the definition of literacy mentions both reading and writing. You are probably familiar with the idea that literacy involves both reading and writing, although traditionally reading has received much more attention in the elementary school. Reading and writing are both processes of composing meaning from text (Pearson and Tierney, 1984). In the case of reading, the text is already present, while in the case of writing, the text must be created.

One of the implications for literacy instruction is that teachers will want to give an equal emphasis to reading and writing, and to look at ways that instruction of one can strengthen learning of the other. For example, if students read biographies, they might be inspired to write biographies of their own.

Although not mentioned in our definition, speaking and listening, the other language arts, also have a crucial role in students' literacy development. Students may read aloud or listen to someone else read aloud. Or they may discuss their ideas about the same text, whether a newspaper editorial or a new novel. When students write, they may meet with the teacher or a peer to talk about their drafts and to get ideas for revision.

The ability to read and write well in standard American English is certainly a goal for all students. However, teachers should be aware of allowing students of diverse backgrounds to use strengths in their home languages as the basis for becoming proficient in reading and writing in English. For example, as shown in chapters 8 and 9, students might read a standard English text but discuss their ideas in their home languages, such as Hawaiian Creole English or Spanish. During the discussion the teacher models the use of standard English to express the same ideas and encourages students to use these new terms and structures.

Constructing Meaning

Third, in our definition of literacy, reading and writing are used to con-struct meaning. This view is consistent with research which suggests that meaning does not reside in the text, but in the interaction among the reader, the text, and the social context (Wixson, Peters, Weber, and Roeber, 1987). A text may be compared to a blueprint, and the reader's job is to interpret and fill in the gaps in order to create meaning (Collins, Brown, and Larkin, 1980). Similarly, with writing, the writer's job is to create a text. Viewing reading and writing as constructive, creative processes takes us away from a mechanistic, skill-by-skill approach to literacy instruction.

Viewing reading and writing as constructive processes also reminds us of the importance of the background knowledge that students bring to the task. Readers' background knowledge strongly influences their interpreta-tion of a text (Anderson and Pearson, 1984). In multicultural classrooms, teachers may find that students arrive at what appear to be unusual inter-pretations of a particular text. These varying interpretations may result, not from careless reading, but from differences in the background knowl-edge or cultural schemata students bring to the reading task.

The influence of cultural schemata on text interpretation is illustrated in a study conducted by Steffensen, Joag-dev, and Anderson (1979). The subjects were adults residing in a university community; half were from the United States, while half were from India. The subjects read two letters, one describing a wedding in the United States and one a wedding in India. Subjects recalled more information from the letter describing an event in their own country, and were able to make more culturally appropriate inferences about that text. When it came to the letter describing an event in another country, subjects made more interpretations that a native of that country would regard as inappropriate.

For example, the letter about the Indian wedding described the two events for guests that followed the wedding. Indian subjects were aware of the two events, a feast and a reception, while American subjects collapsed the two into a single event. The letter about the American wedding stated that the bride was going to wear her grandmother's wedding dress. American subjects recognized the connection to family tradition shown by the wearing of an heirloom dress. In contrast, one Indian subject described the gown as "too old and out of fashion," because in Indian weddings, the bride's wearing of a fashionable new sari is an indication of the financial status of her family. Clearly, American and Indian subjects interpreted the letters in terms of different cultural schemata or frameworks of knowledge.

The effects of different cultural schemata upon reading comprehension are also shown in a study conducted by Reynolds, Taylor, Steffensen,

Shirey, and Anderson (1982). They asked eighth grade students to read a letter that included the following passage:

> Classes went at their usual slow pace through the morning, so at noon I was really ready for lunch. I got in line behind Bubba. As usual the line was moving pretty slow and we were all getting pretty restless. For a little action Bubba turned around and said, "Hey Sam! What you doin' man? You so ugly that when the doctor delivered you he slapped your face!" Everyone laughed, but they laughed even harder when I shot back, "Oh yeah? Well, you so ugly the doctor turned around and slapped your momma!" It got even wilder when Bubba said, "Well man, at least my daddy ain't no girlscout!" We really go into it then. After a while more people got involved — 4, 5, then 6. It was a riot! People helping out anyone who seemed to be getting the worst of the deal. All of sudden Mr. Reynolds the gym teacher came over to try to quiet things down.   (p. 358)

What do you think the passage describes? From the perspective of most readers from mainstream backgrounds, the passage appears to be about a fight or physical aggression in a school cafeteria. That is the way the passage was interpreted by the European American students in the study. However, the African American students in the study recognized that the passage described an instance of **sounding**, a form of ritual insult and verbal play practiced mainly by teenage boys in many African American communities.

These studies suggest that teachers need to encourage students to explain their interpretations of text so that the reasons behind their interpretations become evident. In some cases, the cultural schemata of students from diverse backgrounds may give them insights about a text that the teacher and other students do not have.

Printed Text

Fourth, our definition of literacy ties literacy to a **printed text** (Snow, 1983), which distinguishes the way we are using the word *literacy* from the way it is often used as a synonym for knowledge, as in "cultural literacy" or "computer literacy." Literacy in our definition refers to a person's ability to work with printed text, that is, to read and write. However, there are times when a person is not reading or writing text but seems to be using a form of literacy. Think about a situation in which students are discussing a story read aloud by the teacher. Students have not done any of the reading themselves, but they are using their ability to interpret a text. Is this literacy? Or consider a situation in which two students are working together to compose a story. One of the students is coming up with new ideas, while the other is writing the words down on paper. Is the student who is generating the ideas showing literacy?

We would suggest that these situations both involve literacy, even though students are not reading the text themselves, and one of the students is not putting words down on paper. The teacher's reading aloud of literature and collaborative writing are both excellent occasions for literacy learning. However, students also need to be involved in reading on their own and writing on their own. This is important if they are to develop the skills of fluent, independent reading, and of fluent, independent writing.

At the same time, teachers should be aware that school literacy activities, which usually emphasize individual performance, differ significantly from literacy activities in the community and workplace. In settings outside of school, literacy is often carried out in a collaborative manner. For example, Fingeret (1983, cited in Guthrie and Greaney [1990]) shows that neighborhood literacy may involve individuals in the joint reading of income tax forms, bank statements, bills, and other materials. It is likely that children also collaborate to use literacy in settings outside of school, although there is little research on this topic.

Social Context

Finally, our definition of literacy states that reading and writing are used in ways appropriate to the requirements of a particular **social context**. A social context is any of the situations someone may experience in settings such as the school, home, neighborhood, workplace, shopping mall, or elsewhere, whether alone or with other people. When someone reads or writes, those acts of literacy are taking place in some social context. The reading of a newspaper at home, while surrounded by family members, is an example of literacy taking place in a particular social context. Taking notes at the library on information needed for a term paper is another example of literacy in a particular social context. Still another example is seen when two first graders read a book together in the classroom library corner.

The idea of social context is especially important when it comes to the literacy instruction of students of diverse backgrounds. The social contexts of the home and community often prepare students of diverse backgrounds to learn in ways quite different from those expected by the school, as explained in chapters 6 and 7. Also, as discussed later in this chapter, students of diverse backgrounds often experience literacy in social contexts vastly different from those typically found in schools. Culturally responsive instruction, as defined in chapter 1, involves changing the social context of instruction so that lessons can be more effective for students of diverse backgrounds. The teacher's goal is to enable students of diverse backgrounds to use literacy successfully in mainstream social contexts, as well as in the contexts of their homes and communities.

Meeting Requirements

What does it mean for literacy to **meet the requirements** of a particular social context? Many social contexts in a society such as the United States call for the use of literacy. Literacy is required to read street signs, to look up phone numbers in the telephone directory, and to complete the application for a driver's license. To accomplish each of these tasks successfully, the individual must possess certain knowledge and skills or be prepared to seek help from others.

To read most newspaper articles easily, one must be able to comprehend text written at a tenth- to eleventh-grade level (Wheat, Lindberg, and Naumann, 1977). Taking notes requires the ability to identify relevant points and write them down in just a few words. To read a book together, first graders must know how to handle books (hold them right side up, turn pages), to track print, and to appreciate illustrations.

The requirements for literacy may vary even when the printed text remains constant. For example, I may read a novel for my own enjoyment, without reflecting much about it. But if the same novel were assigned reading for an English course, I would probably read it in a different manner. I might link what I am reading to points discussed in class, compare and contrast the novel with others read as part of the same course, and jot down questions that come to mind.

There is not just one way to read or just one way to write. The literate person is one who can read or write in ways that meet the requirements of the various social contexts in his or her worlds. For example, a parent reading a storybook to a child will read aloud with expression, saying every word. At the office, the same adult might scan a memo quickly and silently, perhaps just to find out about the time and location of a meeting.

We may judge different forms of reading and writing to be appropriate or inappropriate, on the basis of the requirements of the social context. Our expectations and sense of what is appropriate may even cause us to overlook certain types of literacy entirely. In a study of an elementary school in an African American neighborhood in Philadelphia, Gilmore (1983) discovered that students used literacy in certain ways that teachers did not acknowledge. For example, students often wrote notes to one another, but teachers did not see the composing of these notes as writing. Similarly, teachers did not recognize the spelling and decoding skills girls showed when they participated in "doin' steps," a distinctive type of street rhyme. Gilmore concludes that, because only officially sanctioned activities count as literacy in school, teachers are often unaware of the full range of literacy skills students of diverse backgrounds may possess. Gilmore's research highlights the role that power relationships between teachers and students, reflecting those in the larger society, may play in endorsing some forms of literacy while dismissing others.

As Gilmore suggests, even within the school itself there may be different literacies associated with the different worlds of teachers and students. Discussing this idea in a more general way, Erickson (1984) writes that

. . . the notion of literacy, as knowledge and skill taught and learned in school, is not separable from the concrete circumstances of its uses inside and outside school, nor is it easily separable from the situation of its acquisition in the school as a social form and as a way of life. The school can be seen as an arena of political negotiation that embodies individual and group interests and ideologies. It is reasonable to expect that various kinds of literacies might represent a variety of interests and be embedded in a variety of belief systems.   (p. 525)

Teachers need to be aware that literacy may take many forms. While teachers will want to acquaint all students with mainstream forms of literacy, they will want to be aware that other forms of literacy may also be significant in the lives of students of diverse backgrounds.

Community Differences in Literacy

Teachers working in multicultural settings will find it especially important to understand how literacy may vary depending on the social contexts of students' homes and communities. The manner in which literacy may vary from community to community is illustrated in research conducted by Shirley Brice Heath (1983). She describes the nature of literacy in two communities, Trackton and Roadville, only a few miles from one another in the Piedmont Carolinas. Both are working-class communities. Trackton is an African American community. It was once a farming area but residents now work in the textile mills. Roadville is a European American community where families have worked in the textile mills for four generations. As Heath shows, each community has its own literate traditions.

Literacy in Trackton

Trackton homes often contain newspapers, advertisements, church materials, homework, and school notices. Besides the Bible there are likely to be no books except those from the school or church. Trackton parents do not buy either special toys or books for their children. They do not create reading and writing tasks for their children or consciously demonstrate reading and writing for them. Yet children develop literacy skills in their encounters with the environment. They learn to identify labels on soups, cereals, and other items and to read price tags. Preschoolers have a sense of the print in newspapers and know, for example, that the print in a headline at the top of the page is bigger than the print in the story beneath it.

Literacy events in Trackton tend to involve a process of social negotiation and to be public and group-oriented. Talk is an integral part of literacy events. Authority does not reside in the printed text but in the meanings that are negotiated as the text is discussed in terms of the group's experiences. One example involves the reading of the evening newspaper. Obituaries are read and discussed in terms of possible connections to the deceased, his or her relatives, place of birth, church, or school. There is active discussion about the individual and those who are likely to have known him or her.

Another example involves circulars or letters informing people of recreational, medical, educational, and other services that have become available. One day Lillie Mae received a letter about a day-care program and decided she wanted to enroll her two-year old son. Lillie Mae initiated a discussion by standing on her front porch and reading aloud the first paragraph of the letter. Neighbors on their porches and in their yards joined in the conversation, which lasted for almost an hour. They discussed specific points, such as how Lillie Mae might obtain a copy of her son's birth certificate, and shared their knowledge about day-care programs. Lillie Mae drew relationships between the text and the experiences shared by the group and came to a final synthesis of meaning, which she checked with some members of the group.

In Trackton the generally accepted procedure is for reading materials to be interpreted as part of a group process, rather than individually. Heath notes:

> In general, reading alone, unless one is old and very religious, marks an individual as someone who cannot make it socially.   (p. 191)

Writing follows similar patterns. Women write down phone numbers and addresses, appointments, and the dates of school holidays; some write notes to the school and to local merchants; and a few write letters to relatives. Men appear to do less writing, except perhaps in connection with tax preparation and church activities. The preparation of written materials such as church bulletins and schedules is negotiated during meetings and no individual takes sole responsibility for any writing tasks. In short, community literacy activities in Trackton tend to be public, social events in which members of the group work together to synthesize information from the text with their collective experiences.

Literacy in Roadville

Different patterns are seen in Roadville. Homes have an abundance of reading materials, including magazines, newspapers, advertisements, church circulars, and children's books. Parents read books to their children at bedtime, and children are allowed to participate actively in this event, for example by making the sounds of the animals or by responding to questions such as "What is it?" and "Who is it?" This pattern shifts as children reach the age of three or so, when adults begin to encourage them just to sit quietly and listen. As children near the age for entering kindergarten, parents give them workbooks and assist them in writing their names, coloring within the lines, matching shapes and letters, and so on. Parents convey to children that these are things they need to know before they go to school.

In Sunday school as well as at home, children are taught to listen passively and respond to questions with the right answers. Answers to questions that come from books are assumed to have just one correct answer, because authority and meaning are believed to reside in the written word, not in the individual's experiences and interpretation.

Reading is much talked about in Roadville, but few people do much reading or take action based upon the reading they have done. For example, Jay Turner praises reading and subscribes to three magazines, but he spends his evenings watching television. Women clip recipes and ideas for home decorating that they save with the intention of reading over "someday." The use of patterns for dressmaking is the one area in which women rely upon and follow written instructions.

Women write letters to family members to keep in touch and share news about friends and relatives. Because those exchanging letters know each other so well, letters take the form of "conversations written down." (p. 213) Women also send greeting cards and thank-you notes, and children are taught to write thank-you notes. When greeting cards, notes, and letters are received, they are shared orally, especially among women and children. For example, a mother may read a letter aloud to her children, or a child may be informed that he or she has received a birthday card in the mail. Roadville residents also write notes, for example, to explain a child's absence from school, to remind children of their chores, or to outline the plan for a church meeting. Men write checks and make notes for preparing income tax forms, but they write lists and notes much less frequently than women.

> Each community has its own literate traditions.

Heath's research in Trackton and Roadville shows how literacy is carried out differently in different communities. There are fewer reading materials in Trackton but a more collaborative, interpretive approach to literacy. Reading has a higher value in Roadville, in terms of people's statements but not necessarily their actions. Parents in Trackton and Roadville have different beliefs about how their children will learn to read and write. However, as Heath discovered, neither community's literacy concepts and practices matches well with the concepts and practices of school literacy. This issue is pursued in chapter 5, which discusses Heath's work further.

The point is that Heath's research shows how literacy in the home and community is very much a part of people's culture. Different cultures or subcultures, such as those of Trackton and Roadville, incorporate different beliefs about literacy and have different customary uses for literacy.

Practical Implications

Teachers need to be aware that when students from diverse backgrounds participate in school literacy activities, they are in essence being socialized into the literacy practices of a different culture, the culture of the school. Furthermore, the culture of the school tends to be primarily a reflection of mainstream culture. As shown in chapter 1, in classrooms with students of diverse backgrounds, there are many possibilities for mismatches between the culture of the school and the culture of the home. In school literacy instruction we should seek to develop students' ability to read and write through approaches that do not threaten their cultural identity or violate their cultural values.

Ferdman (1991) writes:

> In the context of literacy education, the issue has to do with what is experienced by the student as "owned" and what is experienced as "not owned" by his or her group. To which texts and to which writing tasks does the student engage in a relation of "us" or "ours" and to which as "they" or "theirs"? (pp. 107-8)

On the one hand, when students perceive reading and writing tasks and materials to reaffirm their cultural identity, they are likely to become more deeply involved and to construct their own personal meanings. On the other hand, when students feel that school literacy tasks and materials deny or devalue their cultural identity, they are likely to show indifference or resistance.

Redefining School Literacy

As part of putting new patterns of literacy instruction in place in schools, we need to consider how school literacy may be redefined to affirm the cultural identities of students of diverse backgrounds. Several possible steps toward redefining school literacy appear promising.

Types of Texts

First, school literacy can be redefined in terms of the types of texts students read. In the past, students were often taught to read using texts that reflected only mainstream culture. Such ethnocentric texts served to affirm the cultural identity only of students from mainstream backgrounds. Today the texts students read should include many works of literature reflecting the varying perspectives of authors from diverse backgrounds, such as *Roll of Thunder, Hear My Cry* by Mildred Taylor (1976) and *Dragonwings* by Laurence Yep (1975). Reading multicultural literature is one way for students of diverse backgrounds to affirm their own cultural identity and to develop an appreciation for the cultural heritage of others (Martinez and Nash, 1990), as discussed further in chapter 11.

Instruction Centered on Meaning

Another step toward redefining school literacy involves changing the nature of instructional activities. In the past, reading and writing activities often centered on the learning of low-level skills, such as decoding, spelling, grammar, and literal comprehension (associated with transmission models of instruction, to be discussed in chapter 3). Reading and writing were treated as mechanistic processes instead of active, constructive processes. Today instruction should center on students' efforts to make meaning from text, whether in reading or in writing, and skills should be taught in the context of this meaning-making (in keeping with constructivist models of instruction, discussed in chapter 3). The basis for meaning-making is students' prior experience and knowledge. As a primary means of instruction, the teacher seeks to involve students in a dynamic process of discussion about texts, whether written by the students themselves or by others, in which students draw upon their background experience and knowledge. This approach to instruction is also discussed in more detail in chapter 3.

School literacy may be redefined through:
  Types of texts;
  Instruction centered on meaning;
  Writing based on students' experiences;
  Culturally responsive instruction;
  Critical literacy.

Here is an example of a text and instructional activities that show school literacy redefined to affirm the cultural identities of students from diverse backgrounds. Students read *Family Pictures* by Carmen Lomas Garza (1990), which describes scenes from the author's childhood growing up in a Mexican American community in Texas. The cultural schemata some Mexican American students in the class may bring to this text enables them to make many connections to their own lives, and to appreciate nuances and details that elude students from other backgrounds. Differences in comprehending and appreciating the text can and should be discussed among the students and teacher. Certainly, students of all backgrounds can benefit from trying to understand the author's childhood experiences and comparing and contrasting them with their own. Students may then draw and write about family pictures of their own, as the class continues its discussion of family and community customs, activities, and values.

Writing Based on Students' Experiences

Still another step in redefining school literacy is to make central the writing students do about their own experiences and from their own perspectives. This is consistent with the principles of the process approach to writing and the writers' workshop (Graves, 1983). Students should be allowed to choose the topics they want to write about and the forms or genres in which their ideas can most effectively be presented.

Nancie Atwell (1987) gives the example of a Vietnamese student who was struggling to write about a dream of her mother's. Her first drafts were in prose. While Atwell respected the student's rights as an author, she did not take a laissez-faire attitude; she provided the student with guidance and offered options. Atwell suggested the student try poetry, but she did not force the issue. Eventually the student did decide to frame her thoughts as a poem, and both teacher and student were pleased with the results.

Writing about their own experiences and from their own perspectives provides students with the opportunity to gain a better understanding of their own lives. The pieces written by students of diverse backgrounds are multicultural texts from which other students and the teacher may learn.

Teachers may be surprised by students' choices but should be prepared to reflect upon whether their students do not have some insight they lack. The following example illustrates the situation of a teacher who failed to accept other perspectives. As part of a unit on explorers, a Native Hawaiian student in the ninth grade chose to write about the Polynesian voyagers who first discovered and settled the Hawaiian Islands, instead of about the first contact with the islands made by a European, the British explorer James Cook. Through his reading, the student learned that at several periods between about 900 and 1400 A.D., Polynesians made the voyage back and forth between Hawaii and the Marquesan Islands and Tahiti, using sophisticated skills of non-instrument navigation. As a Polynesian, he felt a sense of pride in the accomplishments of these explorers. When the student turned in his paper, his teacher accused him of "rewriting history" and gave him a failing grade. The student's research was accurate, but the teacher evidently saw his job as that of reinforcing a mainstream perspective on history and so failed to appreciate and learn from the understandings the student introduced. The student and his family correctly perceived this incident as a example of how schools typically honor the accomplishments of some groups but ignore the accomplishments of others. In keeping with the theory of structural inequality, as discussed in chapter 1, this is an example of how schools serve to maintain the power relations between dominant and subordinate groups.

Culturally Responsive Instruction

School literacy may also be redefined through culturally responsive instruction. School literacy activities can be adjusted to follow the form of activities familiar to students in the home and community. For example, as discussed in chapter 1, students may work on reading and writing activities collaboratively, rather than individually, to build on strengths gained through home experiences with sibling caretaking. Or classroom discussions may take a culturally responsive form, rather than following mainstream rules for discussion. For example, with Native Hawaiian children, teachers find it effective to conduct literature discussions following the interactional rules for talk story, a Hawaiian community speech event (Au, 1980). These and other adaptations, and the subject of culturally responsive instruction, will be covered in detail in chapters 6 and 7.

As part of culturally responsive instruction, teachers may explore with their classes the ways in which students and their families use literacy at home and in the community. Students and their families may use literacy in sophisticated ways which are not necessarily familiar to teachers from mainstream backgrounds. Knowledge of these uses of literacy may give teachers ideas about how classroom literacy activities may be adapted to relate to the literacy skills students already have or may want to have. In any event, teachers will have increased their knowledge of their students' lives. For example, teachers may not be aware of the degree of responsibility students from diverse backgrounds have in their households, particularly if both parents must work at one or more jobs (Delgado-Gaitan and Trueba, 1991).

Trueba (1984) describes some of the home literacy activities of Alma, a 12-year-old Mexican American girl. Alma's younger sister, Carmen, had Down syndrome and attended a special school. Each day Carmen's teacher wrote a brief report on Carmen's progress in a diary. So that her mother would be able to understand the report, Alma translated the teacher's message from English to Spanish. Her mother then dictated a reply in Spanish, which Alma translated and wrote down in English. With her mother's permission, Alma opened mail written in English and explained its contents in Spanish. Alma and her sisters assisted her parents with filling out forms and documents, although they often made mistakes in these tasks.

A teacher familiar with Alma's responsibilities at home might introduce some classroom literacy activities to strengthen the skills Alma and other students could use to assist family members with forms and documents. Skills of document literacy, such as reading bills and completing applications, often receive scant attention in the elementary grades but could be immediately useful to students like Alma.

Critical Literacy

Still another step is to expand our views of school literacy to include a critical reading of the world and the word, in the sense intended by Paulo Freire (1985), a Brazilian educator noted for his work in using education and literacy to help members of subordinate or oppressed groups to achieve freedom. Freire proposes that reading involves a constant movement between the reading of words and the "reading" of reality. Reading entails a critical perception of the world and the transformation of the world through practical action. This type of literacy is called **critical literacy**. Henry Giroux (1988) and other proponents of critical literacy challenge the view that students' acquisition of literacy in school is simply the process of mastering the technical skills of literacy and of learning the mainstream academic knowledge represented in works such as the "great books." Developing a critical literacy in schools is a way of helping students understand the nature of inequalities in society, how some groups are privileged over others, and to empower students to work toward positive changes in their own lives and in society.

Critical literacy requires not just that teachers accept students' experiences but that they help students of diverse backgrounds understand their own experiences, as well as the experiences of others, in terms of the dynamics of the larger society. According to Giroux (1987):

> At issue here is understanding that student experience has to be understood as part of an interlocking web of power relations in which some groups of students are often privileged over others. But if we are to view this insight in an important way, we must understand that it is imperative for teachers to critically examine the cultural backgrounds and social formations out of which their students produce the categories they use to give meaning to the world. For teachers are not merely dealing with students who have individual interests, they are dealing primarily with individuals whose stories, memories, narratives, and readings of the world are inextricably related to wider social and cultural formations and categories. The issue here is not merely one of relevance but one of power. (p. 177)

Redefining school literacy should involve all of the steps described above, to the degree that the teacher feels ready and able to attempt them. Each of these steps takes us forward toward new patterns and away from old patterns that have often blocked the school literacy success of students from diverse backgrounds.

Summary

An expanded definition of literacy goes beyond skills to include people's willingness to use literacy, the connections between reading and writing, the dynamic process of constructing meaning (including the role of cultural schemata), and the importance of printed text. Social context is a particularly important concept for teachers to consider, both in terms of understanding literacy and of understanding how typical school literacy lessons might need to be adjusted to be more beneficial for students of diverse backgrounds. Patterns of literacy use and beliefs about literacy may differ from community to community, as shown in the examples of

Trackton and Roadville. Literacy practices are very much a part of culture. For the benefit of students of diverse backgrounds, school literacy should be redefined to highlight the study of multicultural literature, instructional practices that involve an active process of meaning-making, writing instruction that makes students' background experiences central, culturally responsive instruction, and the development of critical literacy.

Application Activities

1. What are some of the major ways you and your family and friends use reading and writing in everyday life? To answer this question, keep notes for a week on your own literacy activities, as well as the literacy activities of your family and friends.

2. Reflect on the views of reading and writing communicated to you through your own school experiences. Assess the impressions you were given about reading and writing in terms of the expanded definition of literacy presented in this chapter.

Suggested Readings

Freire, P. (1985). "Reading the World and Reading the Word: An Interview with Paulo Freire." *Language Arts*, 62(1), pp. 15-21.
Gilmore, P. (1984). "Research Currents: Assessing Sub-Rosa Skills in Children's Language." *Language Arts*, 61(4), pp. 384-91.
Heath, S.B. (1980). "The Functions and Uses of Literacy." *Journal of Communication*, Winter, pp. 123-33.

chapter 3

Instruction: Advantages of Constructivist Models

1. Discuss research on children's literacy learning and explore a definition of instruction based on this research;

2. Compare and contrast constructivist and transmission models of instruction;

3. Highlight possible advantages of constructivist models of instruction in the school literacy learning of students of diverse backgrounds

4. Explore the need to adapt constructivist models to the needs of students of diverse backgrounds.

The Nature of Literacy Learning

This chapter examines new models of instruction that appear effective in promoting the school literacy learning of students of diverse backgrounds. One of the assumptions in these models of instruction is that literacy learning begins in the home, not the school, and that instruction should build on the foundation for literacy learning established in the home.

Research suggests that knowledge of the functions of literacy, such as the use of literacy to maintain social relationships, precedes knowledge of the forms of literacy, such as the names of letters of the alphabet (Taylor, 1983). Even before they enter preschool or kindergarten, children have experiences with literacy that can serve as the basis for further growth in reading and writing. For example, three- and four-year-olds often draw pictures and scribble messages, showing early signs of writing. They also interact with books and magazines, showing early signs of reading.

Emergent literacy is the term generally used to refer to the early signs of reading and writing shown by young children, before they begin to read and write in ways recognized by most adults (Teale, 1987). Use of the adjectives *emergent* or *emerging* reminds us that children are always in the process of becoming literate, probably from the time they are just a few months old.

Several in-depth studies have looked at the home literacy events experienced by children of diverse backgrounds, particularly before they enter school. One of these studies, Heath's (1983) research with working-class African American and European American families, was discussed in chapter 2.

Anderson, Teale, and Estrada (1980) conducted research involving low-income African, European, and Hispanic American families in the San Diego area. The results revealed nine different types of literacy events (Teale, 1986): daily living activities, entertainment, school-related activities, work, religion, interpersonal communication, participating in information networks, storybook time, and literacy for the sake of teaching/ learning literacy. On the whole, these events were highly social in nature, involving considerable use of talk and relatively little direct reference to the printed text. Most literacy events served a particular purpose, such as paying bills, being entertained, or transmitting information, and did not involve the use of literacy for its own sake. The young children in these families witnessed these events but became physically involved with the text only during school-related and storybook events.

Taylor and Dorsey-Gaines (1988) conducted an in-depth study of four African American families in an inner-city neighborhood they called Shay Avenue. Children in each family were perceived by their parents to be successfully learning to read and write. Adults in the Shay Avenue families used literacy in many different ways. For example, Jerry discussed his favorite poems and shared lists of the books he had read and intended to buy. Ieshea received and replied to letters from family and friends almost every day, and saved poems and articles she clipped from the newspaper. All families made extensive use of literacy in their dealings with public agencies, reading and filling in forms and providing documentation. The researchers' observations left no doubt that the children in these families were growing up in literate homes.

> Families, regardless of ethnicity and socioeconomic background, include young children in a range of literacy events.

In a review of these and other studies of home literacy, Sulzby (1991) concludes that all families, regardless of ethnicity and socioeconomic background, include young children in a range of literacy events. Participation in family life gives all students knowledge of some of the functions, or purposes, served by literacy. Home literacy events serve a variety of social functions and seldom center on literacy for the sake of learning literacy. The specific uses of literacy may vary from family to family and from community to community, but the evidence suggests that young children from diverse backgrounds receive ample exposure to literacy in their homes.

The idea that young children's literacy is emergent and has its roots in family life has important implications for literacy instruction in multicultural classrooms. The concept of emergent literacy suggests that all children come to school with certain experiences and interests in literacy, and that as teachers, we should seek to recognize and to build upon these experiences and interests. The concept of emergent literacy reminds us that literacy begins in the home, not the school, and that school literacy instruction should seek to make connections to the lives children have beyond the walls of the classroom.

Successive Approximation

The notions of successive approximation, meaningfulness, and supportiveness are especially important in the school literacy learning of students of diverse backgrounds. As discussed in chapters 6 and 7, students of diverse backgrounds often have home experiences that differ significantly from school expectations for literacy. This is why the teacher plays such a critical role in bridging the gap between home and school and in promoting students' literacy development.

In the home, young children appear to grow into literacy in much the same way as they learn to speak, without formal instruction (Teale, 1987). Children learn to speak by engaging in meaningful acts of communication with those around them, and by constructing their own ideas about the principles of language (Wells, 1986). Evidence that children construct their own ideas about language, rather than merely imitating the speech of adults, is shown in their use of "goed," "foots," and other forms that adults do not use. In many of these instances children are showing a good understanding of the regularity in the English language, such as use of the *-ed* ending to mark the past tense.

The process of learning to speak has been described as one of **successive approximation**, in which children engage in the full process of speaking and gradually refine their efforts (Holdaway, 1979). When babies are learning to speak, adults do not criticize them for failing to pronounce words such as *bottle* or *flower* correctly. Rather, when the baby says, "Ba-ba," the parent is likely to say something like, "Bottle, does baby want her bottle?"

Holdaway (1979) and others have argued that the process of learning to read and write should be viewed like the process of learning to speak. When children are learning to read and write, they should engage in the full processes of reading and writing during meaningful acts of communication. Their efforts to read and write should be seen as acts of successive approximation, in which they are gradually moving from emergent literacy toward conventional literacy, and then toward increasingly sophisticated understandings. Children are not belittled for making errors, although, when it is appropriate, they should be taught the skills to advance beyond those errors.

It is important for teachers in multicultural classrooms to remember that, for *all* students, including those of diverse backgrounds, literacy learning is a process of **successive approximation**. Sometimes teachers assume that becoming literate through a process of successive approxima-tion is a luxury to be allowed only those students for whom they have high expectations. Often, these are students from mainstream backgrounds. Teachers give these students the benefit of the doubt, for example, by waiting longer for them to correct a reading error or to answer questions (Allington, 1983). When working with students for whom they have low expectations (often, students from diverse backgrounds), teachers are likely to intervene quickly with the correct response, without giving students the chance to come up with answers on their own. Or teachers may teach a scripted skill lesson rather than giving students the opportunity to do their own reasoning. In essence, when they do not guide students to think through ideas on their own, teachers unwittingly deny students the chance to expand their understandings about literacy.

Teachers must be aware that all students, including those of diverse backgrounds, are learning to read and write through a process of succes-sive approximation. All students, especially those of diverse backgrounds, should be given ample opportunity to construct their own understandings of reading and writing. Students of diverse backgrounds will not develop high levels of literacy if instruction is based on rote memorization or drill on skills in isolation.

Meaningfulness and Functions of Literacy

Meaningfulness indicates that the starting point for literacy learning lies in knowledge of the functions of literacy, not in the forms of literacy or specific skills. In school, students of diverse backgrounds need from the beginning to be involved in meaningful, motivating communication experi-ences, such as the reading of storybooks and the writing of messages to their families and classmates. Through these experiences they will become familiar with school functions of literacy. Once school functions of literacy have become meaningful to them, and with the teacher's guidance, stu-dents will be able to master the forms of literacy (such as spelling and word reading strategies) associated with various tasks.

Supportiveness

The notion of **supportiveness** means that teachers need to strike a delicate balance between stepping back and giving students the space to construct their own understandings of reading and writing, and stepping in with the support they need for further growth in literacy. You saw above how the adult rephrased and expanded upon the baby's request for the bottle. Similarly, the teacher needs to be aware of providing support for the student's future development as a reader and writer.

In the following example, you see a teacher striking the proper balance between respecting the progress the child has made and providing the honest feedback needed to encourage growth. This writing conference was conducted by Dawn Harris Martine in her second grade classroom in Harlem, New York City (Center for the Study of Reading, 1990). Damien, the student in the conference, was a quiet student who had spent much of the first half of the year drawing, rather than writing down his ideas. When Damien drafted this story, Martine was delighted.

Damien:	(reading aloud from his draft) Once there lived three sheep. They lived in a barn. They kept on asking for food and the farmer sent them away. Then they saw some straw on the floor. Then — then one of the pigs made a house. A wolf came and said open up this — it is me. Me who? said the pig.

Martine realized that Damien had borrowed his story line from the tale of the three little pigs, but that was fine with her. She also noticed that the characters in the story switched from sheep to pigs. Here is what she said when Damien had finished reading his draft aloud.

Teacher:	All right. You know what this reminds me of?
Damien:	What?
Teacher:	This kind of reminds me of the — the three pigs. It's kind of like the three pigs story, right?
Damien:	Yeah.
Teacher:	And like what happened was it even reminded *you* of the three pigs story because you started off with sheep. You said the sheep kept asking the farmer for food and he sent them away. And then all of a sudden the sheep became pigs. (Martine continues enthusiastically.) So were they pigs because they kept eating all the food? They were like piggies? (She changes to a conspiratorial tone.) It's okay, you know, to write a story like a story you heard before. Lots of authors do that and they just change the names and everything else, so that's fine.

Martine made up a plausible reason for the shift from sheep to pigs and assured Damien that his story was perfectly acceptable. Later, to conclude the conference she asked him to decide whether he wanted his characters to be sheep or pigs, and helped him follow through with his choice. In short, she skillfully provided both reassurance and instruction to further Damien's growth as a writer.

> Teachers need to strike a delicate balance between stepping back and giving students the space to construct their own understandings, and stepping in with the support they need for further growth in literacy.

Instruction and Constructivist Models

The definition of instruction to be used in this book draws upon research on the nature of literacy and literacy learning and the ideas of Vygotsky. **Instruction** is defined as:

> helping the student to become interested and involved in a meaningful activity, then providing the student with the support needed to complete the activity successfully.

This definition of instruction grows out of a school of thought known as **social constructivism**. Models of literacy instruction consistent with this definition are known as **constructivist, process,** or **transactional** models. The whole language philosophy (for example, Weaver, 1990) is an educational application of social constructivist thought that has become particularly influential in schools. The roots of social constructivism and of constructivist models of instruction may be traced to frameworks in a range of fields, including philosophy, linguistics, and the history of science (Applebee, 1991).

At the heart of constructivist models of instruction is the notion that learners must actively construct their own understandings. The constructivist model may be contrasted with transmission models of instruction, which assume that skills and knowledge can somehow be transmitted or passively absorbed (Weaver, 1990), as discussed further later in this chapter.

Within the constructivist perspective, the work of Vygotsky (1978, 1981) has special significance to our discussion of literacy instruction. Vygotsky asserted that learning is basically a social process that takes place through the interactions between children and others in their environment. Gradually, the child internalizes the skills and knowledge acquired through these social interactions. Vygotsky (1981) stated that

> any function in the child's cultural development appears twice, or in two planes. First, it appears in the social plane, and then on the psychological plane. First, it appears between people, as an interpsychological category, and then within the child as an intrapsychological category.   (p. 163)

For instance, in the area of language, children learn to express themselves by engaging in interactions with adults or more capable peers. Adults or peers provide the support children need to communicate.

In a multicultural kindergarten classroom in which I was observing, the teacher began the day with a writers' workshop. Ronald, one of the students, always did drawings showing events involving his family and friends. Although some of the other students used invented spelling along with their drawings, Ronald relied on drawings alone to communicate his message. One day when it was Ronald's turn to share, the teacher helped him to tell the class the story behind his drawing:

Ronald: My brother (inaudible) the eel.

Teacher: Tell us about the eel. What is the eel doing?

Ronald:	My friend caught the eel.
Teacher:	Good, Ronald, what else?
Ronald:	I ran away.
Teacher:	Why did you run away?
Ronald:	I was scared.
Teacher:	Of what?
Ronald:	The eel.
Teacher:	You ran away because you were scared of the eel. And when you ran away where did you go?
Ronald:	Home.
Teacher:	You went home.
Ronald:	I went home.

In this example the teacher and other students were genuinely interested in hearing Ronald's story. But when Ronald hesitated to say much, the teacher asked questions to elicit further information. As Ronald's story unfolded, the teacher pieced his phrases together ("You ran away because you were scared of the eel") to model the kind of language he might use to tell his story. By collaborating with the teacher, Ronald was able to share an exciting story with the class. As the year went on, with the assistance of the teacher and other students, Ronald began to use invented spelling to label his drawings. At first, he wrote just a letter for the initial sound in a word, such as *B* for *brother*. By the end of the year he was able to compose sentences using invented spelling.

The kind of help provided by the teacher in the example above is referred to as **scaffolding** (Cazden, 1988), which is help provided while the child is engaged in a meaningful task. The child does everything he can, and the adult provides the assistance needed so that the child can complete the task successfully. In this example, the teacher gave Ronald the help he needed to tell the story behind his drawing. In other interactions she also encouraged him to make the connection between sounds and letters.

Vygotsky suggested that a child learns through interactions that take place in the **zone of proximal development**. He defined the zone of proximal development as

> the distance between the actual developmental level as determined by independent problem solving and the level of potential development as determined through problem solving under adult guidance or in collaboration with more capable peers. (Vygotsky, 1978, p. 76)

In other words, there are certain parts of the task the child can do independently, for example, when telling a story to classmates. There are other parts of the task that the child can attempt with adult guidance. Those parts of the task that the child can manage only with adult guidance are said to be in the zone of proximal development, or in the area most likely to be affected by instruction. Beyond the zone of proximal development there may be parts of the task that the child cannot yet manage at all, even with adult assistance. In short, the zone of proximal development defines the area in which instruction can be of greatest benefit to the child.

The idea of the zone of proximal development suggests that adult guidance or scaffolding should be both temporary and adjustable. That is, the adult should provide just the degree of assistance the child needs, but no more, so that the child assumes as much responsibility for the task as possible. In this example, the teacher provided Ronald with quite a bit of prompting, but as the school year progressed Ronald was able to tell his stories with less and less help. The process by which the child does more and more, and the adult less and less, is called the **gradual release of responsibility** (Pearson and Gallagher, 1983). The teacher gives students the help they need to complete a task successfully and, over time, gradually releases responsibility to students, by decreasing the amount of help provided.

Applying the Definition to Literacy Instruction

Now that you understand some of the thinking behind the definition of instruction, let's see how this definition applies to the specific case of literacy instruction. Constructivist models of instruction assume that students will learn literacy by engaging in the full processes of reading and writing, in a purposeful, largely self-directed manner. This is consistent with research in the home and community, cited earlier in this chapter, which shows that adults use literacy in a variety of ways as part of carrying out their everyday lives, and that there is little literacy only for the sake of literacy.

Through involvement in the full processes of literacy, and with the assistance of teachers, students gradually construct their own understandings of the hows and whys of reading and writing. In this sense, they learn to read by reading and to write by writing. While students' growth may follow broad developmental trends (for example, Clay, 1975), constructivist models do not rely on the teaching of specific skills in a set sequence.

In constructivist models, teaching proceeds from the whole to the part. In the terms of the whole language philosophy, language and literacy are kept whole or treated as full processes, rather than dissected into skills (Goodman, 1986). For example, in the process approach to writing, children begin by drawing or writing on topics of their own choosing. They are encouraged to use invented spellings when first putting their thoughts down on paper (for example, a kindergarten student may write *GM* for *grandma*). After a student has produced a draft, the teacher and peers assist him in making revisions, and then in editing and publishing his piece as a little book. Spelling, capitalization, punctuation, and other skills are taught as part of editing.

In other words, constructivist models include instruction in specific skills, but skills are not taught for their own sake. Rather, skills are taught at the point when they are likely to be useful to the child, as part of an authentic literacy task. In the example above, conventional spelling is taught when the child is editing the text of a book to be shared with his classmates and family.

> In constructivist models, teaching proceeds from the whole to the part.

Constructivist models of literacy instruction generally include discussions of literature, either in small, teacher-led groups or in literature circles (Harste, Short, and Burke, 1988). While teachers generally help students to begin the group's meetings and may continue to influence the course of discussion, students are encouraged to share their own responses to the literature. Students often keep response journals in which they write about their reactions to the story. Finally, students may decide upon a project to share their reading with classmates, for example, creating a large book poster or acting out a scene from the story.

Transmission Models

Constructivist models of instruction can perhaps be better understood in contrast to transmission models. These models are also called **skills** or **mastery models** of instruction (Farrell, 1991) and are based largely on the theories of Carroll (1963) and Bloom (1976).

In transmission models the complex tasks of reading and writing are broken down into what are judged to be their component skills. It is believed that students will become proficient readers and writers if they master these component skills. Typically, students are given lessons on these skills in a set, seemingly logical order.

The processes of reading and writing are transmitted to students through instruction in individual skills. In other words, teaching proceeds from the part to the whole. In reading, skills begin with letter discrimination and move on to letter names, letter sounds, sight words, and then sentences made up of combinations of known words. In writing, students might begin by learning to print letters of the alphabet, spell short words, and compose sentences containing a target word. Reading instruction, in particular, tends to center on the use of workbooks and worksheets filled with multiple-choice or short-answer skill exercises.

Advantages of Constructivist Models

Teachers who use constructivist models of literacy instruction are able to overcome many of the weaknesses seen in transmission models, particularly as they affect the learning of students of diverse backgrounds. A first advantage is that constructivist models recognize that literacy is always embedded in particular social contexts. As discussed earlier, literacy is not carried out in the abstract but is part of the social world of individuals, families, and communities. It follows that literacy instruction should not be viewed as a matter of teaching skills in the abstract, but rather as a matter of engaging students in meaningful reading and writing activities. This view is consistent with the definition of instruction, which highlights the importance of students' interest and involvement in meaningful activities.

In contrast, transmission models of instruction ignore the fact that literacy is always embedded in particular social contexts. Wong Fillmore (1986) found the absence of a meaningful context for classroom literacy activities to be especially damaging to the language progress of Hispanic second-language learners. Also, transmission models of instruction aim to teach skills such as "central theme" in the abstract, without regard for the social context. Yet different themes for a story may be inferred, depending on the nature of the text, the individual reader or community of readers, and the social situation (Au, 1992). Other skills may vary in a similar fashion.

A second advantage of constructivist models is that they encourage students to explore the functions of literacy. With students of diverse backgrounds, there may be differences between the typical uses of literacy in school and at home. Students can benefit from the opportunity to learn about school functions of literacy, and to come to an understanding of the varied uses of literacy.

One example of an authentic school literacy context is seen in the use of dialogue journals. Lindfors (1989) recommends the use of dialogue journals in classrooms with students who are learning English as a second language (dialogue journals will be discussed in more detail in chapter 10). Lindfors found that students could use dialogue journals to explore many different functions of writing, including the use of writing to teach, to inquire, to joke, to inform, and to compliment.

As students explore the functions of literacy, such as through dialogue journals, the teacher provides them with support aimed at improving their abilities. In the case of dialogue journals, the teacher responds in writing to the students. As the dialogue progresses, the teacher does not correct the students' writing but models conventional forms in her own written responses. Gradually, through engagement in this meaningful process of communication, students' writing moves closer and closer to conventional forms. Of course, students' progress may be speeded if the teacher makes note of the writing skills likely to be useful to students, provides explicit instruction in these skills, and helps students to apply them (Reyes, 1991).

Transmission models of literacy instruction, in contrast, do not deal with the functions or purposes people have for using literacy. Instead, transmission models center on teaching the forms or skills involved, such as letter sounds, and place little or no emphasis on the various functions of literacy, such as reading for enjoyment.

When using transmission models of instruction, teachers frequently fail to make certain that students understand the underlying functions of literacy, and the relationship of skills to these functions. Without an understanding of the functions of literacy, students of diverse backgrounds may conclude that reading and writing in school are merely routines to be carried out for the purpose of advancing to the next grade. They may also come to define reading and writing in terms of the low-level skill activities that take up the majority of the language arts period (Allington, 1983).

This negative situation is well-illustrated in the following interview, conducted with a second grade student in a school with a highly structured skills-oriented curriculum.

Teacher: What is reading?

Student: It's like when you, when the teacher ask you questions and you have to answer them back and when you have to read sometimes, read directions and stuff, and sometimes it be like a group and they read and stuff, and like that.

Teacher: Okay. What do people do when they read?

Student: They read the story and sometime it be questions they have to answer.

Teacher: Okay. Why do we read?

Student: Why do we read?

Teacher: Um-hmm.

Student: It's part of a minimal skill so we can get to third grade.

Teacher: Any other reasons?

Student: Not that I know of.

Teacher: When you're at home, you told me [before] that when you're at home you like to read. You're not reading for minimal skills at home.

Student: I read to get to third grade and stuff.

(Weaver, 1990, p. 32)

As this interview suggests, there is often a wide gap between the purposeful reading and writing children experience outside of school, and the dull and seemingly pointless routines typically associated with transmission models of literacy instruction. All too often, school experiences in transmission models of instruction narrow rather than broaden students' literacy horizons (Taylor, 1983).

A third advantage of constructivist models is that they are student-centered rather than skills-driven, and so can take account of the fact that students may pursue literacy through highly individual paths. Research by Graves (1983) and others, for instance, shows that children follow strikingly different paths in learning to write. Constructivist models allow us to recognize that students may differ in terms of their home literacy experiences, language backgrounds, cultural schemata, and personal interests as readers and writers. All of these factors may influence the course of students' literacy development.

Yet the assumption in transmission models of instruction is that all students will learn to read and write in the same manner, by mastering skills in the same set sequence. Many different paths to literacy may be followed by children from diverse backgrounds, as well as children from mainstream backgrounds, and transmission models generally do not have a place for either individual or group differences in preferred paths to literacy.

In constructivist models, students' sense of their own directions as literacy learners can be acknowledged and fostered. Students can be given the opportunity to set their own goals for literacy learning and to determine the literacy activities they would like to carry out. For example, a fifth grade boy in a multicultural classroom wrote that he would like to use more interesting words in his writing and to read a wider variety of books at home. In following through on his self-determined goals, he revised a piece he was writing to include new vocabulary terms and he began to read some science fiction.

Teachers should certainly take the initiative to design activities to broaden students' horizons, but the process of literacy learning will proceed best if students have a considerable say about classroom activities. Giving students a say is an effective means of making students' needs and interests central to classroom literacy instruction. Students may, for example, choose the particular novel they want to read and discuss. They may decide as a group how they would like to go about sharing their novel with the rest of the class. They may write on self-selected topics during the writers' workshop and decide about the form in which their work will be published.

In a multicultural classroom where a student-centered philosophy prevails, the teacher's challenge is to create literacy settings in which all students can win acceptance and be recognized for their accomplishments, however varied. Another way of putting this idea is to say that the classroom must become a literate community (Cairney and Langbien, 1989; refer also to chapter 5) in which readers and writers support and applaud one another's learning. In such an atmosphere the diversity in students' backgrounds and differing contributions to the literacy resources of the classroom can be seen as a cause for celebration.

A fourth advantage of constructivist models is that they recognize the place of the distinctive life experiences and cultural schemata of students of diverse backgrounds, in the process of constructing meaning from text. While transmission models tend to be focused on products or outcomes, constructivist models emphasize the processes of thinking and meaning-making in which readers and writers engage (Applebee, 1991). Texts and situations are subject to a variety of interpretations, depending on the knowledge and perspective of the reader. Meaning is not thought to reside solely in the text, or solely in the mind of the reader, but in the dynamic interaction or transaction among the reader, the text, and the social context (Gavelek, 1986). In this view, a text may have a conventional or canonical interpretation, but personal, individual responses to literature are seen as the heart of the reading process (Rosenblatt, 1978).

Transmission models leave little room for the differing background knowledge or cultural schemata that students of diverse backgrounds may bring to their reading and writing (as discussed in chapter 1), because it is assumed that literacy is largely a matter of right and wrong answers. For example, a text may be seen to have only one "main idea." Transmission models generally deny students and teachers the opportunity to understand the varying perspectives that may be brought to the interpretation and composing of texts.

Schools' reliance on standardized tests, which are based on the use of multiple-choice items and single "right answers," tends to sustain the use of transmission models of instruction. Most of the items in standardized tests evaluate students' knowledge of specific skills or facts, rather than their knowledge of the full processes of reading and writing. Ascher (1990) writes:

> Inside urban classrooms, without academic resources comparable to schools serving more affluent students, testing has too easily become a way of passing blame for inequality in offerings and resources onto teachers and students. As [they have become more] important, mandated tests have tended to narrow instructional practices to measurement-driven curriculum, or to teaching directly for improvement on test scores. They reinforce the drilling of "basic" skills, in which many urban schools were already over-invested, while ignoring the higher-order skills that enable real learning and that our society presumably needs.   (pp. 22-23)

When standardized test scores are the only measure of students' literacy learning, teachers may feel compelled to turn to transmission models as a seemingly efficient way of teaching students the specific skills covered by the test (Smith, 1991). In these situations, the main goal becomes the raising of test scores, and the literacy learning needs of students of diverse backgrounds over the long term can receive little attention.

To summarize, constructivist models of literacy instruction offer at least four distinct advantages over transmission models, in terms of potential benefits to students of diverse backgrounds. Constructivist models encourage us to embed literacy instruction in meaningful social contexts. They remind us of the importance of allowing students to explore the functions of literacy. They prompt us to look first at students' needs and interests, and then to teach skills as they are needed. Finally, constructivist models call our attention to the place of different life experiences and cultural schemata in the meaning making process.

Differences Between Instructional Models

Constructivist models:

1. Learners actively construct their own understandings.
2. Teaching proceeds from the whole to the part.
3. Literacy is embedded in social contexts.
4. Students are encouraged to explore the functions of literacy.
5. Instruction is student-centered; individual differences are taken into account.
6. Instruction emphasizes the processes of thinking; recognizes the place of students' life experiences and cultural schemata.
7. Instruction allows for cultural diversity.

Transmission models:

1. Skills and knowledge can be transmitted or passively absorbed.
2. Teaching proceeds from the part to the whole.
3. Literacy is taught as skills in the abstract, without regard for social context.
4. Little or no emphasis is placed on the functions of literacy or the relationship of skills to these functions.
5. Instruction is skills-driven; little emphasis is given to individual or group differences.
6. Instruction focuses on product; little recognition given to students' life experiences and cultural schemata.
7. Instruction may reflect the values of the mainstream, to the exclusion of other cultures.

Skill Instruction within Constructivist Models

A question that frequently arises about constructivist models concerns the instruction of specific skills. While they are student-centered rather than skills-driven, constructivist models and the whole language philosophy certainly recognize a place for the teaching or highlighting of specific skills (Weaver, 1990). For example, in reading students may be taught about letter sounds, the sequence of events in a story, and the difference between a main idea and supporting details. In writing they may be taught spelling patterns, punctuation, and how to write an interesting lead.

In constructivist models, however, a particular skill is taught in the context of meaningful reading and writing activities and only when it appears that students do not already know how to use the skill and will find it useful. Here is an example taken from a first grade classroom. Malia was writing a story about her new baby sister using the invented spelling *SASR* for *sister*. The teacher added the word *sister* to a sheet of paper labeled "My New Words," which Malia kept in her writing folder, and reminded her to look at this sheet to see how *sister* was spelled. For a time Malia referred to this sheet to check her spelling of *sister*, and after a week or so she knew the conventional spelling.

A second example is taken from a fourth grade teacher's experiences with her students in the guided discussion of a story. The story opened with a flashback, and students became confused about the sequence of events in the story. The teacher taught the students about flashbacks by helping them construct a timeline showing the sequence of events in the story, including those covered in the flashback.

Both of these examples illustrate the point that, in constructivist models of literacy instruction, skills are taught in relationship to students' needs and interests. Skills are not taught in the abstract, or in isolation, apart from situations in which students can come to understand their usefulness.

Teachers in multicultural classrooms who have moved from transmission to constructivist models generally find that, in comparison to previous classes, their students become better at applying word identification and other skills. Students' ability to apply skills is enhanced even though teachers report spending less time on skill instruction than they did when following transmission models (Bird, 1989; Routman, 1991). Skill instruction thus takes less time but appears to be more effective, because skills are being taught in contexts meaningful to students.

Transmission Models and Students of Diverse Backgrounds

In their emphasis on a set path for literacy learning and single "correct" answers, transmission models are likely to reflect only the values, ideas, and experiences of the mainstream. Because of this bias, transmission models of instruction tend to exclude the values, ideas, and experiences of students from diverse backgrounds. In this sense, transmission models may be criticized for imposing dominant group norms on subordinate group students, or for tending to fit better with the literacy learning needs and expectations of students from mainstream backgrounds, than with those of students from diverse backgrounds.

With a heavy emphasis on skills, usually taught apart from attention to the functions of literacy, transmission models frequently lead to students spending up to 70 percent of reading instructional time completing skill sheets (Anderson, Hiebert, Scott, and Wilkinson, 1985). As a result, students may become bored and disenchanted with reading instruction.

However, despite their boredom, students from mainstream backgrounds, in comparison to students from diverse backgrounds, are more likely to persist with skill activities, to cooperate with teachers, and to remain in school. The reason, according to D'Amato (1987), is that students from mainstream backgrounds usually have a good understanding of the structural relationships between doing well in school and success in later life. They gain this understanding from experiences in their families, where they can infer, for example, that graduating from high school and then from college usually enables a person to get a good job.

Students from diverse backgrounds, on the other hand, may not be familiar with these structural relationships. Since they may have less awareness of how schooling may affect their life prospects, these students may see little or no reason to remain in school. The tendency to leave school, or to be less cooperative or to make less of an effort, is strengthened if students' school experiences are boring and negative.

D'Amato argues that teachers must try to make school experiences meaningful, interesting, and rewarding for students of diverse backgrounds, so that students will continue to be motivated to do well in school. School learning must be made immediately meaningful and rewarding to students, because of the lower likelihood that students' motivation to do well in school will be sustained by their knowledge of long-term structural relationships. Meaning and interest are central to constructivist models of literacy instruction, but not to transmission models.

In addition to improving students' motivation, constructivist models may also improve students' achievement. Certainly, the widespread use of transmission models of instruction has not led students of diverse backgrounds to levels of literacy achievement comparable to those attained by students of mainstream backgrounds, as seen, for example, in results of the National Assessment of Educational Progress, reported in chapter 1. Furthermore, it can be argued that use of transmission models is potentially harmful to all students, including those of mainstream backgrounds, since the majority of high school students nationwide do not develop the ability to read and interpret complex texts in a thoughtful manner (Weaver, 1990).

An alternate point of view, advocating the use of transmission models with students of diverse backgrounds, is presented by Gersten and his colleagues (Gersten and Woodward, 1985; Gersten and Keating, 1987), among others. These authors advocate the direct instruction of specific skills through use of programs such as DISTAR, a highly structured and scripted approach.

The point of view taken in this book is that there is definitely a place for instruction in specific skills. However, because literacy is much more than specific skills, as suggested in chapters 1 and 2, it is inappropriate to place instruction of specific skills over and above instruction that leads students to an understanding of the functions and uses of literacy in school and in their own lives. The broad scope of literacy instruction will be explored further in chapter 4. Furthermore, it has been suggested that instruction in specific skills will be most beneficial to students if it takes place in the context of real reading and writing, which motivates students to see the value of specific skills.

Issues of Diversity

As discussed above, constructivist models of instruction have many strengths when used in multicultural settings. In fact, teachers in many multicultural classrooms have experienced success with constructivist models and with the whole language philosophy (for example, Bird, 1989). However, to date very little of the research and writing about constructivist, process models, and the whole language philosophy has directly addressed issues of diversity and power relationships.

Lisa Delpit's work (1986, 1988) is a rare exception. In Delpit's analysis, conventions of literacy, such as the written grammar of standard English, are part of mainstream American culture, or what she terms the "culture of power." The rules or codes of the culture of power are acquired by students from mainstream backgrounds through interactions with their families. These same codes often are not acquired by students of diverse backgrounds because their families are usually outside the culture of power. As a result, students of diverse backgrounds come to school with knowledge of the codes of cultures other than the culture of power.

If students of diverse backgrounds are to have access to opportunities in mainstream society, schools must acquaint them with the rules and codes of the culture of power, such as the grammar of standard English. Teachers may need to make some rules explicit to students. Delpit compares the situation to the problems faced by anyone entering a culture with which he or she is unfamiliar. She writes:

> When I lived in several Papua New Guinea villages for extended periods to collect data, and when I go to Alaskan villages for work with Alaskan Native communities, I have found it unquestionably easier — psychologically and pragmatically — when some kind soul has directly informed me about such matters as appropriate dress, interactional styles, embedded meanings, and taboo words or actions. I contend that it is much the same for anyone seeking to learn the rules of the culture of power. Unless one has the leisure of a lifetime of "immersion" to learn them, explicit presentation makes learning immeasurably easier. (Delpit, 1988, p. 283)

In constructivist or process models of instruction, Delpit notes, teachers must be aware of the possible need to provide explicit instruction in skills to students from diverse backgrounds. She hypothesizes that some teachers who adhere to constructivist models of instruction may be reluctant to provide students with explicit skill instruction because they do not want to appear authoritarian. However, Delpit warns, not making skills and requirements explicit to students of diverse backgrounds may put them at a serious disadvantage. She states:

> Although the problem is not necessarily inherent in the method, in some instances adherents of process approaches to writing create situations in which students ultimately find themselves held accountable for knowing a set of rules *about which no one has ever directly informed them.* (p. 287; italics added)

Delpit describes how students of diverse backgrounds may feel cheated because they believe that knowledge has deliberately been withheld from them. She implies that, in some instances, the absence of explicit instruction may be viewed as one means by which the dominant culture seeks to place subordinate-group students at a disadvantage.

> Not making skills and requirements explicit to students of diverse backgrounds may put them at a disadvantage.

Delpit makes it clear that students' literacy learning will *not* be improved by the direct instruction of skills in isolation, drill-and-practice activities, and a return to transmission models of instruction. Rather, skill instruction appears to be most effective when it takes the form of mini-lessons taught in the context of meaningful activities, as Siddle (1988, quoted in Delpit, 1988) found in research in a writing class for African American students. This study also suggests that skills improve when students have the opportunity to interact with the teacher, for example, in student-centered writing conferences.

Although Delpit sees a great deal of value in process approaches, she points out that the product of students' literacy efforts is important as well.

> Teachers do students no service to suggest, even implicitly, that "product" is not important. In this country, students will be judged on their product regardless of the process they utilized to achieve it.   (p. 287)

In other words, students should have the skills to make their published writing, oral reports, and other products acceptable when judged by the standards of the culture of power.

Delpit's analysis is related to the idea mentioned in chapter 1, that the goals of literacy instruction should be the same for all students, those of diverse and mainstream backgrounds alike. However, the means by which teachers help students achieve these goals may well be different, a point to be discussed in chapters 6 through 9, on cultural and language issues.

Also, it is not a question of replacing the codes of students' home cultures with the codes of the culture of power. Rather, it is a matter of taking an additive stance (Cummins, 1986), of broadening students' repertoire so they are able to function effectively in mainstream settings, as well as in their homes and communities. This view is consistent with Trueba's position, presented in chapter 1, that individuals can be successful both in their relationships to the mainstream and in their relationships to their own ethnic community.

Reyes (1991) sounds another note of caution about constructivist approaches and the application of the whole language philosophy. She criticizes whole language on the grounds that it may result in a "one size fits all" approach to literacy instruction. She warns that we need to avoid the assumption that all students will become literate through the same set of instructional activities, structured in the same way for all. In a study of Hispanic, bilingual sixth grade students, Reyes examined the use of dialogue journals and literature logs (logs in which students wrote about the books they were reading). Reyes found that while students engaged in meaningful communication with the teacher in their dialogue journals, they did not make rapid progress in mastering the conventions of writing. In their literature logs, students tended to write simple summaries in just one or two sentences and did not elaborate upon their thoughts or feelings about the book.

Reyes attributes students' lack of progress to several factors. One factor is schools' tendency to emphasize academic instruction in English, without adapting to the needs of bilingual students. This tendency makes it difficult for students to use strengths in their home language as the basis for developing literacy in school.

Another factor identified by Reyes is the lack of explicit teacher assistance to students, a point also highlighted in Delpit's work. Reyes gives the following example:

> The Hispanic second-language learners in this case study sought the teacher's help in selecting books, but Mrs. Sands chose not to impose her "expertise"; instead she exhorted students to keep trying to find books to their liking. A mere invitation to keep looking for an appropriate book without explicit assistance led to some students' failure to complete the task. The teacher was left with the impression that the students lacked motivation to learn. The assumption that all students flourish in classrooms where there is ample freedom to choose activities and where the teacher's role is that of facilitator raises some doubts relative to these second-language learners.   (p. 166)

The observations made by Reyes remind us that constructivist models and the whole language philosophy are not a ready-made solution to the literacy instruction of students of diverse backgrounds. We must be aware that assumptions about classroom literacy activities appropriate in the case of many students from mainstream backgrounds are not necessarily appropriate in the case of many students from diverse backgrounds. Activities may need to be structured differently, or different types of teacher support may be required, to meet students' needs in literacy learning.

In general, constructivist models of instruction can be used to great advantage in multicultural settings. Yet the concerns raised by Delpit and Reyes remind us that teachers need to be observant and tuned in to the needs of their students, if these models of instruction are to be applied to good effect.

Summary

Children can learn to read and write in much the same way that they learn to speak, if they are involved in the full processes of literacy through meaningful, authentic activities. Constructivist models of instruction are more likely to provide children with this opportunity than are transmission models. Constructivist models of literacy instruction assume that students must first become interested and involved in an activity. Then support must be available, from the teacher or peers, so that the student can complete the task successfully. In contrast to transmission models, constructivist models recognize the diversity in students' background knowledge and the different paths they may take to becoming literate. However, criticisms of constructivist models by scholars of color suggest that these models are not ready-made solutions to the literacy learning of students of diverse backgrounds but still require the use of considerable teacher judgment.

Application Activities

1. Make notes while observing a literacy lesson in an elementary or high school classroom. Analyze this lesson in terms of the definition of instruction proposed in this chapter.

2. Reflect on your own experiences with learning to read and write in school. Did you experience constructivist or transmission models of instruction? In retrospect, can you think of any steps your teachers could have taken to make instruction more effective and meaningful for you?

Suggested Readings

Delpit, L.D. (1988). "The Silenced Dialogue: Power and Pedagogy in Educating Other People's Children." *Harvard Educational Review*, 58, pp. 280-98.

Gavelek, J.R. (1986). "The Social Contexts of Literacy and Schooling: A Developmental Perspective." In T.E. Raphael, ed., *The Contexts of School-Based Literacy*. New York: Random House, pp. 3-26.

Goodman, K. (1986). *What's Whole in Whole Language?* Portsmouth, NH: Heinemann.

Weaver, C. (1990). *Understanding Whole Language: Principles and Practices.* Portsmouth, NH: Heinemann.

chapter 4

The Literacy Curriculum: Students' Goals and the Teacher's Philosophy

―――――――――― CHAPTER PURPOSES ――――――――――

1. Describe how teachers can establish a dialogue to discover the literacy goals students have for themselves;
2. Show how the use of student portfolios might help students set their own goals, and teachers to assist students in achieving their goals;
3. Discuss how a classroom literacy curriculum might look from a constructivist perspective;
4. Explain why ownership of literacy is an especially important consideration in literacy curricula for students of diverse backgrounds;
5. Make connections among the concepts of ownership, the composite classroom culture, and the classroom as a community of learners.

The previous chapter dealt with the nature of literacy learning and the process of literacy instruction. This chapter zeroes in on the question of what to teach, or to what ends teachers should direct their instructional efforts.

Students' Own Goals

From a constructivist perspective, the teacher's intention is to help students set their own goals for literacy learning and to monitor their own progress in achieving these goals. The idea is that students themselves should ultimately be in charge of their own literacy learning, not the teacher. Thus, in constructivist models of instruction, the starting point for literacy learning should be the students themselves, not the objectives listed in a curriculum guide or scope and sequence chart.

Putting students and their own goals at the heart of the literacy learning process is one of the new patterns that should lead students of diverse backgrounds to higher levels of achievement. This pattern may be contrasted with the old pattern in which goals for learning are set out skill by skill in a scope and sequence chart, and relatively little attention is given to the specific needs and interests of individual students.

This does not mean that teachers cannot have goals for students beyond those students have for themselves, or that all of the goals listed on typical scope and sequence charts are unimportant. Instead, it means that teachers should begin the process of instruction by looking at the goals students have for themselves, giving priority to students rather than to skills.

Finding Out About Students' Goals

This new pattern, of putting students ahead of skills, is illustrated in the teaching of Yvonne Siu-Runyan (1991). While working in a mountain schoolhouse with third through sixth grade students, Siu-Runyan experimented with a number of different techniques for assessing her students' literacy abilities and learning about their preferences and interests. One of the most valuable techniques was talking to students. She asked students the question, "What would you like to learn next to become a better reader or writer?" In the beginning, students responded to this question with vague answers. But Siu-Runyan continued to ask, and after a month students came up with statements such as the following:

> I want to learn how to read inside my head, instead of out loud.   (Ben, fifth grade)
> I want to learn how to put conversation in my stories.   (Ashleigh, fourth grade)
> I want to learn about other words to use in place of said.   (Mike, fifth grade) (p. 114)

To discover what she could do to facilitate her students' literacy learning, Siu-Runyan asked students these questions:

> 1. What kinds of things do I do that help you as a writer?
> 2. What kinds of things do I do that help you as a reader?   (p. 111)

Again, students responded vaguely at first, but their answers became more definite after they realized their teacher was sincere in wanting to know their thoughts.

> I like the way you talk to me to help me when I get stuck.   (Travis, fourth grade)
> I feel good after I talk to you about my story. You tell me what you like and you help me think about what I want to say.   (Geoff, fifth grade)
> I like when you share your writing with us.   (Lucas, fourth grade) (p. 112)

Portfolios as a Process of Reflection

Siu-Runyan had her students keep literacy portfolios to provide an ongoing record of their experiences with reading and writing. Notice that she did not treat portfolios simply as folders used to collect students' work. Rather, portfolios represented a **process** in which students reflected upon their literacy learning. Siu-Runyan asked students to follow these procedures:

1. Select samples of your best writing and arrange them in some way.
2. In preparation for our conferences about your portfolio, think about why you selected the pieces you did, and what you want to say about them. Think about:
   a. What parts of your piece do you really like and why?
   b. What [were you] trying to accomplish in this piece and [do] you think you were successful?
3. Look at all the pieces you selected for your portfolio and think about what you learned about yourself as a reader and writer by putting together your portfolio.
4. Now that you've thought about your development as a reader and writer, what goals do you have for yourself as a reader and writer?   (pp. 124-25)

D.J., one of the boys in the class, was particularly adept at self-evaluation and at setting goals for his own literacy learning. In reviewing his portfolio, D.J. chose a story entitled "The Season" as his best piece of writing. When Siu-Runyan asked what was good about it, D.J. replied:

> I like the descriptive words I used to show what my character is like. I also like how my story flowed.   (p. 126)

D.J. spoke of what he was trying to accomplish in this piece:

> In the whole piece I was trying to bring his [the main character's] attitude from a pretty bad attitude to a good attitude where he would be always trying and listening. I wanted to show that he was basically a good player with a good attitude, but at first he was too cocky to play with the majors.   (pp. 126-27)

When his teacher asked him if he had learned from writing this piece, D.J. replied:

> I learned how to use experiences from my own life and put it into a story. (p. 127)

At one point D.J. discussed an essay he had written entitled "Why I Love Reading and Books."

> I liked it when I wrote this part: "Books are like friends. You start to read one and you want to read more, just like you want to see your friends more." I like it because it tells what I think about books. When I find a book I really like I want to find out how the story ends, but when it ends, I wish it was still going on. And it's kind of like losing a friend. (p. 128)

D.J.'s comments below highlight some of the benefits students might experience through putting together a portfolio.

> I learned from putting together this portfolio that I like to read and write about things I can relate to, things I know about. It is from these things that I can write about and describe best. I like strong words like verbs that build up what you are describing.   (p. 131)

The portfolios kept by D.J. and his classmates included more information about their writing than about their reading. However, Siu-Runyan offers the following suggestions for collecting data about students' reading:

1. Have students keep track of the books, magazines, news articles, and other materials they read, to provide information about their "reading diet."
2. Have students copy phrases and brief quotations they find notable, to indicate what they attend to while reading.
3. Have students write their thoughts about books that make a strong impression on them, to get an idea about how books influence them.

As mentioned earlier, putting student portfolios at the heart of the assessment process is not just a matter of having students collect their work in a folder. Rather, portfolios provide a basis for students to reflect upon the reading and writing they have done and to consider their goals for the future. When students and teachers meet together to go over work in the portfolios, as they did in Siu-Runyan's class, students share their reflections and goals. By setting their own goals and pursuing activities that lead them closer to these goals, students come to take charge of their own literacy learning. To support students in this process, teachers should acquaint students with a variety of literacy goals, model the process of setting and pursuing goals, and offer suggestions and support.

Siu-Runyan and other teachers who follow constructivist models of instruction believe that literacy instruction should be driven by the goals students set for themselves. As the examples above indicate, students' goals may be quite specific and different from the goals we as teachers might expect them to have. Also, students may have definite ideas about how teachers can support them in their literacy learning.

It is especially important for teachers in multicultural classrooms to listen to students' ideas about their own literacy learning because students from diverse backgrounds may have literacy goals influenced by circumstances outside of school which are unfamiliar to teachers. For example, Alma, the student mentioned in chapter 2, read and translated materials from English into Spanish and helped her parents fill in forms. Students like Alma might be interested in learning to work with documents and other materials needed to deal with government and other institutions. Generally, it is only through open-ended discussions with students that teachers have the opportunity to learn about these other possible goals.

Eliciting Students' Perceptions

Students' perceptions of classroom literacy activities may also be revealing. In a multicultural first grade classroom, a teacher with whom I was working had set up a number of learning centers. She was curious about the children's reactions to the different centers and decided to ask for their opinions.

The children said they liked the art center most, because they enjoyed the projects and liked having something to take home to show their families. Another favorite was the listening center. The children said they liked listening to the tapes and following along in their copies of the storybooks. The children said they did not particularly like the center where they wrote in response to the literature they had read and discussed with the teacher that day. Nor did they like the comprehension center, in which they had to complete worksheets based on the reading of predictable books.

In discussing her conversations with the children, the teacher said the children's responses reminded her of just how difficult reading and writing can be for many first graders. Several of the children said that the response to literature and comprehension activities were "hard work" and required a lot of concentration and effort. The teacher concluded that the activities were effective in engaging the children in reading and writing, but perhaps needed to be varied so the children would find them more enjoyable.

The teacher tried a new activity in the response to literature center. She worked with the children in each reading group to identify different events in the story they were reading, and each child then did a watercolor painting of one of the events. In consultation with the teacher and other students in the group, each child composed a sentence or two to describe the event he or she had painted. The finished paintings and writings were displayed on a wall in the classroom for a time, and the children then took their work home.

At the comprehension center, the teacher decided to stop using worksheets. She explained to me that her reason for using worksheets in the first place was to ensure that the children read and understood the books. This was an old pattern of instruction, consistent with transmission and basal reader approaches (Anderson, Hiebert, Scott, and Wilkinson, 1985), which the teacher had used for many years. However, in this case the worksheets actually seemed to be working counter to her purpose, because the children were concentrating not on reading the books but on completing the worksheets. When she removed the worksheets from the comprehension center, the teacher explained to the children that, from now on, she wanted them just to enjoy the books by reading them alone or with a partner. Without the distraction of the worksheets, the children became much more interested in reading the books and were eager to read aloud to the teacher and visitors to their classroom.

This teacher was able to improve instruction because she was willing to listen to her students' views about classroom literacy activities. On the one hand, listening to students' ideas can lead us to productive new patterns of instruction. On the other hand, organizing classroom literacy learning without input from students tends to perpetuate less productive, old patterns.

Leading Students to New Goals

As indicated earlier in this chapter, students themselves are a first source of goals for teaching. A second source is the teacher's philosophy about literacy and the literacy curriculum as he or she envisions it. In the elementary classroom, not all goals for teaching can or should come from the students themselves, because one of the major functions of school literacy instruction should be to expand students' horizons. Students' own goals are necessarily limited by their previous experiences, so part of the teacher's job is to introduce new literacy experiences that may lead students to formulate new goals.

Here are two examples of literacy experiences that helped to broaden students' horizons. The first comes from Siu-Runyan's (1991) classroom. Her observations in September and October indicated that a number of students were just going through the motions of writing and not writing from a basis of personal commitment to and knowledge about their topics. Siu-Runyan decided to help the students by modeling how literature inspired her to write. She read *The Important Book* (1949) by Margaret Wise Brown to the class, then told them that the book had given her an idea for writing. During writing time, she wrote her own important story about the class. As Siu-Runyan shared her drafts with the students, several were inspired to write important books of their own.

When she read books to the class, Siu-Runyan asked, "What do you think the author had to know or experience in order to write this piece?" After several discussions, students began to realize the importance of writing about topics of which they had personal knowledge. Gradually, superficial stories such as those based on television shows began to disappear.

The second example comes from a multicultural third grade classroom. One day the teacher called my attention to the powerful writing being done by one of the girls. I saw that Tanya was writing a story about her family's old dog who was to be put to sleep over the Christmas vacation. While meeting in a writing conference with Tanya, the teacher realized that the piece could easily be turned into a poem. This led the teacher to give the class a mini-lesson on poetry. Among other things, the teacher addressed the children's misconception that poetry always had to rhyme. Tanya decided not to turn her piece into a poem, but later in the year she and several other students in the class chose to compose poems.

As these two examples illustrate, teachers who work from a constructivist perspective respect the directions students have set for themselves but do not hesitate to provide lessons to introduce literacy understandings and strategies students might find valuable but are not yet using. In the examples, students benefitted from learning to view literature as a possible model for writing and to put their ideas into poetry as well as prose.

> Students' own goals are limited by their previous experiences, so part of the teacher's job is to introduce new literacy experiences that may lead students to formulate new goals.

A Literacy Curriculum as a Frame of Reference

A literacy curriculum can be viewed as providing teachers with a framework for thinking about the various areas in which students may want or need to grow. There is no one set of skills all students must master in order to become proficient readers and writers. However, there are certain understandings and strategies, applied by many proficient readers, with which most students probably should be acquainted. The specific understandings and strategies teachers should teach, and when they should teach them, must depend on the needs and interests of the students. Students will not have a need for all of these understandings and strategies, but they will certainly find some of them helpful.

It may be important, particularly in multicultural classrooms, for teachers to offer students alternatives. For example, teachers might introduce students to the use of both outlines and webs or other graphic organizers for taking notes and planning their writing. Some students, as well as some adults, find it easier to use outlines for these purposes, while others find it easier to use webs. The idea is not to impose strategies on students but to present them with various alternatives and to help them discover what works best for them.

A literacy curriculum, then, is a frame of reference for reminding teachers of the breadth of literacy understandings and strategies students may find useful, and of the affective (emotional) as well as cognitive dimensions of students' growth. By meshing this framework with knowledge of students' own goals and needs, teachers can establish an overall sense of direction for classroom literacy instruction.

To meet the needs of students and teachers in multicultural settings, a literacy curriculum framework needs to reflect a philosophy of education, teaching, and learning, with a special emphasis on issues of diversity. Curricular frameworks are most useful when they are developed through a schoolwide process of discussion, perhaps including parents. Through the discussion process, values and assumptions are clarified and goals for instruction established.

A Sample Curriculum Framework

Our sample curriculum framework is used to highlight aspects of literacy which teachers will probably want to consider when thinking about goals for instruction. Teachers should think about having goals for students in all six aspects of literacy. The one exception is the area of word reading strategies, since goals in this area become unnecessary once students have

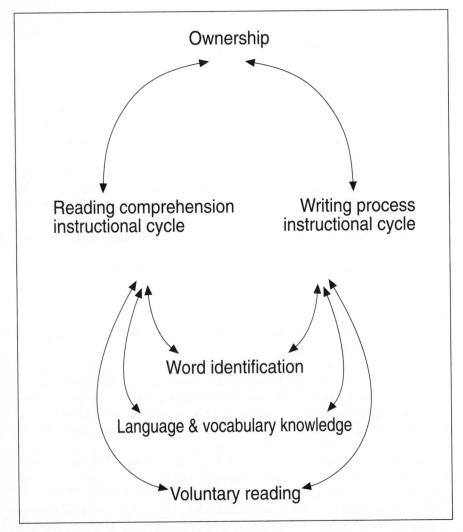

Figure 4.1   Six Aspects of Literacy

become fluent readers. This curriculum framework was developed for use in the Kamehameha Elementary Education Program (KEEP), which serves students and teachers in multicultural classrooms in Hawaii. This curriculum will be explored by looking at how it might work in a particular classroom. This account combines observations made in many different classrooms, and the thoughts attributed here to a single teacher reflect conversations with many different teachers.

Mrs. Nakamura is a third grade teacher in a school in a rural area. About half the students in her classroom are of Native Hawaiian ancestry, while the others are of a variety of ethnicities, including Filipino, Samoan, Portuguese, Japanese, and African American.

Nakamura is familiar with the diagram shown in figure 4-1. She knows that the curriculum encompasses six aspects of literacy (Au, Scheu, Kawakami, and Herman, 1990).

Ownership as the Overarching Goal

The first aspect of literacy, **ownership**, is the overarching goal. Nakamura understands that ownership has to do with her students' valuing their own ability to read and write (Au, Scheu, and Kawakami, 1990). She knows that she must think about her students' motivation and feelings about literacy, as well as about the cognitive strategies they need.

Nakamura watches her students to see if they are developing a positive attitude toward literacy, as well as the habit of using literacy in their daily lives. For example, at the beginning of the year Leilani told Nakamura how much she enjoys writing. Then in November, Leilani showed her a journal she keeps at home, evidence that writing is a daily habit for Leilani, even outside of school.

Nakamura feels that ownership of literacy is a particularly important goal in multicultural classrooms such as hers. Thinking of ownership reminds her that she must provide literacy instruction that builds upon students' own needs, interests, and cultural backgrounds. To develop her students' ownership of literacy, Nakamura has found it helpful to have students

Write on self-selected topics;

Share their writing with the class and receive recognition for the books they publish;

Discuss the relationships between events in novels and events in their own lives;

Decide upon the projects they will complete to show what they learned in a content area unit.

The Writing Process

Nakamura places a great deal of importance on the second aspect of literacy in the curriculum: the **writing process**. She knows that in constructivist or process approaches, writing is seen as a dynamic, nonlinear process involving activities such as planning, drafting, revising, editing, and publishing (Graves, 1983). Nakamura has her students select their own topics for writing, and she learns a great deal about her students through their stories. For example, she saw another side of Kamaka, a rather shy student, in his story about going pig hunting with his father. Nakamura will never forget how Kamaka smiled as he sat in the Author's Chair (Graves and Hansen, 1983) and heard his classmates' glowing comments about his story.

Nakamura commits time every day to the writers' workshop. In her judgment, experiences with the process approach to writing have been the single most important factor contributing to her students' ownership of literacy.

Reading Comprehension

Nakamura also commits time each day to the readers' workshop, when her students read and discuss novels. By having her students work with novels, Nakamura is able to address **reading comprehension**, the third aspect of literacy in the curriculum. Nakamura develops students' reading comprehension by having them respond to literature in a variety of ways. Students' responses to literature include the meanings they construct, the emotions they experience, and the connections they make to their own lives (Martinez and Roser, 1991).

Nakamura believes it is especially important for her students to read multicultural literature. One group read *The Patchwork Quilt* by Valerie Flournoy (1985). Ronette noticed that the quilt in the story looked very different from the quilts her grandmother makes, and she arranged for her grandmother to come to school to explain how a Hawaiian quilt is made.

During the readers' workshop, Nakamura spends her time in guided discussion with the small groups reading different novels. Nakamura believes it is her responsibility as a teacher to sharpen her students' thinking about the literature they read. For example, many third graders can track the sequence of events in the story, but they often need guidance in constructing a theme or inferring the author's message (Au, 1992).

Language and Vocabulary Knowledge

The fourth aspect of literacy, **language and vocabulary knowledge**, involves the ability to understand and use appropriate terms and structures in both spoken and printed English. The first language of many of the students in Nakamura's class is Hawaiian Creole English, the variety of English spoken by many people who are born and raised in Hawaii. Nakamura is aware that her students need to become familiar with standard English if they are to be successful in school. Many of her students use Hawaiian Creole English when conversing informally with peers but tend to use more standard English during group discussions. Nakamura models the use of standard English by paraphrasing students' responses, but she believes that correcting them overtly would keep them from speaking up. Usually, students pick up on her use of standard English and adjust their wording accordingly, as the discussion continues. Perhaps surprisingly, Nakamura finds that her students' writing is almost entirely in standard English with few traces of Hawaiian Creole English. This tells her that her students are sensitive to many of the differences between the two codes.

Nakamura is aware that vocabulary represents students' knowledge of particular topics, and that vocabulary is not a matter of dictionary-style definitions (Mezynski, 1983). She has found that students learn vocabulary best if the new words are all related to a broader topic, so she works on new vocabulary during students' reading of novels or during their work on content area units. Nakamura realizes that there is a limit to the number of words she can teach directly. She thinks it fortunate that many of her students read books independently, at home and at school, because their wide independent reading will allow them to learn the meaning of many new words (Anderson, Wilson, and Fielding, 1988). To help her students along, Nakamura tries to find books they will enjoy reading on their own. She also teaches them the "look in, look around" strategy so that they will be able to infer the meanings of the words they encounter while reading (Herman and Weaver, 1988).

Word Reading Strategies

The fifth aspect of literacy is **word reading strategies**. Nakamura is well aware that her students need strategies to identify and decode words and to read with accuracy and fluency. Nakamura thinks that Marie Clay's (1985) approach to word reading strategies makes a lot of sense. Clay suggests that students need to use three cue systems to identify words accurately: meaning cues, visual cues, and structural cues. About half of Nakamura's students can use the various cue systems quite well. These students stumble only when they come to multisyllable words, such as *masterpiece* and *comfortable*. Sometimes Nakamura models strategies the students could use to decode these words, and sometimes she has a student explain what he or she would do. For the students who are still learning to use all three cue systems in a coordinated fashion, Nakamura provides daily mini-lessons based on words in their reading.

Voluntary Reading

Voluntary reading is the final aspect of literacy in the curriculum. Nakamura understands that voluntary reading, like ownership, has to do with the motivational or affective side of literacy. Nakamura lets her students select the materials they want to read either for pleasure or information. Occasionally, if she feels a student's horizons should be broadened, she makes a specific suggestion. Todd, for example, spent two weeks reading nothing but surfing magazines, so she suggested he try a book about baseball for a change of pace. Each day after lunch, Nakamura sets aside about twenty minutes for sustained silent reading. In the beginning the time allowed was only ten minutes, and some students grew restless after just five minutes. Now the students complain when the time is up. On most days Nakamura takes a few minutes to let volunteers share something about the books they are reading. She has found that listening to their classmates talk about books is an excellent way for students to get ideas about what they would like to read next.

Organizing for Instruction

Although the curriculum has six aspects of literacy, Nakamura does not feel she needs to address each aspect separately. She has a time for a writers' workshop, a time for a readers' workshop, and a time for sustained silent reading, and within this schedule, students have the opportunity to grow in all six aspects of literacy. Instruction in language and vocabulary knowledge and in word reading strategies occurs as part of the writers' workshop and the readers' workshop. For example, in the writers' workshop students are encouraged to use new vocabulary in their pieces, and in the readers' workshop they are helped to learn the meanings of the new words they encounter in literature.

Nakamura is a firm believer in the idea that students learn to read by reading and to write by writing. Involvement in authentic literacy activities improves students' skills. For example, Nakamura finds that the more her students write, the more they become interested in using vocabulary to express their exact meaning. This motivates them to learn more vocabulary, and they take great pride in using new words in their writing.

Assessment and Evaluation

Nakamura's class keeps literacy portfolios and she enjoys meeting with students to discuss their reflections about their growth as readers and writers. At parent conferences, the portfolios help to give parents a clear idea of their children's progress in literacy.

Nakamura has never found the information provided by standardized tests particularly useful, but she is concerned about knowing whether she is doing a good job with her students. For this reason, she keeps in mind the grade-level benchmarks for each of the aspects of literacy, as listed in the curriculum. These benchmarks spell out the level of achievement expected of a hypothetical average student at the end of each grade level. Nakamura knows that these benchmarks are consistent with the state's framework for reading/language arts, recently published reading/language arts programs, standardized tests, and the objectives of the NAEP.

According to the curriculum, here are some of the benchmarks for students at the end of third grade. In the area of ownership, students should be obtaining books from the library and other nonclassroom sources. In the area of writing, students should be writing both personal narratives and reports on content area topics, and they should be aware of conventions such as organizing ideas in paragraphs. In reading comprehension, students should be able to write about a personal connection to a story, and to write a story summary including a discussion of the author's message. A benchmark for language and vocabulary knowledge is that students will identify new and interesting words in a story and make a reasonable inference about the meaning of those words. For word reading strategies, students should read a third-grade passage with 90 percent accuracy. Finally, in the area of voluntary reading, students should have the habit of daily reading, as shown through reading at home and during sustained silent reading and free moments in class.

Nakamura is aware that some of her students, like Mindy and Kamaka, will be able to do all these things and more by the end of the school year. She also knows that other students will not meet the benchmarks. Nakamura understands that the benchmarks are not intended to serve as goals for any individual student, but that they set the standards of achievement she should aim for with the class as a whole.

Sometimes Nakamura wishes that she didn't have to worry about having her students work so hard, although most of them love both reading and writing. However, she wants to be sure she does all she can to help them become good readers and writers. In this community, she knows that over half of the students do not graduate from high school and face a bleak future. Nakamura knows that school is just one influence on her students' lives, but she hopes many of her students will graduate from high school, be able to compete for jobs with students from mainstream backgrounds, become informed citizens, and know something of the world beyond their own community. Because she wants her students to have good opportunities later in life, Nakamura holds her students and herself to the standards represented in the benchmarks.

Nakamura believes that her students have the ability to become excellent readers and writers, and that the whole language philosophy, the writers' workshop, and the readers' workshop will best enable her to give them the support they need. Curriculum changes along these lines lead to new patterns of instruction that can improve the literacy learning of students of diverse backgrounds.

The Importance of Ownership

This chapter began by highlighting the importance of students setting goals for their own literacy learning. Then, in discussion of our sample literacy curriculum and Nakamura's experiences, the concept of students' ownership of literacy was explored. Encouraging students to set their own goals for literacy learning is one way of furthering their ownership of literacy.

Au and Kawakami (1991), building on the work of D'Amato, argue that students' ownership of literacy is an especially important consideration in multicultural classrooms. As discussed in chapter 3, D'Amato (1987, 1988) points out that students who are from mainstream backgrounds generally understand the structural significance of school, or the idea that schooling can lead to better life opportunities. These students perceive the balance of power in the classroom to rest in the hands of the teacher. They need little or no reminding about the importance of doing well in school and becoming a good reader and writer.

D'Amato suggests that students of diverse backgrounds often do not understand the structural significance of schooling, perhaps because few family members have finished high school or college, or because schooling has not led family members to good jobs, due to discrimination or the existence of a job ceiling (Ogbu, 1981). The term **job ceiling** describes a situation in which members of subordinate groups are usually denied good jobs, regardless of their qualifications or level of education.

Students who do not understand the structural significance of schooling do not have any long-term reasons for staying in school. In classrooms with students of diverse backgrounds, then, the balance of power rests in the hands of the students, not the teacher. If classroom activities are uninteresting or structured in ways contrary to the values of students' cultures, students are likely to become uncooperative or to rebel.

To help students of diverse backgrounds take advantage of the possible benefits of schooling, teachers need to show them that classroom activities can be enjoyable and immediately rewarding. Teachers must convince students that school literacy learning can make a difference in their own lives. By making students' ownership of literacy the explicit, overarching goal of instruction, teachers acknowledge their responsibility for making schooling a rewarding experience for students of diverse backgrounds and for making literacy meaningful in their lives.

Ownership and the Composite Classroom Culture

The concept that students' ownership of literacy should be the overarching goal of instruction is related to the concept of a composite classroom culture, discussed in chapter 1. A composite classroom culture is responsive to students' home cultures but is directed toward the goals of academic learning. For example, teachers in classrooms with many Hawaiian students may find the use of peer work groups to be effective, because of the children's home experiences with cooperation and sibling caretaking. For a composite culture to evolve, teachers and students need to adapt to one another's preferred values and styles of interaction and develop shared understandings about how classroom activities should be structured to further learning. The concepts of ownership and the composite classroom culture imply a commitment to helping students of diverse backgrounds attain high levels of literacy through means they find meaningful and motivating.

A practical implication stemming from these concepts is that teachers in multicultural classrooms should not be committed to particular procedures and routines, but should be flexible in working with students to evolve the procedures that will best promote literacy learning. Nakamura, for example, has changed the arrangements in the writers' workshop and readers' workshop from year to year. Among the factors she considers are the needs and interests of the students in the class that year, her own past experiences, and new ideas gained from colleagues and professional reading. However, no matter what arrangements she decides to use, Nakamura always introduces new activities clearly and carefully, making sure students are taught exactly what to do and what is expected of them. The careful introduction of new activities is a topic discussed further in chapter 5.

> The concepts of ownership and the composite classroom culture imply a commitment to helping students of diverse backgrounds attain high levels of literacy through means they find meaningful and motivating.

A Community of Readers and Writers

The concepts of ownership and the composite classroom culture are related to a third concept, that of the classroom as a community of readers and writers. The view of the classroom as a community of learners has been developed through the work of advocates of the process approach to writing and the whole language philosophy (for example, Graves, 1983; Blackburn, 1984; Cairney and Langbien, 1989). These writers emphasize the responsibility all members of the community — students and teachers alike — have for one another's literacy learning. Au and Kawakami state:

> For a classroom to be a community of learners, teachers and students must share similar values about the work they do together every day. While the teacher must communicate her respect for the students as people, she must also communicate a seriousness of purpose. In a community of learners, the emphasis is on cooperation and collaboration and what the class as a whole can accomplish, rather than on competition and individual achievement at the expense of others.   (manuscript p. 7)

Students' participation in the classroom as a literate community depends on the contributions students make as readers and writers, so a focus on academic learning is maintained. Each member has the responsibility of adding to the literacy resources of the community (Blackburn, 1984), for example, by sharing a new book with the class or by participating in a peer writing conference and offering constructive comments.

Au and Kawakami suggest that, when multicultural classrooms are organized as communities of learners, students and their teachers have the opportunity to evolve composite classroom cultures. In a classroom structured as a community of learners, arrangements for learning usually can be varied depending on the nature of the literacy activity and the needs of the learners. For example, children may work alone, in pairs, or in small groups. On some occasions the teacher holds the floor and asks for the attention of the entire class, but on other occasions the children hold the floor.

Greater flexibility in the form and content of instruction is one of the possible benefits of constructivist as opposed to transmission models, which are generally highly prescriptive both about instructional procedures and lesson content. The flexibility permitted when classrooms function as literate communities, focused on supporting all learners, gives the children and teacher the time to experiment and collaborate on the development of a composite culture. For example, the specific procedures teachers and students follow during the writers' workshop and the readers' workshop can evolve and change over time, until arrangements can meet the needs of all students. Further changes may take place as the year goes on. Within the overarching instructional goal of developing all students' ownership of literacy, classroom arrangements are adjusted to provide support for individual students' goals for their own literacy learning.

Through participation in the classroom community of learners, students of diverse backgrounds experience the rewards of their own personal achievement and of their classmates' achievements, which they have helped to bring about. Participation in a literacy classroom community gives students of diverse backgrounds a definite reason for being in school from one day to the next. Classroom communities and classroom organization and management are discussed in the next chapter.

Summary

Within a constructivist framework, there are two complementary approaches to the question of what to teach or to what ends the teacher should direct instruction. The first approach centers on discovering the goals students have for themselves as readers and writers. Engaging students in discussions about their goals and having students keep portfolios of their reading and writing can facilitate the process of students' setting goals for their own literacy. These steps also provide teachers with valuable information.

The second approach involves the teacher developing a vision of a literacy curriculum, since part of the teacher's responsibility is to expand students' literacy horizons by providing them with instruction in areas beyond their existing experiences. Six aspects of literacy formed the framework for a sample literacy curriculum. Ownership of literacy, the overarching goal of this curriculum, appears to be an especially important consideration with students of diverse backgrounds. The concepts of ownership, composite classroom cultures, and the classroom as a community of learners suggest ways that teachers might make classroom literacy instruction responsive to students' interests and rewarding in an immediate as well as long-range sense.

Application Activities

1. For a week, maintain a log of your own reading and writing. Make notes about the processes you go through. Then review your log and write about your own strengths and weaknesses as a reader and writer.

2. Start your own literacy portfolio. Write down at least two goals you have for yourself as a reader and at least two goals you have for yourself as a writer. Discuss what you could do to meet each goal. Describe the evidence you would place in your portfolio to show your progress in achieving each goal.

3. Interview a classroom teacher about his or her goals for students' literacy learning. Compare these goals to the framework shown in figure 4-1. Write an analysis of what you notice when you make this comparison.

Suggested Readings

Au, K.H., J.A. Scheu, A.J. Kawakami, and P.A. Herman, (1990). "Assessment and Accountability in a Whole Literacy Curriculum." *The Reading Teacher*, 43(8), pp. 574-78.

Short, K.G., and C. Burke, (1991). *Creating Curriculum: Teachers and Students As a Community of Learners*. Portsmouth, NH: Heinemann.

Tierney, R.J., M.A. Carter, and L.E. Desai, (1991). *Portfolio Assessment in the Reading-Writing Classroom*. Norwood, MA: Christopher-Gordon.

chapter 5

Classroom Organization: Creating a Literate Community

──────────── CHAPTER PURPOSES ────────────

1. Contrast constructivist and transmission perspectives on classroom management;
2. Explore management issues in the philosophy expressed by a whole language teacher successful in working with students of diverse backgrounds;
3. Discuss ways to establish a classroom community, including the use of peer groups;
4. Highlight typical school practices that appear to hinder the creation of classroom communities and suggest how these practices may be altered for the benefit of students of diverse backgrounds.

The previous two chapters dealt with the process of instruction and the content of instruction. This chapter looks at the organization and management of the classroom reading program, which is seen from a constructivist perspective to involve developing the classroom as a literate community.

Management from a Constructivist Perspective

In traditional classrooms the phrase **classroom management** generally refers to what the teacher should do to control students so they will be attentive to lessons and assignments. Control is a key issue in transmission approaches to instruction, because students are usually asked to sit passively and to provide answers within narrowly defined boundaries.

In constructivist approaches to instruction classroom management is directed toward different ends, since the idea is for students to be *actively* involved in developing their own understandings. Management is used as a means of fostering students' ownership of literacy, and teachers are oriented toward thinking about exerting a positive influence on students, rather than about simply controlling them. If management is seen as influence, then management includes the teacher's relationship with students, students' relationships with one another, and the way the teacher orchestrates the classroom environment and instructional activities to foster students' literacy learning.

This new pattern of management may be contrasted to the old pattern, described briefly above, which equates management with discipline and control externally imposed by the teacher and by commercial programs (Shannon, 1989). In the old pattern classrooms are to be run in an efficient, businesslike manner, and a sense of community is secondary, if it is considered at all.

Constructivist approaches emphasize the teacher's role in leading students toward self-discipline and self-control, so that classroom management ultimately becomes a matter internal rather than external to students. However, as discussed later in this chapter, the style teachers use may vary depending on the background of the students, and teachers in some settings may need to be direct and present themselves in an authoritative manner in order to be effective.

Constructivist approaches rely on purposeful literacy activities. Because students are likely to find these activities interesting and motivating, they find literacy learning to be intrinsically rewarding. In contrast to transmission approaches, there is little or no need in constructivist approaches for extrinsic rewards for reading and writing, such as those that might be provided through token reinforcement systems.

If management is viewed as the means teachers use to influence students' literacy learning, rather than as control, then good management and good instruction can be seen as one and the same. Meaningful, authentic literacy activities hold students' attention and keep them on-task and committed to learning. Management problems are more likely to result when literacy instruction centers on uninteresting activities that fail to hold students' attention. Thus, good management starts by involving students in meaningful activities.

> If management is viewed as the means teachers use to influence students' literacy learning, then good management and good instruction can be seen as one and the same.

The Classroom as a Community

Managing classroom literacy activities is not something teachers undertake to do *to* children, but something they do *with* them. As implied in chapter 4, the basis for management in constructivist, process, or holistic approaches is the development of a classroom community of learners. A sense of community is what enlivens the classroom and makes successful literacy learning a possible for all students.

As Jane Hansen (1987) points out, when we view classrooms as communities of learners we are recognizing the essentially social nature of literacy learning. In previous chapters it was suggested that the school literacy learning of students of diverse backgrounds may depend on their relationships with the teacher. If students and teachers can interact comfortably, teachers have the chance to provide instruction in the zone of proximal development (discussed in chapter 3), and students can make good progress in learning to read and write.

There is an additional advantage in a classroom community, because students' literacy learning can be influenced by peers as well as by the teacher. Peer writing conferences, collaborative learning, paired or partner reading, peer work groups, and peer-guided literature circles are all examples of classroom arrangements based on students working with and learning from other students. Learning can take place more rapidly because there are multiple sources of support and feedback, and students do not need to rely only on the teacher for the help they need.

In a classroom community, Hansen suggests, teachers make the assumption that each student has a wealth of background knowledge and that everyone's background knowledge is different. Teachers recognize that students' knowledge and experiences are just as worthwhile as their own. The teacher's job is to look for the special knowledge or perspective each child has to share, and to encourage each child to be creative and to take risks.

Hansen believes that diversity has special value within the classroom community because it provides challenges that lead students and teachers to new learning. In a classroom community teachers teach students to welcome and to celebrate differences and diverse cultural perspectives. Students learn who can help them come up with a good title, plan illustrations, or find information in the encyclopedia. They learn one another's tastes and interests as readers and writers and so gain greater insight about one another.

When the class has come together as a community, children are remarkably supportive of one another. Hansen gives this example from a first grade class. In February Christopher volunteered to read his published book to the class. All of the children knew that Christopher had never before shared a book with the class, and when he finished, they applauded. It was the first time in the entire school year that the children had applauded, and they did so because they recognized the significance of the event. Christopher had become a full-fledged member of the classroom community, and that was a cause for celebration.

These features of classrooms as communities can be beneficial to students of diverse backgrounds, as they are to all students. In a classroom community all students have the opportunity to be recognized for the knowledge they bring. A variety of talents can be recognized, and each student's progress is supported. Students in classroom communities develop ownership of their own literacy learning and also feel responsible for the literacy learning of others.

Management Philosophy

You now have an understanding of why a sense of community is central to management in constructivist views of literacy instruction. Teachers who manage their classrooms by creating a sense of community have a certain mindset toward their work. As classroom teachers, they assume responsibility for the literacy development of all of their students, rather than passing responsibility on to someone else, such as a remedial reading teacher. They realize that they must begin turning the classroom into a literate community from the first day of school. They have clear goals and strong beliefs about teaching and learning, and the procedures they use to manage their classrooms grow from their goals and beliefs.

The management philosophy of an experienced and successful whole language teacher, Karen Smith, was explored in a year-long study conducted in her sixth grade classroom (Edelsky, Draper, and Smith, 1983). Smith taught a class with twenty-five inner-city students at Laurel School in Phoenix, Arizona. About 75 percent of the students in this school were Mexican American, 15 percent were European American, and 10 percent were African American. Roughly 80 percent of the students qualified for the free breakfast and lunch program. Smith's classroom included many students who had failed two grades in school and some students who had reputations as "bad kids."

Yet Smith succeeded in turning her classroom into a literate community. Students were almost always attending to academic tasks. They were seldom absent from school. At home, parents noticed dramatic increases in students' book reading and story writing. By October even the most reluctant writers were composing entries of a page or more in their journals. All students, even those who had been considered "non-readers," read and discussed works of literature. By the spring students were spontaneously reflecting and commenting on their own writing and on the books they read in terms of such literary elements as point of view and plot.

Edelsky et al. suggest that Smith, in essence, offered students a "deal" on the first day of school. The "deal" she offered them was the opportunity to engage in purposeful reading and writing projects that would be largely under their own control. Beginning on the first day, Smith set the tone for the year by having the students participate in discussions, conduct science experiments, and rehearse the reading they would be presenting to the first graders.

The students recognized that Smith's class would be different, because they detected the absence of traditional classroom practices.

They tentatively accepted Smith's offer, and Smith kept demonstrating her commitment to keeping her end of the bargain. Because Smith was consistent in her beliefs and behavior, the students did not make a counteroffer. After only a few hours on the first day of school, they seemed to be operating within the framework Smith had implicitly proposed, although they were still learning and negotiating details of the system. Students' acceptance of Smith's "deal" was speeded by the fact that the students knew her reputation, since she had been in the school for a number of years. In interviews conducted on the second day of school, students stated that they knew that this year would be "hard" but filled with "fun" projects, such as constructing a haunted house and putting on plays.

Edelsky et al. found that Smith's actions in creating a classroom community were guided by a few goals, principles, and rules. Three overall goals served as the starting point for Smith's management philosophy. She described her goals this way:

1. **To get the students to see opportunities everywhere for learning.**
   "To get them to see learning as more than just books and school, and that out-of-school and fun things have purposes and can provide learning."
2. **To get students to think and take pleasure in using their intellects.**
   "To get them to seek out learning, to pique their curiosity."
3. **To help students learn to get along with and appreciate others.**
   "That they'll see you can get along with all kinds, to accept people, to look at the good in everybody."   (p. 263)

Three additional goals, not directly tied to her stated goals, were inferred from Smith's descriptions of her own actions:

4. To manage the day-to-day environment smoothly so other goals could be accomplished.
5. To get students to relate to and identify with the teacher.
6. To get them to be self-reliant and sure of themselves, and to trust their own judgments.   (pp. 263-64)

All goals were associated with certain values. These included:

Respect (respect others; consider needs of others; see the good in all; all are equal but special; children's ideas are important);

People are good (people are well-intentioned; people are competent; people are sensible);

Interdependence;

Independence;

Activity and work (work is enjoyable; work is purposeful; work is real, serious, good; being busy is good);

Originality.   (p. 265)

Interdependence referred to working cooperatively and relying on others, while independence referred to working individually and being self-reliant. Originality had to do with students' doing their own thinking.

You can see how Smith's goals and values are related to the idea of the classroom as a community of learners, in terms of her emphasis on students' respect for one another as well as on their commitment to learning. In contrast to what would be expected in a traditional, transmission-oriented classroom, Edelsky et al. found that Smith made no interview comments reflecting the values of compliance and conformity, such as keeping quiet or keeping on schedule.

When the association between Smith's goals and values was examined, it was found that goals concerning people and relationships (getting children to identify with the teacher, building self-reliance, getting along with others) were reinforced by the values of respect, independence, interdependence, and the goodness of people. Goals having to do with functioning and work (managing the environment, learning is everywhere, and using the intellect) were supported by work values (work is good; originality). Sorting values by goal categories suggested that Smith was probably pursuing goals in two main areas: "relationships" and "schoolwork and learning." In short, Smith placed a strong emphasis on academic learning and understood that learning could only take place within the context of positive teacher-student and student-student relationships.

Four implicit rules were identified in Smith's classroom. These were:

1. Do Exactly as I Say
2. Use Your Head
3. Do What's Effective, and
4. No Cop-outs.   (p. 265)

These rules were implicit because Smith did not state them as such but frequently invoked them through the demands she made on students.

The "Do Exactly" rule was often invoked during the first days of school when the teacher was giving directions and indicating what the students should or should not do. For example, on the third day of school, when Smith asked the students to sit on the floor, several tried to bring their chairs with them. Smith took the opportunity to make her exact meaning clear:

> If I say "Floor," I don't want chairs. If I say "Chairs and floor and table," I want chairs, floor, and table.   (pp. 266)

While the teacher was giving certain explicit directions, she was also moving the students toward independence right from the start. Two rules, "Use Your Head" and "Do What's Effective," reflected this push toward independence. The teacher employed the "Use Your Head" rule to remind students of their responsibility for independent work, both in and out of school, although she did at times provide them with considerable assistance. She told the students:

Make good use of your time. You know what to do. You're on your own. (p. 266)

The "Do What's Effective" rule meant that students could use their own judgment about how to handle specific situations. For example, they could enter the classroom at will in the morning, instead of lining up and waiting for the bell to ring. They could sit wherever they wanted during films, as long as they could see.

"No Cop-Outs" meant that students had to be responsible for coming up with their own answers. Smith did not punish students for not knowing answers, but she kept pushing them to find answers for themselves. For example, the following exchange took place when Richard and Irene were working on a science project:

Smith: What else is needed so the wind won't destroy it?
Richard: I don't know.
Smith: No, 'I don't knows!' (p. 266)

In this and other instances, the "No Cop-Outs" rule appeared to be linked with goals of self-reliance and using the intellect.

This study by Edelsky et al. confirms that teachers who use constructivist approaches see close relationships between management and instruction. They establish a system of values and behaviors that lead students toward positive, respectful relationships with the teacher and with other students. Karen Smith had just a few broad goals, rooted in personal values, which led to a few sensible rules. In effect, she and the students had entered into an agreement in which she provided them with the opportunity to engage in challenging yet rewarding literacy activities. To keep their part of the agreement, the students committed themselves to working hard, trying their best, and taking responsibility for their own work.

Establishing the Literate Community

Regie Routman (1991), a language arts resource teacher in a district with many students of diverse backgrounds, makes the point that management in whole language classrooms is a matter of teachers sharing responsibility with students. This is a gradual process, and it may take up to two months even for experienced teachers to feel that their classrooms have become collaborative communities. Here are some of the steps Routman's colleagues take to achieve a smooth-running classroom community.

Karen Shiba, a first grade teacher, finds that establishing a classroom community requires consistency and routine. She proceeds slowly during the first months of school as she introduces procedures and makes her expectations clear to the students. She introduces a new learning center only when the classroom is running smoothly and children are working well on their own and ready for something new. Daily shared reading experiences contribute to the sense of community in Shiba's classroom.

Children are attracted by the literature, poems, songs, and chants and further motivated by the text innovations and other literacy activities that allow them to work together, show their creativity, and experience success.

> Establishing the classroom community requires consistency and routine.

Fourth grade teacher Joan Servis starts building a sense of collaboration and community during the first week of school. She begins by demonstrating what she wants students to do, then asks them to carry out the activity by working in pairs. In pairs, the students work on activities such as peer conferencing, note taking, and responding in a literature log. After students have worked in pairs for several weeks, they are asked to carry out the same activities in cooperative groups of three or four.

In building a classroom community, Servis follows five general procedures. First, she gets students in the habit of evaluating their own performance. Whenever students finish working together, for example on a math assignment, they reflect on their behaviors, either orally or in writing. Under Servis' guidance, the students think about how they might improve the way their group is working together. Gradually, Servis gives the students more and more responsibility for monitoring their own work.

Second, she emphasizes cooperation. The students discuss specific behaviors that promote respect and cooperation, such as listening to one another and taking turns. Students are encouraged to help each other, for example, by assisting one another to complete work in their reading logs. Servis checks their work only when everyone in the group has finished. By then their work has usually been completed successfully, since students who needed assistance were helped by their peers.

Third, Servis praises positive behaviors, orally and in writing, so that students are aware of what they are doing well. Praise may serve different functions with different groups of students. In classrooms with Native Hawaiian students, for example, the teacher's liberal use of praise wins students over to the teacher and helps them see the teacher, as well as peers, as someone to turn to when they need help (Jordan, 1985). However, Native Hawaiian students are sensitive to signs that some children are being favored over others, so teachers must be careful to distribute praise evenly (D'Amato, 1988).

Fourth, Servis makes sure that students have a clear understanding of the task. She issues specific instructions and provides repeated demonstrations of what students are supposed to do. She monitors the understanding of each student and checks to see that each group has a spokesperson.

Fifth, Servis moves from teacher modeling to student modeling of appropriate behaviors. She finds that students must have the opportunity to demonstrate their understanding of how classroom activities are to be carried out. For example, several students may be selected to demonstrate appropriate behavior in the classroom library, while the rest of the class observes. When the students have finished their demonstration, the teacher leads the class in a discussion about appropriate and inappropriate behaviors.

Importance of a Systematic Approach

The teachers with whom Routman works find it best to introduce and demonstrate only one new activity at a time. Although a deliberate, systematic approach to establishing classroom routines generally takes six weeks or longer, this initial investment in time is rewarded as the year goes on. In fact, Routman advises, "For teachers who feel routines have not been well established, it works well to think of the current week as week one, and just start again." (p. 423)

As Routman shows, effective management, leading to the development of a classroom community, is a matter of the careful introduction of routines. Teachers make clear their expectations for students' behavior, and students receive the support they need to be successful. Students are not expected to enter the classroom already knowing about self-evaluation, cooperation, and other complex behaviors necessary for full participation in the literate classroom community. Students may be familiar with some of these behaviors to a certain extent, due to home experiences, but that does not mean their knowledge will automatically transfer to school contexts. Thus, students are introduced to or reminded of the necessary behaviors through a process of teacher modeling, student modeling, and guided and independent practice.

Routman's book provides a wealth of information about classroom management and organization consistent with the whole language philosophy, including examples of classroom schedules, room arrangements, and suggestions for learning centers. Other examples of schedules and suggestions for organizing the classroom at the beginning of the year may be found in Crafton (1991).

Earning Students' Respect

As the accounts of Edelsky et al. (1983) and Routman (1991) indicate, the creation of a classroom community depends largely on the teacher's efforts. Students must be actively involved from the start, but it is largely through the teacher's directions, modeling, instruction, and guidance that the community is formed. Before the teacher and students can come together in a community, the teacher must win the students' respect and ensure their willingness to cooperate.

What can teachers do to win the respect of students of diverse backgrounds? Delpit (1988) reminds us that the effectiveness of a particular teaching or interactional style can only be judged within the context of a particular community and culture. For example, teachers differ in the extent to which they behave in a direct, authoritative manner. Consider the following situation. The teacher notices that a child has left a pair of scissors on the table, instead of returning them to the shelf where they belong. A middle-class, European American teacher might say:

Is this where the scissors belong?

or

Don't you want this area to look nice and neat?

In contrast, an African American teacher would be more likely to say:

Put those scissors on that shelf.

Students from mainstream backgrounds are likely to recognize "Is this where the scissors belong?" as a command to put the scissors away. However, Delpit suggests that some students from diverse backgrounds may not realize what teachers expect, when teachers state their expectations in the form of indirect requests or questions. In Heath's (1983) research, both African American and European American students from working class communities had difficulty seeing that teachers intended their indirect requests to serve as direct commands.

When the child does not put the scissors away, the teacher might think the child is deliberately disobeying, when actually the child has not understood what the teacher wants done. Delpit states:

> If veiled commands are ignored, the child will be labeled a behavior problem and possibly officially classified as behavior disordered. In other words, the attempt by the teacher to reduce an exhibition of power by expressing herself in indirect terms may remove the very explicitness that the child needs to understand the rules of the new classroom culture.   (p. 289)

In other words, teachers working with some students from diverse backgrounds may need to make statements in a direct manner, so that requests and expectations are clear to students.

Teachers may also fail to win students' compliance and respect for other reasons, Delpit suggests, having to do with the manner in which teachers present themselves to students. Many African American children expect the teacher to act like an authority figure, not like a "chum." Children are likely to misbehave and take advantage of the situation if teachers do not make it clear that they are in charge.

While many students from mainstream backgrounds automatically regard teachers as authority figures, many students from diverse backgrounds do not share this perception (Delpit, 1988; D'Amato, 1988). Instead, students from diverse backgrounds may expect teachers to earn their respect by behaving in an authoritative manner. Delpit points out that African American students may be proud of their teachers' "meanness," or their ability to manage a class, make high academic demands, and prod students to do their best. She writes:

> The authoritative teacher can control the class through exhibition of personal power; establishes meaningful interpersonal relationships that garner student respect; exhibits a strong belief that all students can learn; establishes a standard of achievement and "pushes" the students to achieve that standard; and holds the attention of students by incorporating interactional features of Black communicative style in his or her teaching.   (p. 290)

Similar conclusions are reached by D'Amato (1986), who uses the metaphor of a "smile with teeth" to describe the style of teachers effective in working with Native Hawaiian students. The smile in the metaphor refers to the value students attach to "niceness," to teachers treating them with kindness. The teeth in the metaphor refers to the value students attach to "toughness," to teachers showing that they can take charge of the classroom, bring misbehaving students into line, and command respect.

In short, teachers working in multicultural settings should be aware that it may be more difficult to win the respect of students of diverse backgrounds than the respect of students of mainstream backgrounds. Often teachers must earn the respect of students of diverse backgrounds by presenting themselves in a manner consistent with students' perceptions of what it means to act like an authority figure. In some settings with students of diverse backgrounds, teachers' ability to create a classroom community may be undermined if they do not make their expectations clear, if they permit students to misbehave, or if they act in other ways that signal to students that they are not taking charge in the classroom.

> Often teachers must earn the respect of students of diverse backgrounds by presenting themselves in a manner consistent with students' perceptions of what it means to act like an authority figure.

Expanding the Concept of Community

Since students from different cultural groups may have different perceptions about how teachers should present themselves, there can be no one set of rules for teachers to follow in interacting with students, making their expectations clear, and guiding the formation of the classroom community. In all cases, however, it is important for teachers to be knowledgeable of the community beyond the school and of the values of the students' community and home culture.

Barrera (1992) points out that students of diverse backgrounds are likely to experience all of the benefits of belonging to a classroom community only if teachers expand the notion of community to include the communities in which students live. She writes:

> The professional reading/language arts literature of the past five years is replete with invitations to teachers to forge "communities of learners" in the classroom and school, an idea which reflects attention to the new notions of literacy and literacy learning as *social* processes. Unfortunately, in schools where teachers also talk about creating communities of readers and writers . . . the concept of "community" often appears to be school-bound. There usually is little teacher awareness that the students are already members of different communities around the school in which literacy is practiced as a social *and* cultural process and includes varying forms of literature.   (manuscript p. 8)

If all students are to feel welcome within the classroom community, that community must in part reflect the values of students' homes, as well as the values of the school and mainstream society. As discussed earlier, students of diverse backgrounds often find school a puzzling and alien environment because of differences between the culture of the school and the culture of the home. A classroom community for students of diverse backgrounds will need to be a composite classroom culture featuring culturally responsive instruction (as discussed in chapters 1 and 6), as well as multicultural literature (as discussed in chapter 11).

"Acting" and Peer Group Dynamics

In previous chapters the importance of adapting classroom literacy instruction to be responsive to students' home experiences was emphasized. Research suggests that students' experiences with the peer group also need to be considered in the organization and management of literacy instruction.

The importance of peer group dynamics is highlighted in research conducted by John D'Amato (1988) with Native Hawaiian students in the primary grades. D'Amato's work emphasizes the fact that students cannot and do not leave the world of peers behind when they enter the classroom.

The young Hawaiian children D'Amato studied had elaborate peer group structures that they maintained through a process of rivalry. Rivalry requires that children contend with one another through verbal and physical means, to show that they are as good as their peers. It is a means of establishing equality, mutual respect, and affection. Rivalry differs from classroom competition, which requires that players try to show that they are better than others. Also, because most competitive classroom situations are under the control of the teacher, children cannot work to maintain a sense of equality among their peers. When relationships of equality are threatened, children are likely to unite in resistance to teachers.

Children carry rivalry into the classroom through a process called "acting." At the beginning of the school year, "acting" generally takes the form of playing tricks on the teacher, in a show of group solidarity and resistance. D'Amato gives the following example of "acting" based on observations in a third grade classroom in September. The teacher asked two boys to move a table, and then turned to the blackboard. The first boy began a game by running at the table, sliding across the top of it on his stomach, and landing on the floor on the other side. The second boy imitated him, and three other boys eventually joined in.

"Acting" begins in a playful spirit at the start of the school year, as this example suggests. However, "acting" has the potential to escalate and to become disruptive to classroom learning. "Acting" intensifies and takes on an increasing hostile tone in classrooms where the delicate dynamics of rivalry are upset because teachers put students in situations where they are forced to compete openly against one another.

For example, D'Amato describes how a second grade teacher caused the leader of one of the boys' groups to lose face in a classroom situation.

> The teacher selected a boy to help her demonstrate the idea of nonverbal communication. She hugged the boy, and at once the room rocked with laughter. As it subsided, another boy pointed out, derisively, that the teacher "loved" the boy who had been hugged. Until this point, the second graders had been "acting" only in playful ways. Relationships were becoming frayed, but open conflict had not developed. It happened, however, that the boy who had been hugged was the leader of one of the gangs; the boy who had teased him was the leader of the rival gang.   (p. 538)

To maintain his status, the boy who had been hugged entered into a dispute with the teacher about a knowledge claim she had made. Eventually, he and several other students succeeded in disrupting the lesson. D'Amato continues:

> The situation broke apart along the line of opposition between boys and girls. The boys shouted out a chant of "boo for the girls, boo for the girls," and the girls returned a chant of "boo for the boys." The lesson never recovered, and the teacher cried before it ended.   (p. 539)

In classrooms with many Native Hawaiian students, the teacher's challenge is to develop classroom activities which channel the process of rivalry constructively. D'Amato suggests that this can be achieved by organizing many activities in a small group format. When students are allowed to work in small groups, they have the chance to work out peer group relationships without conflicts and problems of status being made public. Working in small groups, as opposed to reciting before the entire class, provides all students with many opportunities to prove themselves to peers. Also, teachers do not put themselves in the position of having to direct students' every move and so are less visible as targets for the process of "acting."

The "open" features of talk story-like reading lessons, discussed in Chapter 7, also support rivalry, according to D'Amato. Although the teacher may call on a particular child, that child does not have to speak. Having the option of speaking or not allows children to save face if they do not have an idea to share. Similarly, children who have ideas to contribute do not have to wait to be called on by the teacher. Because talk story-like reading lessons permit overlapping speech, several children can respond to each question the teacher asks. D'Amato suggests that these "open" features of lessons allow children to regulate their answering to keep even with other children, and so to meet the requirements of rivalry in a constructive manner.

Organizing Peer Work Groups

Research by D'Amato (1988) and Jordan (1985) suggests that elementary students of diverse backgrounds may benefit from the opportunity to learn in peer work groups. According to Phelan, Davidson, and Cao (1991), high school students of diverse backgrounds are also more likely to be successful in classrooms with a high degree of student-student interaction. In these classrooms students help and are responsible for one another, as they are in peer settings, and they do not have to make the transition to a completely teacher-dominated setting.

Fordham (1991) describes examples of the constructive use of peer group dynamics with African American students. The key feature of these programs was what Fordham labels **group sanctioned learning**. The first program, for high school students, utilized class/team competitions. Students were not involved in individual competition but were motivated to compete for the benefit of their class or team. In the second program, at the University of California, Berkeley, students were able to achieve at much higher levels once they were involved in support groups. Similarly, research by Philips (1972) suggests that many Native American students may learn effectively in peer work groups.

Cultural Differences and Peer Teaching-Learning Interactions

Like other instructional approaches, the effectiveness of peer work groups may be strongly affected by cultural differences. In their work with Native Hawaiian students, Vogt, Jordan, and Tharp (1987) found that high levels of peer interaction and helping occurred when peer work groups consisted of groups of four or five students, mixed by sex and by achievement level.

When Vogt et al. attempted to use these same arrangements with Navajo students, they did not see the expected patterns of mutual assistance. Instead, students tended to ignore one another and did not seek or offer assistance, even when it was plainly needed. Vogt et al. discovered why the chosen arrangements did not work:

> There is a separation of sexes in Navajo culture, both in roles and for purposes of interaction, a separation that begins to take effect around the age of eight, the age of the students in our class. Boys are admonished not to "play with" their sisters, and girls with brothers. In a small community this means almost everyone, since it extends to clan relations. By puberty this is extremely important, and by adulthood male and female roles are clearly defined and separate. (p. 284)

After experimenting with several different arrangements, Vogt et al. found that teaching-learning interactions would occur if students were placed in groups of two or three with others of the same sex, all working on the same task.

In classroom observations, I have found that peer teaching-learning interactions may appear quite different, depending on the cultural backgrounds of the students. When seated with peers, many young, Native Hawaiian students tend to speak freely about their work. When in need of help, they will make their questions known to peers and, if ignored, persist in their requests. Generally, all those seated nearby know the status of one another's work. In a similar vein, students feel free to offer one another advice and will persist in their efforts to help, even if the targeted student initially refuses assistance. Students are obviously involved in one another's learning, as they call out to one another, lean over to check on each other's work, and exchange papers, all the while engaged in a nearly unbroken chain of conversation.

In classrooms with young, Yup'ik Eskimo students, my experience has been that teaching-learning interactions look quite different in form. The students I observed did not openly seek or offer assistance, but glanced sharply at one another's work from time to time. These quick glances enabled them to monitor one another's progress (Lipka, personal communication). They made few comments to one another. When students noticed that others were in need of help, however, they made statements suggesting that correction was needed. In other words, the Yup'ik students seemed to seek and offer help in a more subtle, less obviously intrusive manner than the Native Hawaiian students.

Practical Implications

In short, teachers in classrooms with students of diverse backgrounds must be aware of the importance of peer dynamics in the formation of the classroom community. Teachers may learn about peer dynamics through their own observations of students, through conversations with community members or with other teachers, and through reading the results of research on this topic.

Teachers must not simply work around peer dynamics but mobilize peer dynamics to further literacy learning. Students of diverse backgrounds are likely to benefit if teachers provide systematic instruction in small groups and organize them in collaborative small groups to work independently. Teachers should understand that peer work groups may need to be organized differently, and that peer teaching-learning interactions may take different forms, depending on the students' cultural background.

Factors Hindering Development of a Classroom Community

Teachers and students need the right conditions to develop a shared understanding of values and of their roles and responsibilities within the classroom as a literate community. Research points to a number of common school practices that can keep students and teachers from joining together to form a literate community. These practices, old patterns that hinder the literacy learning of students of diverse backgrounds, include pull-out programs, tracking and fixed ability groups, and a lack of time for literacy instruction.

Pull-out Programs

Frequently, students of diverse backgrounds are removed from the regular classroom to participate in one or more special programs. For example, a third grader whose home language is Spanish might participate in an ESL (English as a Second Language) program which requires that he be out of the classroom for forty-five minutes a day. On the basis of his scores on a standardized test, the student might also qualify for remedial reading instruction, which removes him from the classroom for another forty-five minutes a day. Including transition time, the student may be out of the classroom for nearly two hours a day.

Being isolated from classmates deprives students of the positive models of language and literacy and the assistance provided by capable peers in the classroom. When students do not have the opportunity to participate in the same literacy activities as their classmates, they fail to develop the strategies and background experiences that allow them to contribute and belong to the classroom community. Other students who remain in the classroom also pay a price, because they are deprived of the opportunity to learn from and work with students who participate in pull-out programs. Often students are stigmatized by participation in pull-out programs, and this situation creates divisions in the class, the very opposite of the accepting, respectful atmosphere sought in a classroom community.

Classroom teachers, who bear primary responsibility for students' literacy development, need to make a special effort to strengthen the connections that students of diverse backgrounds have to the classroom community. First, while students are in the classroom, their literacy accomplishments should be celebrated by all. Second, teachers might explore the possibility of establishing close, ongoing communication with specialist teachers to provide students with consistent literacy instruction following constructivist models. Too often, students receive one form of instruction in their regular classrooms and very different forms of instruction in pull-out programs, which usually follow transmission models of instruction (Allington, 1991). Teachers might also determine whether it is possible for specialist teachers to come into the regular classroom to work with students, rather than to remove students from the room.

Tracking and Fixed Ability Groups

Tracking is another practice likely to be detrimental to the creation of a classroom community and to the literacy learning of students of diverse backgrounds. One form of tracking is that of assigning students to reading classes on the basis of reading test scores or reading ability. For example, consider the situation in which the sixth grade students in four home-rooms are regrouped for reading instruction. The result is a high group, two middle groups, and a low group, each assigned to one of the four sixth grade teachers for reading instruction. Because reading instructional time is limited to only an hour a day, the teachers and students have little time for reading and writing, for getting to know one another well, and for forming a supportive, literate community.

Tracking is detrimental to students' literacy development for other reasons, too. First, it is based on the false assumption that reading ability is fixed, and not a function of the instructional situation. Thus, it leads teachers to have lower expectations for many students. Second, tracking tends to deprive students from diverse backgrounds of high-quality instruction, since many students from diverse backgrounds are usually consigned to the lower groups. A substantial body of research has demonstrated that the quality of reading instruction in groups deemed to be of low ability is inferior to the quality of instruction given to higher groups (Allington, 1991). For example, teachers tend to emphasize oral reading and isolated skill instruction with low-group students, while they emphasize silent reading and reading for meaning with high-group students. In other words, low-group students are often subject to transmission approaches to instruction, which are unlikely to be effective in teaching them to read. Third, tracking lowers the self-esteem of students caught in the low groups, resulting in lower levels of motivation, confidence, and learning (Barr, 1989).

Within the classroom, there are also practices that may prevent the creation of a classroom community. Obviously, the use of fixed ability groups, a form of tracking, will have the same detrimental effects described above. While it is highly important for teachers to meet with students in small groups, the composition of these groups should not be determined solely on the basis of presumed reading ability. Barr (1989) suggests that it may make sense at times to group students by ability in the primary grades, when students differ considerably in decoding ability and therefore in the ability to read a particular text. However, by the fourth grade, when most students have become fluent decoders, placing students in fixed ability groups is difficult to justify.

To avoid the detrimental effects of tracking, flexible groups, intended to provide students with instruction on particular skills, may be formed (Cunningham, Hall, and Defee, 1991). Students may also be grouped on the basis of interests. For example, the teacher offers students a choice of three different novels, and all those who chose a particular novel then become part of the same discussion group. Or students decide upon five different sea creatures to be studied and form five groups to work collaboratively on their reports.

Lack of Time for Literacy Instruction

Another problem at the classroom level is a lack of time for literacy learning and instruction. Typically, schools in low-income communities (including many schools with students of diverse backgrounds) allocate less time for literacy instruction than schools serving middle-income communities (Allington, 1991). The reasons for this situation are not clear, but the effect is that students of diverse backgrounds often have less time to learn to read and write than students of mainstream backgrounds.

Conducting a writers' workshop (as described in chapter 10) requires from thirty to forty-five minutes a day, and students often want even more time to write. Conducting a readers' workshop, with teacher-guided as well as peer-guided small group discussions, may take an hour a day or more. In short, a minimum of one and a half to two hours a day will generally be required for literacy instruction.

One way of lengthening the time for literacy instruction is to incorporate reading and writing in the content areas (including science, social studies, and math) into the same block of time, thus eliminating the need to set aside separate times for each subject. Many whole language teachers are moving toward schedules that integrate the teaching of reading, writing, and content areas (for specific classroom examples, see Mills and Clyde, 1990). For example, the teacher might choose a science topic such as the environment, and have students read both fiction and nonfiction selections and write reports. The advantage of this approach is twofold. First, it may create more time for students to read and write, and second, it may help students see that reading and writing can help them learn about content area topics. The approach can be beneficial to students of both diverse and mainstream backgrounds.

In short, a variety of factors may hinder the ability of teachers and students to create a literate classroom community. Teachers and administrators need to explore alternatives to pull-out instruction, so that students of diverse backgrounds can spend more time in the regular classroom and have a better opportunity to become contributing members of the literate community. Teachers also need to think of ways to avoid tracking and the detrimental effects of categorizing students of diverse backgrounds and setting them apart from their classmates. Finally, there is the need to allocate adequate time for literacy instruction and for the shaping of the classroom as a literate community.

Summary

In constructivist approaches, management of classroom literacy instruction is interpreted in terms of influence rather than control. The concept of the classroom as a literate community is central, and teachers' influence is directed at guiding students to form a classroom community. As illustrated in the case of Karen Smith, teachers who follow holistic and constructivist models of instruction have a clear and consistent management philosophy, involving an emphasis on students' academic learning and a recognition of the importance of positive social relationships in supporting literacy learning. Cultural differences come into play in the creation of a classroom community. Students from different communities and cultures may have different ideas of how teachers should conduct themselves in the classroom, in order to be perceived as proper authority figures, and appropriate arrangements for peer teaching-learning interactions may vary significantly. Finally, in their efforts to create a classroom community, teachers may need to counter established school practices such as pull-out programs, tracking, and a lack of instructional time, which are likely to have a divisive effect on the classroom community.

Application Activities

1. Think back to your own elementary and secondary school experiences. Describe any uses of tracking or fixed ability grouping that you recall. Discuss the effects of these practices on you and your classmates.

2. In a local elementary school, find out about any programs aimed at assisting students experiencing difficulty with reading and at assisting students who speak English as a second language. Are these pull-out or in-class programs? What instructional approaches are used? How is communication handled between the classroom teacher and the specialist teacher?

3. Do you recall a teacher in elementary school who was particularly effective at helping students to make academic progress? Describe

what you believe to be that teacher's management philosophy. Also describe what the teacher did in the classroom to help students learn.

Suggested Readings

Mills, H., and J.A. Clyde, eds. (1990). *Portraits of Whole Language Classrooms: Learning for All Ages*. Portsmouth, NH: Heinemann.

Short, K.G. (1990). "Creating a Community of Learners." In K.G. Short and K.M. Pierce, eds., *Talking About Books: Creating Literate Communities*. Portsmouth, NH: Heinemann, pp. 33-52.

Routman, R. (1991). *Invitations: Changing as Teachers and Learners K-12*. Portsmouth, NH: Heinemann.

chapter 6

Patterns of Interaction: Adjusting to Cultural Differences

————— CHAPTER PURPOSES —————

1. Explain the concept of gatekeeping and how teachers may inadvertently serve as gatekeepers;
2. Through two examples, show how differences between the culture of the school and the culture of the home can hinder the school literacy learning of students of diverse backgrounds
   a. Sharing time;
   b. Styles of questioning;
3. Describe the approaches teachers can use to overcome cultural differences in interactional style;
4. Discuss culturally responsive instruction, composite classroom cultures, and strategies for dealing with cultural differences.

Culture and Related Concepts

In chapter 1 the idea of invisible culture was introduced. You learned that culture can be seen as a system of values, beliefs, and standards that is learned, shared, adapted to particular circumstances, and continually changing. A related concept is that of culturally responsive instruction, or instruction that is responsive to the values and standards for behavior of students' home culture and also directed toward the goals of academic achievement. When teachers use culturally responsive instruction, they help students affirm their cultural identities while expanding their knowledge through school literacy experiences.

As discussed in chapters 1 and 5, composite classroom cultures result from the mutual adaptation of students and teachers to one another's values and styles. This process of mutual adaptation can lead to the classroom becoming a community of learners. In a composite classroom culture, students of diverse backgrounds and their teachers have reached a shared understanding about the importance of literacy learning and have an open line of communication, which enables them to decide upon the activities that will best promote students' literacy learning as a group and as individuals.

In settings with many students of diverse backgrounds, differences in **interactional style** often need to be bridged in order to bring about culturally responsive instruction, composite classroom cultures, and classroom communities of learners. Bridging these differences is one of the new patterns that may allow teachers to work more effectively with students of diverse backgrounds. A failure to acknowledge the existence of differences in interactional styles, which leads to a failure to adjust instructional situations, is one of the old patterns that appears to prevent students of diverse backgrounds from achieving at high levels in school.

Power Relationships and Gatekeeping

Cultural differences as reflected in interactional style become an issue because of the power relationships between dominant and subordinate groups. Erickson and Shultz (1982) and Gumperz (1976) point out that, in complex societies such as the United States, individuals are placed from time to time in **key situations** or **gatekeeping** encounters.

An example of a key situation, that studied by Erickson and Shultz, is a college student's meeting with a counselor who will guide his decisions about future course work, schooling, and employment. If the student and the counselor are following the same rules for face-to-face interaction, the session is likely to go quite smoothly and the student will receive helpful advice and moral support. This is apt to happen if both the student and the counselor participate in the mainstream culture, or if the two are from similar cultural backgrounds.

But suppose that the student and counselor are from different cultural backgrounds, and each is following his or her own set of rules for interaction. In this case there may well be misunderstandings. For example, Erickson and Shultz demonstrate that European American counselors in a junior college setting tended to misread the listening behaviors of African American students. Students did not nod their heads and make noises such as "Um-hmm" according to the pattern expected by the counselors, but timed their head nods in a way appropriate in African American culture. As a result, counselors thought that students were not concentrating on the advice they were giving, and so they persisted in explaining the same point. For their part, students interpreted the counselors' tendency to dwell on the same point as "talking down" to them and highly insulting. The students and counselors did not realize that they were dealing with a mismatch in interactional styles and so inferred other motives for one another's behavior.

In face-to-face interactions misunderstandings can result even from matters as seemingly insignificant as the timing of head nods. Yet these small matters may have lasting consequences. Counselors, job interviewers, and others who are in a position to provide or deny social opportunities act as gatekeepers, often letting through the gates those of backgrounds similar to their own, while keeping those of different backgrounds out. Since in many situations gatekeepers are from mainstream backgrounds, the outcomes of gatekeeping encounters tend to be favorable for those from mainstream backgrounds and unfavorable for those from diverse backgrounds. To an individual acting as a gatekeeper, the decisions seem logical and objective, because they are based in part on the ease with which rapport and understanding were reached during face-to-face interaction. Thus, although many gatekeepers probably do not intend to discriminate against applicants from diverse cultural backgrounds, the fact is that they often do so unknowingly.

Teachers as Gatekeepers

In school, literacy lessons put teachers in the position of gatekeepers. This happens because, during lessons, teachers may interact well with some students and so facilitate their literacy learning, but interact poorly with others and so hinder their literacy learning. Because many teachers, like most other gatekeepers, are from mainstream backgrounds, they are less likely to be familiar with the interactional styles of students from diverse backgrounds. Many teachers are unaware that the difficulties they experience when conducting lessons may well be the result of mix-ups in communication that result from differences in interactional style. Instead, teachers may tend to attribute the problems that students experience during lessons to flaws in the students' intellect or character. For example, a teacher may decide a student is just naturally slow to learn, unmotivated, lazy, or inattentive.

Clearly, the circumstances just described fall into the familiar old pattern of assuming that the problem lies in the students rather than in the situation. When teachers make the mistake of believing that the problem is in the students rather than the situation, they lower their expectations for students' learning and offer them less challenging activities. Like their teachers, students of diverse backgrounds are frustrated when lessons are marred by miscommunication. Thus, students tend to withdraw, act out, and behave in other ways that lead them to learn less. Then when students' progress stalls, teachers feel confirmed in having lowered their expectations.

Teachers need to break this vicious cycle. To do so, teachers first need to understand the nature of mismatches in interactional styles and why they come about. Second, teachers need to be aware of how they can overcome these mismatches.

Sharing Time

Our first example comes from research conducted by Sarah Michaels (1981; 1986). Michaels' study took place in the first grade classroom of a teacher called Mrs. Jones. Half the students in this class were African American and half European American. Michaels focuses on "sharing time," which is also called "show-and-tell," a common activity in primary classrooms. Every day, the teacher called upon volunteers to give a narrative account about an important event (for example, a birthday party) or a formal description of some object (for example, a new coat).

Michaels identifies sharing time as a key situation or gatekeeping en-counter in the classroom. During sharing time, the teacher helps students learn to use discourse much like that they will encounter in books or use when they write. This literate discourse is quite different from the oral language children bring to school. For example, writers are expected to describe situations clearly and in some detail. They are not supposed to assume that the reader already knows all about the situation being de-scribed. In contrast, in oral discourse speakers usually rely to a greater extent on cues in the setting or on the background knowledge they share with their listeners. For example, they do not have to describe an object in detail if the listeners can see it in front of them.

Sharing time is part of the culture of many schools and generally reflects mainstream expectations and norms for interaction. During shar-ing time, teachers use questions and comments to help children speak in a literate style. Children's success at acquiring literate discourse, then, depends to a large extent on their ability to interact successfully with the teacher. If the children are from mainstream backgrounds and have inter-actional styles similar to that of the teacher, they will usually be successful. However, if the children are from diverse backgrounds with interactional styles different from the teacher, they may well be unsuccessful during sharing time.

Teachers seem to have definite requirements for the type of account they expect children to share. For example, Jones expected children to name and describe objects, even those in plain sight, and to assume the audience had little or no background knowledge about the event and its context. One of Jones' main requirements, the one to be discussed here, was that children stick to a single topic.

Topic-Centered Style

The European American children in the class had little difficulty meeting these requirements. They used a sharing style Michaels calls **topic centered**. Their accounts were focused on a single topic or closely related topics, were ordered in a linear fashion, and led to a resolution. Here is an example of a topic-centered account. (Conventional punctuation has been substituted for the notations in Michaels' transcripts, which show timing, stress, pitch, and other linguistic features.)

Mindy:	When I was in day camp we made these um candles.
Teacher:	You made them?
Mindy:	And uh I — I tried it with different colors with both of them but one just came out, this one just came out blue and I don't know what this color is.
Teacher:	That's neat-o. Tell the kids how you do it from the very start. Pretend we don't know a thing about candles. OK. What did you do first? What did you use? Flour?
Mindy:	Um . . . there's some hot wax, some real hot wax that you just take a string and tie a knot in it. And dip the string in the um wax.
Teacher:	What makes it uh have a shape?
Mindy:	Um you just shape it.
Teacher:	Oh you shaped it with your hand. Mm.
Mindy:	But you have, first you have to stick it into the wax and then water and then keep doing that until it gets to the size you want it.
Teacher:	Okay, who knows what the string is for? (pp. 431-32)

Michaels points out how well Jones was able to collaborate with Mindy. For one thing, Jones timed her questions so that they occurred just as Mindy had completed a thought. Questions were timed so that Mindy did not perceive them as interruptions. Jones moved her level of questioning from general to specific until she reached the level at which Mindy could respond appropriately. For example, she cued Mindy to start her description of making the candles by telling about the materials used ("What did you use? Flour?"). Finally, Jones' comments and clarifications built on what Mindy had started to say ("Oh you shaped it with your hand."). In short, Jones was able to help Mindy fashion an account following the rules for sharing time, and Mindy learned something about how to present an account using literate discourse.

Topic-Associating Style

In contrast to the European American children, the African American children in the class used a sharing style Michaels calls **topic associating**. The topic-associating style, in which episodes follow a theme, has a logic different from that of the topic-centered style but one that is equally valid (Cazden, 1988). In the topic-associating style, children present a series of episodes linked to some person or theme. These links are implicit in the account and are generally left unstated. However, Jones did not have the cultural knowledge to understand the topic-associating style, so she could not discern the topic of the discourse or predict where the child's narrative was headed. As a result, she often mistimed her questions and ended up cutting children off.

It should be emphasized that Jones was sincerely interested in helping topic-associating children learn to share in what she regarded as a more appropriate style. To this end she started asking the children to share about "one thing," that is, to stick to a single important or interesting topic. What Jones did not realize was that, from their own point of view, children who used the topic-associating style *were* sharing about one thing.

Here is an example of a topic-associating child's sharing turn, which begins with the teacher reminding the child to share "some one thing that's very important."

Deena:	Um. In the summer, I mean, w-when um I go back to school, I come back to school in September, I'ma have a new coat, and I already got it. And it's um got a lot of brown in it. And when um, and when I got it yesterday, and when I saw it my mother was, was going somewhere, when I saw it on the couch and I showed my sister, and I was readin' somethin' out on, on the bag and my sister said
	|_____|
Child:	|Um close the door.|
Deena:	My big sister said, Deena you have to keep that away from Keisha, 'cause that's my baby sister, and I said no. And I said the plastic bag because um when um sh-when the um she was um (with me), wait a minute, my cousin and her
	|_____|
Teacher:	|Wait a minute. You stick with your coat now. I said you could tell | one thing. That's fair.
Deena:	This was about my |c—
Teacher:	|OK, | all right, go on.
Deena:	|This was— and today, and yesterday when I got my coat, my cousin ran outside and he ran to, tried to get him, and he, he, he start — an' when he get in, when he got in my house, he layed on the floor and I told him to get up because he was cryin'.
Teacher:	Mm — what's that have to do with your coat?
Deena:	H-he, becau— he wanted to go outside, but we couldn't. (exasperated)
Teacher:	Why?
Deena:	Cause my mother s— wanted us to stay in the house.
Teacher:	What does that have to do with your coat?
Deena:	Bec— um uh
Child:	(whispers)
Deena:	Because, I don't know.
Teacher:	OK. |Thank you very much, Deena.

Children: |(talking)

Teacher: OK, do you understand what I was trying to do. Deena, I was trying to get her to stick with one thing. And she was talking about her

Children: Coat.

Teacher: New

Children: Coat.

Teacher: coat. It sounds nice, Deena.   (pp. 435-36)

The connections in Deena's account (among her cousin, her baby sister, and the coat) are not readily apparent. If Jones had been able to collaborate with Deena as she did with Mindy, perhaps Deena would have been able to verbalize the connections. But Jones was unable to time her comments appropriately. She twice interrupted Deena in the middle of a clause, and she asked her questions three times. Deena's train of thought may well have been disrupted by Jones' attempts to help her move toward a topic-centered style of sharing. Deena did not have the opportunity to learn to present her account using literate discourse, because Jones was unable to build on what she was saying.

From her conversations with Jones, Michaels knew she assumed that there was no connection among Deena's coat, her cousin, and her baby sister. Jones believed Deena and the other children who shared in this fashion did not plan their accounts in advance. She thought they just wanted to keep talking and so would say whatever came to mind.

Michaels wanted to understand the children's perspective, so she decided to play the tape of the sharing turn for Deena and to interview her about what she was trying to communicate. During the interview Deena clarified many of the previously unstated connections in her account. According to Deena, her cousin was "a *bad* little boy" who came into the house with dirty hands, which he started to put on her coat. Her baby sister entered the picture and because the plastic bag over the coat might be dangerous, Deena had to keep it away from her. Her coat had caused Deena to be concerned about both her cousin and baby sister, although for different reasons.

What is important, Michaels concludes, is that teacher and child were unable to collaborate, so it was not possible for the account to be clarified and expanded as the child was attempting to present it. Jones saw herself as trying to help Deena to share in an appropriate manner, but Deena saw Jones as actively interfering with her efforts. Michaels states:

> Moreover, during the interview Deena expressed a keen sense of frustration about being interrupted during sharing time. She saw this as an indication that the teacher was simply not interested in what she had to say, explaining, "she was always stoppin' me, saying' 'that's not important enough,' and I hadn't hardly started talking!"   (p. 439)

Cazden (1988) points out that sharing time is one of the few occasions in the school day when children have the chance to talk about their personal experiences and to bring their lives at home into the classroom. From this point of view, Deena's perception that the teacher was not interested in what she had to say is especially disturbing. Although far from their intent, teachers may unwittingly send children of diverse backgrounds the message that their experiences are less important than the experiences of other children.

Influence of Teachers' Cultural Backgrounds

There is ample evidence to suggest that teachers' ability to understand and appreciate topic-associating (or episodic) as well as topic-centered narratives is influenced by their cultural backgrounds. For example, Michaels (1981) observed that the African American instructional aide in Jones' class seemed able to follow the intentions of topic-associating children and to ask appropriate questions that helped them to expand upon and organize their accounts. Michaels and Cazden (1986) report that African American graduate students were better able to understand the thread in topic-associating narratives than were European American graduate students. They also suggest that the topic-associating narratives shared by Deena and other African American children appear to show elements of African American rhetorical style. For example, Smitherman (1977) describes how the narratives of African American adults may follow a style of relating many episodes that appear to wander away from the "point," only eventually to converge. While highly prized by African Americans, this style is likely to be exasperating to European Americans.

Adjusting to a Topic-Associating Style

The sharing time research conducted by Michaels and Cazden highlights the importance of teachers being responsive to cultural differences in the form and style of children's speaking. Awareness of cultural differences is an important first step. The next step is for teachers to make a conscious effort to understand the situation from the child's point of view and to adjust their instructional efforts accordingly.

Michaels (1986) describes the case of a teacher who understood the topic-associating style and used her knowledge successfully during a writing conference. Antonia, an African American student in the combination first/second grade class, had composed the following draft:

> I have a cat and my cat
> never go to the bathroom
> when my cousin eating over
> my house and we went to
> the circus my cousins
> names are LaShaun Trinity
> Sherry Cynthia Doral.
> (p. 114)

As Michaels watched, the teacher asked Antonia to read her draft aloud. When the child had finished reading, the teacher responded, "Boy, you've got a lot of cousins!" For the next few minutes she chatted with Antonia about her family. Then the teacher paused and asked in a thoughtful tone, "Just one more thing . . . what do your cousins . . . have to do with the circus . . . and your cat?" Antonia replied confidently, "Oh, my cousins always eat over my house, and they sleep over my house too. And one day last week, we all went to the circus." "Ooooh, I see," said the teacher, nodding her head and smiling. (p. 114)

In a discussion with Michaels, the teacher indicated that she had recognized that Antonia's writing was probably an example of topic-associating discourse. She commented, "You know, it's a whole lot easier to get *them* to make the connections clear, if you assume that the connections are there in the first place." (p. 115)

This teacher was able to understand a different style of discourse and to interact appropriately and constructively with a child who used it. She showed Antonia that she valued her writing and chosen topic. Near the end of the conference, the teacher gently signaled to Antonia that she was interested in having her make the connections in her writing explicit, one of the requirements of literate discourse. Because she has established rapport with Antonia and understands something of her cultural perspective, the teacher will be able to help her gradually to improve her writing to meet conventional expectations.

Styles of Questioning

Our second example of differences in interactional patterns centers on styles of questioning and comes from research conducted by Shirley Brice Heath, as mentioned in chapter 1. As part of her long-term study, Heath (1982) worked with children from the African American community she calls Trackton, and with their teachers. Heath explored the idea that Trackton students' difficulties in school stemmed in part from their lack of familiarity with the kinds of questions they were expected to answer in school. Like Michaels' research on sharing time, Heath's research explored the possibility that cultural differences in styles of discourse were causing teachers and students to experience communication difficulties.

Teachers' perceptions of these difficulties were reflected in statements such as the following:

> The simplest questions are the ones they can't answer in the classroom; yet on the playground they can explain a rule for a ballgame or describe a particular kind of bait with no problem. Therefore, I know they can't be as dumb as they seem in my class.
> I sometimes feel that when I look at them and ask a question, I'm staring at a wall I can't break through. There's something there; yet in spite of all the questions I ask, I'm never sure I've gotten through to what's inside that wall.   (p. 108)

When Heath observed the teachers at home, she found they asked their own children many questions. The teachers and other adults in these families saw young children as conversational partners and used questioning as a means of interacting with them. For example, two-year-old Missy was asked 103 questions in a 48-hour period. Almost half of all the utterances directed to her were questions.

The majority of questions posed to Missy were known-answer questions, those for which the questioner already had the information being requested. For example, while Missy and her mother were looking at an album of family photographs, her mother pointed to a picture of the family dog, Toby. She asked Missy two known-answer questions:

What does Toby say?
Where does Toby live?

Missy dutifully answered both questions. Heath concluded that the teachers and other adults in their families used questions to socialize children and to teach them such behaviors as what to attend to when looking at books, how to label objects, and how to name the attributes of an object (such as its color).

Questioning in Trackton

The questioning experience of young children in Trackton was very different from that of the teachers' children. Heath found that adults questioned children far less, apparently for two reasons. First, Heath discovered, "Trackton adults did not attempt to engage children as conversational partners until they were seen as realistic sources of information and competent partners in talk." (p. 114) Second, Trackton adults almost always had someone else to talk to, so mothers and young children were rarely alone at home together. In other words, young children did not have to serve as conversational partners for adults, because there were generally other adults or older children around.

Trackton adults did not ask children known-answer questions. Instead, they asked analogy questions that required children to compare one thing to another. For example, seeing the flat tire on a neighbor's car, an adult asked, "What's that like?" The child responded, "Doug's car," which had never been fixed. (p. 116) Adults did not ask children questions about the attributes of objects, such as, "What color is the flower?" As one grandmother told Heath, "We don't talk to our chil'un like you folks do; we don't ask 'em 'bout colors, names, 'n things." (p. 117) During a reading lesson in a third grade classroom, a boy from Trackton stated the same idea:

Teacher: What is this story about?
Children: *(silence)*
Teacher: Uh . . . Let's see . . . Who is it the story talks about?
Children: *(silence)*

> **Teacher:**   Who is the main character? Um . . . What kind of story is it?
>
> **Child:**   Ain't nobody can talk about things being about theirselves!
>   (p. 105)

Adjusting Questioning in School

In collaboration with Heath, teachers began to adjust the curriculum to reflect the experiences and questioning style familiar to Trackton students. For example, in social studies lessons about the community, teachers used photographs showing public buildings and scenes of several local communities and the surrounding countryside. Instead of asking questions about the identity or attributes of objects in the photographs, teachers posed questions such as:

> What's happening here?
>
> Have you ever been here?
>
> Tell me what you did when you were there.
>
> What's this like? (pointing to a scene or an item in a scene)   (p. 124)

The teachers found that Trackton children participated in lessons much more actively, showed a higher level of interest, and shared considerable information from their own experiences.

During certain lessons the teachers taped the children's responses. They later added to the tapes typical school known-answer questions requiring the naming of objects and their attributes, along with answers provided by children proficient at answering this kind of question. The tapes were placed at a learning center. Trackton students enjoyed listening to the tapes, probably because they could hear questions and responses similar to those favored in their own community. By listening to the conventional school questions and answers that were also on the tapes, Trackton students learned about the standard forms of classroom discourse. After a while, teachers asked certain Trackton students to help with the questions and answers added to the tapes. Then Trackton students were able to hear themselves successfully responding to conventional school questions.

Besides working with the tapes, teachers discussed with their classes different kinds of questions and the types of answers each required. For example, a *who* question could be answered with a single word, but a *why* question would probably need to be answered with many words, equivalent to a sentence or even a paragraph when written. Heath adds:

> Teachers and students came to talk openly about school being a place where people "talked a lot about things being about themselves." Students caught onto the idea that this was a somewhat strange custom, but one which, if learned, led to success in school activities and, perhaps most important, did not threaten their ways of talking about things at home.   (p. 125)

Culturally Responsive Instruction

Michaels' study of sharing time and Heath's study of questioning styles suggest how teachers can move toward making instruction responsive to the cultures of students of diverse backgrounds. [In chapter 3 you learned about current views of instruction and how many students learn school literacy largely through interactions with teachers and capable peers. In this chapter you have been introduced to the notion that teachers may act as gatekeepers.] In effect, when teachers are highly successful in interacting with some students (as Jones was with Mindy), they can do much to open the gates to school literacy. When teachers are largely unsuccessful in interacting with other students (as Jones was with Deena), they can do much to close the gates to school literacy.

The research of Michaels and Heath suggests, first, how important it is for teachers to begin with the assumption that students' actions are inherently logical, even though the logic they are following may be quite different from our own. Second, these studies suggest that we may benefit from learning more about the discourse and interactional styles of students' homes and communities. Both researchers discovered that teachers could act upon the knowledge gained and by doing so, improve classroom conditions for themselves and their students. In effect, when teachers act to broaden the rules for what is acceptable in the classroom, in terms of how students speak and write about their lives and how they answer questions, they are moving toward creating a composite classroom culture. They have changed the culture of the classroom to be responsive to students' home cultures.

But notice that we have not dropped our pursuit of academic goals. Rather, we recognize the importance of adjusting the means by which academic goals are met. For example, teachers of the Trackton students added content and questions that would make social studies lessons more meaningful. However, they also sought to familiarize Trackton students with the kinds of known-answer questions they needed to be able to answer to participate successfully in conventional lessons. Teachers signaled to students that ways of speaking in the home were respected in school, but that other ways of speaking would also be learned. Teachers maintained high expectations for students' literacy learning, even as they made instruction culturally responsive.

Understanding and acting upon knowledge of cultural differences is not, of course, a single or final remedy. We must also be aware of the larger social, political, historical, and economic contexts that generate and sustain conditions of inequality among groups and communities (Bennett and Pedraza, 1984; Ogbu, 1987). In this sense, cultural differences in discourse and interactional styles are just one manifestation of larger societal and historical conditions, reflecting the power relations among groups within American society.

> Teachers can signal to students that ways of speaking in the home are respected in school, but that other ways of speaking will also be learned.

Composite Classroom Cultures

Still, the concepts of culturally responsive instruction and the composite classroom culture offer implications for the classroom and the possibility of change. Recall the ideas about culture presented in chapter 1. When teachers seek to provide culturally responsive instruction, they are taking steps toward creating a composite classroom culture, one that meets school goals for literacy learning but is also responsive to students' cultural backgrounds. The composite classroom culture is an adaptation to the complex situation created by the interaction between the requirements of school literacy learning, which largely reflect mainstream values, and the needs and interests of students of diverse backgrounds.

The composite classroom culture is continually evolving, as teachers and students make adjustments to one another. The composite classroom culture is something both teachers and students must learn, through a process of experimentation and trial and error. In a sense, teachers and students are creating the composite classroom culture and initiating one another into this culture at the same time.

In multicultural settings communication problems do not disappear merely as a result of teachers having classroom experience with students of diverse backgrounds, or as a result of students' continual exposure to conventional school practices. For example, as their comments indicated, teachers were well aware of the reluctance of Trackton students to answer conventional school questions. For their part, students may be aware of different styles of interacting but not of the consequences of using one style or the other. Michaels, for example, learned that Deena apparently knew that Jones' idea of "good" sharing talk involved a relatively brief account with a beginning, middle, and end. Throughout the school year, though, Deena preferred to give accounts in her own style. Similarly, Heath reports how, after just a few weeks in preschool, Lem, a Trackton 4-year-old, generated strings of known-answer questions as he played "teacher." However, even after years of exposure to these questions in school, he and other Trackton students continued to be reluctant to respond to known-answer questions, until the teachers tried the changes described earlier.

Clearly, composite classroom cultures involve both teachers and students in the process of learning and changing. It is never easy to break out of old patterns, and the creation of a composite classroom culture requires the time, effort, and commitment of teachers and students alike.

Dealing with Cultural Differences

Perhaps the importance of teachers taking the first step toward working with students to create a composite classroom culture can be better understood by looking at the full range of strategies available to teachers and students who must deal with the stress caused by cultural differences. Jacob and Sanday (1976) suggest that individuals may pursue one of five strategies:

1. Contact with individuals of the other culture is avoided.
2. Contact is kept to a minimum or regulated to areas where differences are minimal.
3. Contact occurs regularly, but misunderstanding and misinterpretation lead to open conflict and hostility.
4. Contact occurs regularly, but the individual changes his operating culture to incorporate the standards of the culture of the individuals who hold the balance of power in the contact situation.
5. Contact occurs regularly, and all involved in the interaction work toward the development of a composite public culture.   (p. 98)

Jacob and Sanday believe that the first four strategies place a heavy burden on the student. Strategies 1 and 2 make school literacy learning virtually impossible, because students do not have the opportunity to participate in lessons and to interact sufficiently with teachers. Strategy 3 leads students to feel threatened and to resist the effects of schooling, as discussed in chapter 1. Strategy 4 denies the values of diversity and implies that it is only students of diverse backgrounds, not teachers and schools, who need to do the learning. An underlying assumption in this strategy is an acceptance of the dominant culture and a rejection of all others. In essence, students are asked to sacrifice their cultural identity as the price for school success (Fordham, 1991). Strategy 5, in which teachers and students work together to create a composite classroom culture, is the one advocated here. It allows students both to affirm their cultural identities and to strive for high levels of literacy and academic achievement. It allows teachers and students to affirm the value of diversity. It seems to be the only strategy that puts both teachers and students in a win-win situation.

Summary

Life opportunities in a complex society like that of the United States may depend on individuals' performances in key situations with gatekeepers. Teachers may inadvertently serve as gatekeepers during literacy lessons when they are more successful in interacting with some students than with others. Two examples were presented of situations in which cultural differences appeared to be hampering the school literacy learning of students from diverse backgrounds. In Michaels' work on sharing time, teachers were able to collaborate effectively with students who used a topic-centered style of discourse, but not with those who used a topic-associating style. In her work on questioning styles, Heath found that students were uncomfortable with the kinds of questions usually asked in school, due to the questioning patterns preferred in their homes and community. In both cases, once teachers learned about the cultural differences that were creating problems, they were able to use their knowledge to interact in a different, more positive manner with students. School literacy learning depends to a large extent on just such positive interactions between teacher and student. When teachers adjust to cultural differences in students' styles of interactions, they are moving toward culturally responsive instruction. The strategy of working collaboratively with students, in a process of mutual adaptation, leads to the development of composite classroom cultures in which students of diverse backgrounds have improved opportunities for literacy learning.

Application Activities

1. Pay close attention to the face-to-face interactions you experience over the next week or two. Write briefly about ones in which you have difficulty communicating. What were these interactions like? How did you feel?

2. Have you ever had difficulty communicating with someone from a different cultural background? If so, describe the experience. Discuss what you think you might do in the future to help communication flow more smoothly.

3. Suppose that you are a classroom teacher experiencing difficulty communicating with students who are from cultural backgrounds unlike your own. Describe the steps you might take to analyze and then to remedy the situation.

Suggested Readings

Cazden, C.B. (1988). *Classroom Discourse: The Language of Teaching and Learning*. Portsmouth, NH: Heinemann.
Heath, S.B. (1982). "Questioning at Home and at School: A Comparative Study." In G. Spindler, ed., *Doing the Ethnography of Schooling: Educational Anthropology in Action*. New York: Holt, Rinehart and Winston, pp. 102-31.
Michaels, S. (1981). "Sharing Time": Children's Narrative Styles and Differential Access to Literacy. *Language in Society,* 10(3), pp. 423-42.

chapter *7*

Patterns of Interaction: Achieving a Balance of Rights

————————— CHAPTER PURPOSES —————————

1. Highlight the importance of two themes:
   a. Interacting successfully with students;
   b. Giving students the opportunity to construct their own understandings of literacy;
2. Discuss the concept of the participation structure and how participation is usually structured in classrooms;
3. Consider why typical classroom rules governing participation in mainstream classrooms do not work with many students of diverse backgrounds;
4. Present positive examples showing how teachers and students may achieve a balance of rights in interactions.

This chapter continues the discussion begun in chapter 6 of how teachers can interact successfully with students of diverse backgrounds to promote their literacy learning.

Being in Tune with Students

Earlier chapters explored the idea that successfully accomplished teacher-student interactions are likely to be key to the school literacy learning of students from diverse backgrounds. In chapter 6 you learned of the importance of teachers being able to communicate effectively with students, in order to collaborate with or actively involve them in lessons. In chapter 3 you saw that instructional interactions must give students the opportunity to construct their own understandings of literacy. These are the two themes to be developed in this chapter: the importance of interacting successfully with students and of giving them the opportunity to construct their own understandings of literacy.

Let us begin with the first theme. To conduct effective lessons, teachers must strive to be in tune with their students. That is, teachers and students must have a shared understanding of the rules governing face-to-face interaction in that particular lesson setting. In classrooms with students of diverse backgrounds, it may be a mistake for the teacher to assume that students share mainstream assumptions about how face-to-face interaction should be carried out. As shown in chapter 6 in the examples of sharing time and questioning styles, students may be following a logic related to practices and values of their own home and community, not of the school and the dominant culture. If teachers wish to be in tune with students, they may find it helpful to be aware of assumptions about the patterning of interaction in both the mainstream culture and other cultures. Teachers being in tune with students is one of the new patterns that offer the promise of improving the school literacy learning of students of diverse backgrounds.

Conventional Classroom Recitation

In schools, the prevailing pattern of interaction is what can be called **conventional classroom recitation**. This pattern begins with the teacher initiating the sequence. A student responds, and the teacher then evaluates the student's response. This three-part sequence of teacher initiation, student response, and teacher evaluation has been described by many researchers (Sinclair and Coulthard, 1975; Mehan, 1979; Cazden, 1988) and may be observed in classrooms everywhere, ranging from the preschool to college levels.

Here is an example of recitation in a junior high classroom:

Teacher:	What kinds of books are on the back wall?
Student:	Periodicals.
Teacher:	No. Cox, what kind of books are on the back wall?
Student:	Fiction.
Teacher:	What else, Misha?
Student:	Biographies.
Teacher:	If I wanted to know where George Washington was born, can I find that out from the encyclopedia?
Class:	[in unison] Yes.

(Brown, 1991, pp. 22-23)

The teacher initiates the sequence by asking about the books on the back wall. The first student responds, and the teacher evaluates this response with a "no." To initiate the second sequence, the teacher calls on Cox and repeats the question. Cox gives the answer "fiction." By continuing with another question, this time addressed to Misha, the teacher signals that Cox's answer is acceptable and, at the same time, initiates the third sequence.

Just about everyone has participated in or conducted discussions structured in exactly this fashion. Conventional classroom recitation is very much a part of the culture of schools and a reflection of mainstream norms for how lessons should be conducted. Often, as in the example, the teacher uses known-answer questions. More often than not, these questions call for responses of just a word or two and do not require students to do much thinking. An obvious difficulty with these questions is that they usually do not give students much opportunity to construct their own understandings of literacy, but instead focus their attention on guessing about the answer the teacher wants to hear.

> Conventional classroom recitation imposes a structure for participation that may not be appropriate for students of diverse backgrounds.

Research on the Warm Springs Reservation

Conventional classroom recitation imposes a structure for participation that may not be appropriate for students of diverse backgrounds. To make this idea clear, let us consider Susan Philips' (1972) work in classes of Native American students on the Warm Springs Indian Reservation. Philips developed the concept of the **participation structure** (she uses the term **participant structure**) or arrangements for interaction. Conventional classroom recitation, described above, represents a certain kind of participation structure. Erickson and Shultz (1977; 1982) suggest that different participation structures involve different rules for speaking, listening, and turn-taking, and give individuals certain communicative rights and obligations. For example, in conventional classroom recitation, one of the rules for speaking is that only the child called upon by the teacher may answer. The teacher has the right to ask the questions, and the students have the obligation of answering.

In reservation classrooms, Philips noticed that students experienced difficulty when, in keeping with the rules for conventional classroom recitation, the teacher closely controlled who would speak and when. Students did not volunteer to answer and frequently refused to speak in front of the class. In contrast, students were comfortable in a participation structure in which they worked independently and could initiate interactions with the teacher, either by raising their hands or by going over to speak with the teacher at her desk. They also spoke more in a structure that allowed them to work in small, student-run groups, indirectly supervised by the teacher.

You recall that Trackton students were also reluctant to speak during classroom lessons, although in somewhat different circumstances and for somewhat different reasons. Students' reluctance to speak is significant because it indicates that there has been a breakdown in student-teacher communication, and repeated breakdowns may result in a lower degree of literacy learning.

Philips attributed Warm Springs students' reluctance to speak in certain classroom situations to differences between classroom participation structures and those in the community. First, in the classroom teachers set themselves apart from the other participants, the students, when they directed and planned activities. In community events students were accustomed to seeing the group as a whole work together. For this reason, in the classroom students tended to see themselves as within the same group, while they regarded the teacher as an outsider.

Second, teachers saw themselves as leaders with the right to issue instructions. Similarly, they felt that students were obliged to comply with their instructions. In the community, though, students learned that leadership was not based simply on holding a particular position and that individuals had the right to choose whom they would follow.

Third, classroom activities seldom included all students, while community activities were open to all who wanted to participate. Furthermore, teachers determined the degree of students' participation, for example, whether they were to recite in front of the class. In the community individuals decided upon the degree to which they would participate, after having determined in private that they were capable of performing successfully.

In short, Philips demonstrated that students were more willing to speak during classroom participation structures that had features like those of community participation structures. Philips suggested that communication would flow more smoothly if teachers gave students the right to determine when they would speak. If students had this right, they would probably volunteer to speak when they decided they could perform capably. Philips also suggested that teachers allow students to organize themselves to accomplish tasks within a small group.

When Philips (1985) conducted observations in classrooms just outside the reservation, she found that teachers were less likely to acknowledge and build upon the responses of Native American students than the responses of European American students. Part of the breakdown in communication seemed to be a matter of timing. Philips observed that, before giving a reply, Native American children and adults typically waited slightly longer after a person had stopped speaking than did European Americans. During lessons Native American students often gave their answers just as teachers were asking the next question. Because teachers had already started to say something else, they rarely acknowledged the students' answers.

Philips cuts to the heart of the matter when she suggests that we need to go beyond looking at cultural differences or cultural conflict in the classroom to consider a deeper issue:

> *The extent to which the teacher's interpretive framework is dominant in that context.* Teacher and student do not meet on an equal basis and work out

between them what is meaningful, or what is right and wrong. It is the teacher who defines what is meaningful, what is appropriate, what is true and what is false. She does so within a framework of classroom procedure that derives from white middle-class culture, and she derives her authority to define what is real and meaningful from the power structure that sustains that culture.   (p. 316; italics in the original)

Philips' comments highlight the manner in which power relations between dominant and subordinate groups underlie the problems of cultural differences in the classroom. These problems, which can slow the school literacy learning of students of diverse backgrounds, result from the imposition of classroom procedures that embody only the values of the dominant culture or the mainstream.

Participation structures, or the structures of face-to-face interaction, are a reflection of cultural values. Conventional classroom recitation, the main participation structure used in classrooms, gives the teacher the right to call upon students and tightly control the course of the lesson. In the Warm Springs community, as described earlier, students were taught the values of individual autonomy, self-determination, and a non-hierarchical style of leadership. Teachers' use of conventional classroom recitation, then, ran counter to the students' values. When the teacher called upon students to recite in front of the class, without giving them the option of volunteering or preparing in advance, students tended to feel cornered. Teachers' singling out of individual students in this manner has been called the **teacher spotlight effect**. Non-Native American teachers are generally in the habit of turning the spotlight on students by calling on them in front of the group, while Native American teachers generally avoid spotlighting (Erickson and Mohatt, 1982).

Breathing Room

In literacy lessons in multicultural classrooms, it seems important to give students **breathing room**, or the autonomy to shape the situation to some extent. Giving students breathing room allows teachers and students to achieve a **balance of rights** in which both parties can feel comfortable and literacy learning can proceed (Au and Mason, 1983).

Some teachers see it as their responsibility to organize and control every aspect of the learning situation without any input from the students, a perception reinforced by the transmission model of instruction. This perception is in striking contrast to the views shown by the Native Alaskan teachers described in the following account by Carol Barnhardt (1982):

> In one instance, a teacher is sitting at her desk getting her papers and books ready for a reading lesson. Five children in the reading group are already at the reading table. They are busy reading aloud the words on the board, opening their books, talking with each other and getting up and down in their chairs. The students are in essence doing reading activities without the teacher, and

they have a tempo well established before she comes on the scene. . . . [The teacher] sits down at the table, opens her book, puts her hand toward the board and begins talking using the same rhythm that was established by the children. There is no attempt on the teacher's part to change the pattern already established by the students. It is a very smooth entrance into the group and there is no time or energy lost in the transition.

When relating this incident to a friend, who is also a Native Alaskan teacher, she expressed surprise that *any teacher would want to set the pace for the students*. She said that she felt far more comfortable coming into her classroom *after* the students had been there for a while, and indicated that she would feel frustrated if she didn't have a sense of where the students' "heads were at" before she started each day.   (p. 155; first set of italics added)

The two Native teachers described by Barnhardt have a strong sense of what it means to be *in tune* with their students and to give them the breathing room they need (for another good example, see Lipka, 1991). As you noticed in the description of the first teacher's classroom, the children had actually started with reading activities before the teacher moved from her desk to their table. This is a good example of giving students breathing room. The teacher gave the students the chance to shape the learning situation, but she did not allow them to stray from the tasks of literacy learning. In fact, students became engaged in literacy tasks even without the teacher's intervention.

> In literacy lessons in multicultural classrooms, it is important to give students "breathing room," or the autonomy to shape the situation to some extent.

Talk Story-Like Reading Lessons

Another example of the problems created by conventional classroom recitation is seen in reading lessons taught to young students of Native Hawaiian ancestry. Teachers with little experience with Hawaiian children often try to control turntaking by calling on the children to speak one at a time. They try to enforce the rule that only the child called upon should answer. These procedures do not work well with these children, as shown in the following sequence taken from a small group reading lesson. The teacher has written several sentences on the chalkboard and wants one of the children to read aloud the third sentence, "A grasshopper is green." (Brackets mark overlapping speech. Nonverbal behaviors are in parentheses. X indicates an unidentified child.)

Teacher: Now, is there a volunteer for the (Annabelle raises her hand)
            [third sentence?

Annabelle?:	[Happier?
Annabelle?:	Hopper
Teacher:	I see — a hand is up over here. Annabelle, good, what is — (T. points at Annabelle. T turns to board, points. Annabelle lowers her hand.)
Tony?:	Green
Teacher:	Can you read this one? (Eloise looks away.)
Tony:	Oh I know. A guess —
Teacher:	Just a minute. (Leroy raises his hand.)
Samuel:	A grass.
Leroy:	[I know. T. leans toward Tony, puts arm forward, turns and looks at Tony.)
Teacher:	[Is your name Annabelle? Are you Annabelle?
Tony:	No.
Teacher:	You — you sound like you're Annabelle. I called Annabelle to read. (T. puts hand to her throat, looks at Annabelle then back to Tony.)

(Au and Kawakami, 1985, pp. 407-408)

This example shows the teacher and children operating within two different frameworks. The teacher is trying to follow the procedures for conventional classroom recitation, in which she initiates the sequence, a single student responds, and she evaluates that student's answer. The teacher calls on Annabelle, but Tony, Samuel, and Leroy all start to speak, either saying part of the answer or indicating that they know the answer. To enforce the rules she wants the children to follow, the teacher asks Tony if his name is Annabelle. Because she feels she must insist upon certain rules for interaction, the teacher puts the focus of the lesson on management and not on reading.

In contrast, teachers successful in teaching reading to Hawaiian children conduct discussion lessons in a style similar to that found in **talk story**, an important speech event for Hawaiian children outside of school (Watson, 1975; Watson-Gegeo and Boggs, 1977). During talk story children present rambling narratives about their personal experiences, usually enhanced with humor, jokes, and teasing. The main characteristic of talk story is **joint performance**, or the cooperative production of responses by two or more speakers. For example, one boy may begin talking about a day when he and several friends went fishing together. Immediately after beginning, he will invite another boy to join him in describing the events of that day. From that point on the two boys will alternate as speakers, assisting one another in telling the story. Others present may occasionally chime in.

Seldom in talk story does any one child monopolize the right to speak, as children are asked to do during conventional classroom recitation. What seems important to Hawaiian children in talk story is not individual performance in speaking, which is emphasized in the classroom, but group performance in speaking. Children who are leaders, those who are well liked by others, usually are those who know how to involve others in the conversation, not those who hold the floor for themselves. The value Hawaiian children attach to group versus individual performance seems consistent with the importance in Hawaiian culture of contributing to the well-being of one's family or friends, rather than working only for one's own well-being (Au and Kawakami, 1985). Conventional classroom recitation may cause difficulties for Hawaiian students because it reflects a different set of values as well as a different style of interaction.

Talk story-like reading lessons seem to be effective because they allow the teacher and students to focus on reading and not on the management of interaction. In fact, when compared to lessons conducted following conventional classroom recitation, talk story-like reading lessons are associated with about twice as much productive academic activity. For example, students mention many more text ideas and make many more logical inferences based on the text (Au and Mason, 1981). Examples of discussion in talk story-like reading lessons are presented in the next section of this chapter.

Experience-Text-Relationship Approach

Teachers successful in working with Hawaiian students combine the use of talk story-like participation structures with a general procedure for guided discussion of text known as the experience-text-relationship approach, or ETR (Au, 1979). Teachers analyze the story and decide upon a theme they feel will help children understand the story as a whole. They think of how the story can be connected to the children's own background experiences, so children will find it meaningful. They also divide the story into segments for silent reading and discussion. The length of the segment may vary from a page or two of a short story to several chapters of a novel, depending on the group of students and the difficulty of the text.

During the **experience** or **E** phase, the teacher begins by having the children discuss background experiences relevant to the story to be read. During the **text** or **T** phase, segments of the text are read silently, and the teacher leads the group's discussion. Finally, during the **relationship** or **R** phase, the teacher helps the children to draw relationships between their background experiences and text ideas.

Jo Ann Wong-Kam decided to have her second graders read "Annie and the Old One" (Miles, 1971), the story of a young Navajo girl (Annie) whose grandmother (the Old One) announces that she must soon return to Mother Earth. This story seemed appropriate because children in many Hawaiian families have a close relationship to their grandparents, much like the relationship between Annie and her grandmother. Wong-Kam decided to pursue the theme of the natural cycle of life and death.

During the *E* phase Wong-Kam began by having her students discuss their relationship with their own grandparents. She learned that the children were very close to their grandparents, and one had experienced what it was like to lose a grandparent.

During the *T* phase Wong-Kam and her students read and discussed the story. She found that the students needed considerable guidance to understand the events in the story and Annie's motives, and she found it useful to create a visual structure (a mapping of causes and effects in the story) to make key points clear. She had to do a lot of questioning and prompting to help the children understand that the problem in the story was not just that the Old One was going to die. The deeper problem was that Annie thought she could keep the Old One from dying, and so the solution needed to come in a change in Annie's way of thinking.

During the *R* phase, when the entire text had been read, Wong-Kam guided the children toward an understanding of the theme, the natural cycle of life and death. As she did throughout the series of lessons, Wong-Kam tried to elicit ideas from the children rather than giving answers away. In this way she required the children to take as much responsibility for text interpretation as they could, but she stood ready to provide additional assistance by asking other questions or by supplying needed information.

Let us look at part of the *R* discussion of "Annie and the Old One." Here Wong-Kam focuses the discussion on the final events in the story, when grandmother takes Annie out into the desert to talk to her about the natural cycle of life and death.

Teacher:	But she also compared it [when she said —
Joey:	[The cactus.
Teacher:	Okay, tell me about the cactus, Joey.
Joey:	Oh, I know about the cactus.
Teacher:	(What did you) find about the cactus?
Joey:	(Reads from text) "The cactus did not bloom forever. Petals dried and fell to earth."
Teacher:	Okay, what is she trying to tell Annie by using that analogy of the cactus?
Ross:	That people die of old age. That people just don't die when they say so.
Teacher:	Well, yeah, okay, that's — that's true. But what did they mean when they said, "The cactus did not bloom forever"?

Ross: That people, they got to die.

Kent: That means that when it starts blooming a life will start, but when it falls the life will end.   (Au and Kawakami, 1986, pp. 70-71)

The videotape of this part of the lesson shows the children conversing with the teacher without raising their hands or vying for turns to speak. There were moments when Wong-Kam called on one child, Joey, and he was the only one to speak. At times, then, interaction in talk story-like reading lessons does resemble conventional classroom recitation. Generally, though, the teacher asked a question and the children got the floor simply by starting to answer. This is what Ross did when he said, "That people die of old age." To move the discussion forward, Wong-Kam rephrased her question. Again without being called upon, Ross began to answer. This time Kent chimed in to clarify and to expand upon what Ross had started to say.

In conventional classroom recitation the teacher determines who will answer. In talk story-like lessons the *students* determine who will answer, although the teacher occasionally calls on children or helps a quiet child to hold the floor. The main purpose in talk story-like reading lessons is for the group to come to a shared understanding of the story being read. Rather than competing against one another, children are collaborating to interpret the story for the whole group's benefit. It makes sense, then, for children who have ideas to speak up, while others who do not have ideas to share at the moment remain silent. Of course, if certain children are not contributing at all, the teacher takes steps to draw them into the discussion. For example, the teacher might say, "Daniel, I bet you have some good ideas, too. Keep thinking, and in a minute I'll give you a turn."

In talk story-like reading lessons, a balance of rights is established between the teacher and students. The teacher has the right to set the topic and to keep discussion focused on the text. The students, however, have the right to decide when they will speak and how many speakers there will be. Often, as you have seen, children collaborate in producing answers to the teacher's questions.

Talk story-like lessons incorporate features of conventional classroom recitation, too. At times teachers may call on a certain child, and that child becomes the lead speaker. Other children may chime in to help that child or take over the floor if their ideas are stronger. Teachers keep the discussion on track through questioning and by repeating or paraphrasing key points made by the children. They use a process of constant eliciting to raise the level of children's thinking and give them the opportunity to construct their own understandings of the text. Talk story-like lessons also have a feature called **equal time**, because the children do as much, if not more, talking than the teacher. In some lessons the longest utterances are by children, not the teacher (Au, 1980).

In one series of lessons, a third grade teacher guided the children in a reading group to interpret a story entitled "Magic in a Glass Jar" (Bacmeister,

1964). The two children in the story, through the help of their grandmother, are able to see a caterpillar turn into a beautiful moth. The teacher, Joyce Ahuna-Ka'ai'ai, planned to work with the theme of learning from grandparents. During the discussion, however, the children collaborated to construct another theme: the importance of letting the moth go free (Au, 1992). This series of lessons and the one described earlier demonstrate the potential of talk story-like lessons to promote students' higher-level thinking about text and the active construction of meaning.

The strength of these lessons seems to come from two sources. First, teachers structure participation in a manner comfortable for students, and second, teachers constantly try to raise the level of children's thinking about text. A teacher once told me that she thinks of "stretching the students' minds" during reading lessons. Children's thinking about their reading also reaches a higher level because of the ideas of the other students.

Many of the classrooms in which talk story-like lessons are given include students who are not of Native Hawaiian ancestry but members of the many other ethnic groups found in Hawaii. These children participate successfully in talk story-like lessons as well, although in some cases they need some time to learn this style of interaction. So while talk story-like lessons seem especially well suited to the backgrounds of Hawaiian children, they seem beneficial for children of other backgrounds as well.

Achieving a Balance of Rights: Another Example

In talk story-like reading lessons, a balance of rights is achieved by the teacher's controlling the topic of discussion, while the children control who will speak and when. In classrooms with other groups of children, there seem to be other ways of achieving a balance of rights in reading lessons. For example, Pamela McCollum (1989) describes reading lessons taught by a teacher she calls Mrs. Ortiz, a native of Puerto Rico who taught a third grade class in San Juan, Puerto Rico. McCollum describes Ortiz as "a facilitator of interaction rather than a director of it." (p. 142) In common with talk story-like lessons, Ortiz's lessons seemed to resemble everyday conversation more than conventional classroom recitation. Ortiz used a procedure McCollum called the **invitation to reply**, which involved asking a question and then allowing children to take the floor without first having to be called on. This is the same procedure observed in talk story-like lessons, as discussed above.

But the balance of rights in the lessons taught by Ortiz seemed to be achieved in a somewhat different way. Ortiz was open to student initiations, and students frequently introduced personal comments into the reading discussion. In the following example, the class is reviewing a story about the Taino Indians, the inhabitants of Puerto Rico when Columbus arrived.

Mrs. O:	Vamos a escuchar a Ricardo a ver lo que él me vá a decir. [Let's listen to Ricardo and see what he's going to tell me.]
Ricardo:	(inaudible)
José:	Sí, Misi, es verdad. [Yes teacher, it's true.]
Ricardo:	(inaudible)
Mrs. O:	Vamos a escuchar a Ricardo. [Let's listen to Ricardo.]
José:	Misi, mi tatarbuelo era de la primera guerra mundial y luchó. [Teacher, my great grandfather was in the First World War and fought.]
Ricardo:	[ ] y que habían muchos, muchos árboles. Que no habían ni carreteras ni lagos ni habían casas. [[ ] And there were many trees. That there weren't any highways nor lakes, not even houses.]
José:	Misi, Misi, Misi [Teacher, Teacher, Teacher]
Mrs. O:	Lo que contó tu abuelo es una realidad. Es muy cierto. OK, vamos a seguir. [What your grandfather told you is true. It certainly is. OK, let's continue.]

(McCollum, 1989, p. 148)

In the sequence above, the teacher encourages Ricardo to speak, and he shares about his grandfather. The teacher acknowledges his statements before turning to discussion of the Taino Indians. McCollum suggests that this pattern of conducting lessons reflects a different social relationship between the teacher and students. In Ortiz's classroom the teacher-student relationship included the sharing of personal information during lessons. There was less of a boundary between personal conversation and reading-oriented conversation. In these lessons, then, it appears that the teacher's acceptance of children's personal experiences may contribute to achieving a balance of rights.

This possible interpretation of Ortiz's lessons finds support in work by Cazden, Carrasco, Maldonado-Guzman, and Erickson (1980), who observed extensively in the Chicago classrooms of two bilingual Chicana teachers. In these first grade classrooms the teachers interacted with their students in a manner consistent with Hispanic community definitions for social relations between adults and children. When speaking with the children, the teachers communicated *cariño* (love or tenderness) by showing concern for the children's well-being and a knowledge of their families.

Cazden (1988) suggests that an intermixing of social talk and talk related to the business at hand, such as the collecting of homework, may be an important feature of establishing a sense of community in these classrooms. Cazden writes, "In Hispanic communities, when people come together to transact any business, it is inappropriate — even rude — to begin the agenda immediately." (p. 177) Ortiz seems to be showing a similar style when she takes the time to have Ricardo speak about his grandfather, before shifting the discussion to focus on the text.

Style or Situation?

Discussion in this chapter has focused on cultural differences in interactional styles and how teachers can adjust to these differences during literacy lessons. However, these differences should *not* be interpreted to mean that students of diverse backgrounds should be characterized as having a certain set "learning style." Rather, cultural differences have been described to stress how classroom situations can be changed to better support children's literacy learning.

Problems with the idea of a fixed "learning style" are made clear in work conducted with Navajo students by McCarty, Lynch, Wallace, and Benally (1991). Some writers have tended to stereotype Native American students as "nonanalytical, nonverbal learners" or as "silent." Given these stereotypes, there was the belief that these students would not benefit from inquiry-based instructional approaches that relied on questioning, speaking up, and inductive reasoning. However, through the use of a social studies curriculum that drew on students' background experiences, teachers discovered that students would respond well to inquiry-oriented activities.

> In one fourth-grade class, for example, students continued their study of communities by researching local institutions and interviewing community members outside of class, later constructing a floor sized replica of Rough Rock complete with personalized family vehicles, homes, and livestock. Individually and in groups, they wrote and discussed personal experience stories about the project and their community. This study, the teacher noted, created high levels of interest and involvement "because I'm interacting with them, and they're not just reading someone else's idea of a community in a book." Moreover, she observed, students' expressiveness in these activities and their willingness to pose and respond to questions transferred to their work in other content areas.   (McCarty et al., 1991, p. 49)

McCarty et al. also suggest that inductive reasoning is often the pattern of learning Navajo children experience outside the classroom.

> When young children learn to herd sheep, for example, their first tasks are to monitor sheep behavior in the company of a caretaker — an older sibling, a parent, aunt, uncle, or grandparent — and to identify what they see the sheep doing. Caretakers help children organize their observations by explaining: "What you see is what sheep eat during the day . . . This is good for them, but if they eat X (a poisonous plant), they can become sick and die." In the context of purposeful sheepherding activity, children may ask, "If the sheep eat X, what will happen?", to which the caretaker is likely to reply, "What do you think will happen?"   (p. 50)

This work reminds us that, while becoming informed about cultural differences, we should be careful to avoid stereotypes that suggest that certain groups of students cannot benefit from literacy learning activities that require their active, constructive involvement. The claim that students of diverse backgrounds cannot benefit from constructivist models of instruction, and instead benefit more from transmission models, appears to arise from observations of students in situations that were (probably inadvertently) constructed to inhibit their participation.

Clearly, cultural differences in the patterning of interaction can cause difficulties in the classroom. However, students and teachers can make adjustments that permit them to communicate openly with one another, for the purposes of advancing literacy learning. In this chapter you have seen three examples of how this type of communication can evolve, with Hawaiian children, with Puerto Rican children, and with Navajo children.

Moving Beyond Conventional Procedures

Malcolm (1989) argues that the problem lies not in the cultural backgrounds of the students but in the constraints imposed by features of conventional classroom recitation and other, related mainstream classroom procedures. He highlights the striking similarities reported worldwide in the classroom behaviors of students from many different cultural backgrounds, including the Australian Aborigine students in his own research. During conventional classroom recitation, students show what Malcolm calls the "shyness syndrome" or what has been called "reluctance to speak" in this book. They also "call out" replies at inappropriate times, as seen also in the lesson of the teacher inexperienced in working with Hawaiian children. Malcolm concludes that teachers must come to value the need for meaningful input from students of diverse backgrounds, over and above the need to maintain conventional classroom procedures. He believes that, if teachers have a receptive attitude, they will come up with creative adaptations in interactional patterns.

Malcolm's analysis may be interpreted to mean that teachers do not need to worry about tailoring patterns of interaction to students' specific cultural backgrounds, which is an impossibility at any rate in classrooms where students are of many different ethnicities. It is important to be aware of cultural differences, and specific information about the patterning of interaction within a number of different cultures can be very helpful. However, what seems most important is that teachers are willing to try alternatives to the strict, unthinking use of conventional classroom recitation as the main way of structuring interaction during literacy lessons.

Cultural background no doubt contributes to teachers' comfort and facility with one style of interaction versus another. However, it is also clear that *teachers can learn new styles of interaction*. For example, teachers inexperienced in working with Hawaiian children generally can learn to use the talk story-like style of interaction in a matter of months (Au and Kawakami, 1985).

A related point is that ethnic or cultural background does not automatically determine the interactional style a teacher will use in the classroom.

Teachers may have cultural knowledge but decide not to apply it in the classroom, for a variety of reasons.

Piestrup (1973), for example, found that African American teachers effective in teaching African American students to read used an interactional style she called "Black Artful." However, not all the African American teachers Piestrup studied used this style, and none of the European American teachers did.

Piestrup describes the Black Artful style in the following manner:

> The Black Artful group used Black speech fluently, directly involving the children in learning reading rather than to establish rapport as an intermediate step. The label Black Artful is used to describe teaching which incorporates a form of rhythmic play unique with Black dialect speakers. It is not the surface features of phonology or grammar that are important, but the rapid interplay with intonation and gesture familiar to Black children as one of the art forms of Black culture. (p. 103)

Teachers who used the Black Artful style pressed their students to achieve at a high level, encouraged students to participate actively in discussions, and took the time to develop students' knowledge of new vocabulary. They emphasized to Piestrup that the abilities of their African American students were often underestimated. Piestrup found that these teachers were in tune with students in ways that other teachers, both African American and European American, were not.

Piestrup's work suggests that knowledge of and participation in a culture does not automatically carry over into one's teaching style. This means that reflection upon cultural differences may be an important activity for all teachers, even those who share their students' cultural background.

Summary

It is important both to pattern interaction in a manner responsive to students' cultural backgrounds, and to use discussions to allow students to construct their own understandings of literacy and to engage in text interpretation and other forms of higher-level thinking. Conventional classroom recitation, which reflects mainstream norms and values, is the participation structure generally used to structure lessons. However, it appears to be an inappropriate means of structuring lessons for students from a number of different ethnic groups, because it violates the norms and values of their home cultures. The experience-text-relationship approach and the use of talk story-like participation structures present possible alternatives to conventional lessons, at least for some groups of students. Effective teachers of students from diverse backgrounds are those who are in tune with students, achieve a balance of rights in classroom literacy lessons, and allow students breathing room and equal time. The approaches teachers use to show that they are in tune with students may vary, depending on the backgrounds of the students. Teachers do not have to be of the same ethnic background as their students to be effective. They can learn new styles of interaction if they are receptive to students, open to change, and willing to give priority to literacy learning rather than to conventional procedures.

Application Activities

1. Observe a classroom lesson in an elementary school and take notes on what the teacher and students say. Also make notes on the nonverbal behavior shown by the students, such as whether they raise their hands and look in the direction of the teacher or another student. What were the rules for speaking, listening, and turntaking in this lesson? Did you observe conventional classroom recitation or another type of participation structure?

2. Conduct a lesson with a group of elementary school students. Audiotape or videotape the lesson. Analyze the lesson to see how you structured interaction. What were the rules for speaking, listening, and turntaking in your lesson? How much of the talking did you do? How much of the talking did the students do?

3. Brainstorm alternatives to conventional classroom recitation. Outline two or more alternative approaches that involve teacher-guided instruction and two or more alternatives that involve groups of students working on their own. Describe what you see as the possible advantages and disadvantages of each approach.

Suggested Readings

Au, K.H., and A.J. Kawakami (1985). "Research Currents: Talk Story and Learning to Read." *Language Arts*, 62(4), 406-11.

Erickson, F., and G. Mohatt (1982). "Cultural Organization of Participation Structures in Two Classrooms of Indian Students." In G.B. Spindler, ed., *Doing the Ethnography of Schooling: Educational Anthropology in Action*. New York: Holt, Rinehart and Winston, pp. 132-74.

Philips, S. (1972). "Participant Structures and Communicative Competence: Warm Springs Children in Community and Classroom." In C. Cazden, V. John, and D. Hymes, eds., *Functions of Language in the Classroom*. New York: Teachers College Press.

chapter 8

Language Differences: Key Concepts and Varieties of English

1. Offer cautions about the use of inappropriate forms of language assessment;

2. Discuss why schools often do a poor job of promoting the literacy learning of students who speak a first language other than standard American English

3. Provide guidelines for the literacy instruction of students who speak nonmainstream varieties of English

4. List questions teachers can use to assess classroom situations, for the purposes of improving literacy instruction.

The present chapter and the next chapter address issues of language. This chapter provides an introduction to the topic through a discussion of key concepts and focuses primarily on the literacy instruction of students who speak nonmainstream varieties of English. The next chapter centers on the literacy instruction of students who speak a first language other than English.

Language as Part of Culture

The starting point for this discussion of language issues is the idea that language is part of culture. In this view a language includes a set of sounds, rules for grammar, and vocabulary. But a language is also seen in terms of its users and the situations in which it is used (Hymes, 1974). If we know a language well, it means we know how to use it appropriately in the company of other speakers who share a common culture, history, and set of values.

If you can view language from this broad, social perspective, you will realize that you have already learned a great deal about issues of language and literacy in the previous two chapters on patterns of interaction. For example, Black English was the home language of the African American students in the studies by Michaels and Heath, and Hawaiian Creole English was the home language of the Hawaiian children in my own research.

In all of the research described, the primary barriers to school literacy learning did not lie in the details of sounds, grammar, and vocabulary. Instead, the barriers were those created by schools' failure to acknowledge and appreciate students' home cultures and to build upon the interactional styles and everyday uses of language with which students were already familiar. From reading these chapters you also have a sense of how some procedures (particularly conventional classroom recitation) are widely used and seem to have a privileged status in schools, not because they are particularly effective for promoting literacy learning, but because they are a familiar part of mainstream school culture.

The terms "home language," "first language," and "native language" will be used interchangeably here. All refer to the language children learn at home when growing up. In many cases children continue to speak this language even after they have become proficient in standard American English, because this language is part of their cultural identity and heritage.

How Schools Hinder Literacy Learning

With this background, let us consider one of the main questions to be addressed in this chapter: Why is it that schools often do such a poor job of promoting the literacy learning of students who speak a nonmainstream variety of English or a first language other than English? The answer seems to lie in schools' tendency to discount the language ability of students of diverse backgrounds and to fail to capitalize upon the language skills they bring from the home. The reasons for this situation are many, but a major reason is that standard American English is the language of power in the United States, and educational gatekeepers tend to regard other languages as inferior and less useful for the purposes of schooling.

Research provides ample evidence that students of diverse backgrounds are skilled language users well equipped to learn to read and write (Rigg and Allen, 1989). But students' school literacy learning is frequently blocked by procedures that dictate a single path to literacy based on the use of mainstream codes, procedures, and materials not designed to tap the language skills and existing knowledge of students of diverse backgrounds. Insistence on these codes, procedures, and materials is one of the old patterns that needs to be broken. Like some of the other old patterns identified in this book, such as the use of conventional classroom recitation, this one stems from the power relations between dominant and subordinate groups.

Methods of assessment and testing connected with this old pattern, such as typical language assessment sessions and standardized tests, tend to be error-prone and largely uninformative when used with students of diverse backgrounds (Figueroa, 1989). Yet the results, however faulty, frequently have profound consequences for children. For example, schools frequently attempt to assess the language ability of kindergarten students as a means of determining the types of language and literacy instruction they will receive. These tests essentially look only at students' knowledge of mainstream language forms and settings.

Yet students who are identified as having "weak language skills" are often placed in the bottom reading group or sent out of the classroom for remedial reading instruction. In either event their language arts instruction generally follows a transmission model and is almost entirely centered on oral reading, skill instruction, and other rote learning activities (Allington, 1991). In general, students do not find this instruction meaningful, fail to progress well in learning to read and write, and develop negative attitudes toward school. Numerous studies have documented this pattern in classrooms with students whose home language is a nonmainstream variety of English and with students whose home language is Spanish or another language other than English (McDermott and Gospodinoff, 1981; Wong Fillmore, 1986; Delgado-Gaitan, 1989). Once placed in this slower track, students remain behind their peers in reading throughout their elementary school careers (Barr, 1989).

Language Assessment in an Intimidating Situation

One of the problems is that language assessment often takes place in situations that many young students of diverse backgrounds find uncomfortable and intimidating. An example of a child's response to such a situation is presented in the transcript below. This interview is representative of hundreds conducted in a school in New York City (Labov, 1972).

A young African American boy enters the room to be greeted by a large, friendly, European American interviewer. The interviewer places a block or a fire engine on a table in front of the boy and says, "Tell me everything you can about this." (The interviewer's remarks are shown in parentheses.)

[12 seconds of silence]

(What would you say it looks like?)

[8 seconds of silence.]

A space ship.

(Hmmmm.)

[13 seconds of silence]

Like a je-et.

[12 seconds of silence]

Like a plane.

[20 seconds of silence]

(What color is it?)

Orange. [2 seconds.] An' whi-ite. [2 seconds.] An' green.

  [6 seconds of silence]

(An' what could you use it for?)

  [8 seconds of silence]

(If you had two of them, what would you do with them?)

  [6 seconds of silence]

Give one to some-body.

(Hmmm. Who do you think would like to have it?)

  [10 seconds of silence]

Cla-rence.

(Mm. Where do you think we could get another one of these?)

At the store.

(Oh ka-ay!)

(Labov, 1972, p. 206)

William Labov, the sociolinguist who conducted this research, attributes the child's poor performance not to his lack of language ability but to the asymmetrical nature of the interview situation. In such a situation, a child is likely to feel that anything he says can be held against him. The child has developed some strategies to avoid saying much in this situation, and he works hard at it. Labov notes that the boy uses a special intonation pattern when he says, "A space ship." This intonation pattern is used by African American children when the answer to a question is obvious and they know they are being quizzed. This pattern is the children's way of saying to the question-asker, "Will this satisfy you?" This interview is a good measure of the child's ability to defend himself in a threatening situation, Labov concludes, but a poor measure of his language ability.

Effects of Changing the Assessment Situation

If children's verbal performance is related to the characteristics of the situation, and not only to their language ability, then it should be possible to change situations to produce better demonstrations of language use. Such an experiment was tried with 8-year-old Leon, a boy who showed a pattern of interview responses much like that presented in the transcript above. To change the situation, Clarence Robins, the interviewer

1. Brought along Leon's best friend, Gregory;
2. Brought along some potato chips;
3. Sat on the floor;
4. Introduced taboo words and topics.

The presence of Gregory and the potato chips turned the situation into something more like a party. When Clarence sat on the floor, he decreased the asymmetry between himself and Leon. The taboo words and topics signalled to Leon that he could speak freely without fear of retaliation.

These changes led to remarkable differences in Leon's verbal performance, as the following transcript illustrates:

CR:	. . . Hey Gregory! I heard that around here . . . and I'm 'on' tell you who said it, too . . .
Leon:	Who?
CR:	about you . . .
Leon:	Who?
Greg:	I'd say it!
CR:	They said that — they say that the only person you play with is David Gilbert.
Leon:	Yee-ah! yee-ah! yee-ah! . . .
Greg:	That's who you play with!
Leon:	I 'on' play with him no more!
Greg:	Yes you do!
Leon:	I 'on' play with him no more!
Greg:	But remember, about me and Robbie?
Leon:	So that's not —
Greg:	and you went to Petey and Gilbert's house, 'member? *Ah haaah!!*
Leon:	So that's — so — but I would — I had came back out, an' I ain't go to his house no more. . .

(Labov, 1972, pp. 211-12)

In a situation made more symmetrical, Leon and Gregory have no difficulty expressing themselves and have so much to say that they keep interrupting one another. Speech samples like these reveal children's use of an assortment of complex grammatical structures. As shown above, Leon uses Black English structures that include negative concord (*I 'on' play with him no more*), the pluperfect (*had came back out*), and negative perfect (*I ain't had*).

These results show how assessment in situations that appear threatening to students of diverse backgrounds can serve to mask their language ability. As seen in earlier chapters, students' language and literacy ability can also be masked in classroom settings that impose mainstream norms for interaction and deny students the possibility of using strengths gained through experiences in the home and community. The practical implication seems to be that much of the time and effort spent in formal assessment and testing would probably be better spent in analyzing and making adjustments to classroom learning conditions. Assessment needs to focus on typical classroom situations and on how well those situations support students' literacy learning. This idea will be discussed at length near the end of this chapter.

> Much of the time and effort spent in formal assessment and testing
> would probably be better spent in analyzing and making adjustments
> to classroom learning conditions.

Language and Power Relations

Research dismisses the notion that the often poor literacy achievement
of students of diverse backgrounds is due to their entering school with a
lower level of oral language ability than their mainstream, middle-class
peers. Studies suggest that students from diverse backgrounds receive extensive verbal stimulation in the home and community (Delgado-Gaitan,
1990; Pease-Alvarez, 1991). For example, in summarizing his observations
of African American children growing up in Harlem, Labov wrote:

> We see a child bathed in verbal stimulation from morning to night. We see
> many speech events which depend upon the competitive exhibition of verbal
> skills: sounding, singing, toasts, rifting, louding — a whole range of activities
> in which the individual gains status through his use of language . . . . We see
> the younger child trying to acquire these skills from older children — hanging
> around on the outskirts of the older peer groups, and imitating this behavior
> to the best of his ability. We see no connection between the verbal skill at the
> speech events characteristic of the street culture and success in the classroom.
> (Labov, 1972, pp. 212-13)

The problem appears to lie not in the child's language ability, but in the
fact that schools generally do not value skill in any language but standard
American English. Yet all varieties of English are equally effective systems
for everyday communication and for complex thought. Linguists have demonstrated that different varieties of English, including Black English and
Hawaiian Creole English, are complete languages, each with its own
complex set of rules for grammar, pronunciation, and vocabulary (Fasold,
1972; Bickerton, 1981).

Linguistic research also confirms that these varieties of English are
readily used for logical thought. In fact, arguments stated by speakers of
Black English can be better reasoned, more convincing, and more concise
than those of speakers of standard American English. For example, a 15-year-
old African American gang member named Larry, an accomplished speaker
of Black English, used about 135 words to present a complex set of six
interdependent propositions on the question of whether one's spirit would
eventually go to heaven or hell. In contrast, a college-educated African
American adult speaking standard English required 100 words to state
just one basic proposition concerning his spiritual beliefs (Labov, 1972).

From a linguistic point of view, standard American English is itself a
variety of English and neither superior nor inferior to other varieties of

English. However, social and historical processes have given standard English greater prestige than other varieties (Labov, 1972). What gives standard or "broadcast" English its special role in the United States is that it is the language of power, the variety spoken by those in the dominant, mainstream groups.

Spanish, Black English, and other languages, which are as effective as standard English for the purposes of reasoning and complex thought, do not have the same privileged status, because they are generally spoken by those from subordinate groups or of diverse backgrounds. Standard English is not a "better" language, but its speakers do hold greater power in American society.

Varieties of English as Languages in Their Own Right

As a reflection of power relations, it is common to encounter the mistaken view that the languages spoken by subordinate groups are inferior or "broken" versions of a dominant-group language. In the United States this misconception often affects schools' views of Black English and Hawaiian Creole English, to cite just two examples, which are erroneously treated as imperfect copies or dialects of standard American English (Sato, 1989).

Smitherman (1984) argues that Black English, the home language spoken by many African Americans, is rightly called a language rather than a dialect. She writes:

> If one considers only words, grammar, and sounds as the essence of language, then Black speech data might tend to look more like a dialect of White English. If one also considers the history and social rules that govern the use, production, and interpretation of the words, grammar, and sounds, then Black speech data more nearly resemble a different language.   (p. 106)

Smitherman reminds us of the importance of teachers viewing language differences in the context of cultural differences, and understanding that languages do not just differ in terms of surface features such as sounds. As discussed in chapters 6 and 7, students' home languages are tied to family and community routines, customs, and values and so are an important aspect of students' cultural identities.

Proficiency in Standard English as a Goal

With regard to school literacy learning, proficiency in standard American English should be seen as a goal, *not* as a prerequisite to becoming literate. When proficiency in standard American English is understood to be a goal rather than a prerequisite, teachers encourage students to use their home language as the basis for becoming literate in school. When standard

English is viewed as a prerequisite, teachers base instruction in literacy on students' ability to speak, read, and write just this code and deny them the opportunity to use their home languages as the means for becoming literate in school.

> With regard to school literacy learning, proficiency in standard American English should be seen as a goal, not as a prerequisite to becoming literate.

Helping students of diverse backgrounds increase their command of standard English will not, in and of itself, improve their ability to think critically, since students' own languages can serve just as well for verbal expression and reasoning. The main reason for emphasizing standard English in school is that a command of standard English is likely to enable students to compete more successfully in mainstream settings, including schools and places of employment, as discussed in earlier chapters.

In theory, students' speaking of home languages other than standard English does not, in and of itself, pose a problem for school literacy learning. Literacy learning is part of language learning, and students' proficiency in any language, especially if they can read and write in that language, provides a solid foundation for future learning.

In fact, speaking a nonmainstream variety of English gives students many language strengths that can be used as the basis for developing literacy in standard English. Lee (1991) found that signifying, a means of using indirect words or gestures in African American culture, could be used as a metaphor to help African American high school students interpret the themes of novels. Delain, Pearson, and Anderson (1985) discovered a direct relationship between seventh grade African American students' skill at sounding (a form of ritual insult that is a popular variety of signifying) and their ability to comprehend figurative language. This research suggests that students who speak Black English and other nonmainstream varieties of English come to the classroom with special strengths in language that are directly relevant to such important literacy outcomes as comprehending literature.

Teachers' Attitudes

Teachers' attitudes may be another factor tending to sustain the old pattern of schools' failure to build on the existing language abilities of students of diverse backgrounds. The negative attitudes some teachers have towards students' home languages may cause students to feel alienated and resentful and eventually lead them to refuse to participate in school literacy activities (Fairchild and Edwards-Evans, 1990).

In the following example, taken from Piestrup (1973), a group of first grade students is reading sentences printed on long strips of cardboard. When it is Lionel's (C1's) turn to read, the teacher spends the time correcting his pronunciation.

(The text being read aloud is in italics.)

T	This one, Lionel. This way, Lionel. Come on, you're right here. Hurry up.
C1	*Dey, —*
T	Get your finger out of your mouth.
C1	*Call —*
T	Start again.
C1	*Dey call, "What i' it? What is it?"*
T	What's this word?
C2	Dey.
C1	Dat.
T	What is it?
C2	Dat.
C3	Dey.
C4	(Laughs.)
C1	Dey.
T	Look at my tongue. *They.*
C1	*They.*
T	*They.* Look at my tongue. (Between her teeth.)
C1	They
T	That's right. Say it again.
C1	They.
T	*They.* OK. Pretty good. OK, Jimmy.

(Piestrup, 1973, pp. 54-55)

As Piestrup points out, the teacher actually disrupts the continuity of the reading lesson by focusing on a surface feature of speech. Lionel's pronunciation is the correct one in Black English and indicates that he understands that the word is *they*. But when the teacher asks, "What's this word?", Lionel and another child (C2) guess instead that the word might be *that*. C4 seems to be enjoying the confusion. In the last line, the teacher's comment of "pretty good" communicates that Lionel's pronunciation is still not acceptable.

In this and other examples, Piestrup shows how teachers can alienate children from school learning situations by subtly rejecting their speech. Teachers can discourage children by constantly correcting their speech and by implying that they know very little. These signals can be sent through words, tone, gesture, and even silence. Piestrup found that children showed their resistance to teachers' negative attitudes by engaging in verbal play apart from the teacher or by withdrawing into a moody silence. Both strategies cut the children off from opportunities to learn to read in school.

Rejecting students' home languages can be tantamount to rejecting the students themselves. When students feel that their language is being denigrated by teachers, their resistance to teachers' negative attitudes increases, their school literacy learning slows, and they eventually drop out of school.

Labov and Robins (1969) suggest that, for a group of 13-to 15-year-old African American boys involved with the street culture, there was no relationship between reading achievement and verbal ability. Schools had failed to help any of these boys, even those with extensive verbal ability, learn to read at higher than the fifth grade level. The boys perceived school as hostile and irrelevant to their lives and turned to gangs instead. Their language abilities, which were rejected by the school, were appreciated by members of their gangs. In a related vein, Fordham (1991) argues that schools put African American teenagers in the position of having to choose between identifying themselves as African Americans and achieving academic success.

Instruction through Meaningful Communication

How can teachers use students' existing language abilities to promote school literacy learning? Teachers of students who speak a nonmainstream variety of English, or a first language other than English, will want to be aware of basing the classroom literacy program on constructivist models of instruction, as discussed in chapter 3. Reading instruction should be focused on the reading of high-quality children's literature, as discussed in chapter 11, with skill instruction growing out of the reading of literature. Writing instruction should be conducted through the writers' workshop and dialogue journals and other authentic, purposeful forms of writing, as discussed in chapter 10.

When interacting with students, teachers will want to have the mindset that they are communicating for the purpose of exchanging ideas, not for the purpose of correcting pronunciation and grammar. While engaged in exchanging ideas with students, teachers can model the use of standard English, including pronunciation, grammar, and vocabulary. The idea of building students' language and literacy abilities through meaningful communication applies whether communication is taking place orally or in writing. The following two examples illustrate this point.

Reading Instruction

This example is taken from a small-group reading lesson taught to a group of second graders, all native speakers of Hawaiian Creole English. At this point in the story, the main character is afraid of what will happen if the frog he has found is used for bait. (T is the teacher; A, V, L, and S are students. Brackets mark overlapping speech. Additional information about nonverbal behavior, such as hand raising, appears in the original.)

T: If you're gonna use it for bait, what do you have to do with that frog? You just throw it in the water?

V: Uh-uh (negative).

A: Put it on a hook.

T: Oh n-o-o-o! He's gonna have to stick it on a hook. (Gestures hooking something with hands, glances at S, then back to A.)

L: And den go like dat, an den dat. (Gestures casting a line.)

T: And throw it in the water,
     [and (also makes gesture of casting)

A: [En den, en mi [ght (?)

S: [The
     fish
     [might come and eat it.

A: [Da fish might come
     and eat it.

   (Au, 1980, pp. 104-105)

As this example shows, the teacher, Claire Asam, welcomes the children's ideas. She paraphrases what the children have said ("He's gonna have to stick it on a hook"), and supplies words for their gestures ("And throw it in the water"), but this modeling and extending of language takes place very naturally during the exchange of ideas about the story. The teacher accepts the children's language and focuses on their thoughts rather than on their pronunciation. She allows students to chime in and build on one another's ideas, in the talk story-like style described in chapter 7.

Writing Instruction

> Standard English does not replace the home language but is available to students as an alternate code, to be used in school and work settings when it is necessary and appropriate to do so.

Delpit (1988) cautions that the goal of teachers is not simply to have students learn to use an alternate code. Teachers also need to be aware of encouraging students to value their home languages and to see relationships between language use and power realities in the United States.

   In this regard, Delpit cites the teaching strategies used by Martha Demientieff, an accomplished Native Alaskan teacher of Athabaskan Indian students. Demientieff's students live in a small, isolated village with a population of under two hundred people. They speak a variety of English known in Alaska as "Village English." To heighten students' awareness of different codes of English, Demientieff identifies examples of Village English in their writing and puts these words and phrases on half of a bulletin board. She labels this side of the board "Our Heritage Language." On the other side of the board she puts the students' writing into equivalent words in standard American English. This side is labeled "Formal English."

Demientieff and the students take a considerable amount of time to enjoy the words and discuss the shades of meaning on the "Heritage English" side of the board. "That's the way we say things," she reminds the students. "Doesn't it feel good? Isn't it the absolute best way of getting that idea across?"

Then, moving to the other half of the board, she informs the students that there are people in the world outside of the village who judge other people by the way they speak and write. She says:

> We listen to the way people talk, not to judge them, but to tell what part of the river they come from. These other people are not like that. They think everybody needs to talk like them. Unlike us, they have a hard time hearing what people say if they don't talk exactly like them. Their way of talking and writing is called "Formal English."
>
> We have to feel a little sorry for them because they have only one way to talk. We're going to learn two ways to say things. Isn't that better? One way will be our Heritage way. The other will be Formal English. Then, when we go to get jobs, we'll be able to talk like those people who only know and can only really listen to one way. Maybe after we get the jobs we can help them to learn how it feels to have another language, like ours, that feels so good. We'll talk like them when we have to, but we'll always know our way is best.
> (Delpit, 1988, p. 293)

Demientieff does many activities to develop the concepts of Heritage (informal) English and Formal English. She compares the speaking of Heritage English to the relaxed informality of a picnic, and the speaking of Formal English to the "dressed up" ways of a formal dinner. The students prepare a formal dinner in their classroom, and they speak only Formal English as they eat with silverware and china. Then they prepare a picnic where they speak only informal, Heritage English.

To sensitize students to differences in written language, Demientieff contrasts the "wordy" academic style of writing with the metaphorical style of Athabaskan. She and the students discuss the idea that a lengthy manner of writing is a feature of book language, while brevity may be preferred in Heritage language. Students write papers in the academic style and confer with Demientieff and their peers about whether their writing is wordy and formal enough to sound like a book. Demientieff then asks students to reverse the process, to summarize their meaning in just a few sentences. At the end students further distill their writing until they end up with a saying short enough to put on the front of a T-shirt. They write their sayings on little paper T-shirts that are hung all over the room. Sometimes they extract the basic message from the texts of other authors.

Demientieff's approach shows how students can be empowered through both an appreciation of their home language and an understanding of standard English. Students' new knowledge of standard English is added to their knowledge of their home language. Standard English does not replace the home language but is available to students as an alternate code, to be used in school and work settings when it is necessary and appropriate to do so. As this example suggests, an approach like that used by Demientieff may enable students of diverse backgrounds to have the best of both worlds.

Assessing the Learning Situation

In the old pattern described at the beginning of this chapter, it was assumed that learning problems were somehow related to factors within the student, such as "weak language skills" and the speaking of a home language other than standard English. As you now know, research does not support the assumptions of this old pattern. Many studies demonstrate that students of diverse backgrounds come to school with considerable language ability and, in view of their language ability alone, should not have any difficulty learning to read and write.

In the new pattern teachers assume that students of diverse backgrounds have ample language ability and can learn to read and write well, given the proper circumstances. When students experience learning difficulties, teachers recognize that the problem lies in the situation rather than in the students. They reflect upon the learning situations within the classroom and make adjustments in these situations until they find the conditions in which students can make satisfactory progress in learning to read and write.

As implied in earlier chapters, there are a number of factors to be considered when seeking to adjust classroom situations to meet the literacy learning needs of students from diverse backgrounds. In analyzing classroom situations, teachers might ask questions such as;

Did students find the activity interesting, motivating, and meaningful?

Did students have a chance to share their ideas about the activity?

Was the activity adjusted on the basis of students' suggestions?

These questions relate to our discussion in chapter 3 of the importance of the motivational, affective dimension in literacy instruction.

The following questions stem from our discussion in chapter 4 of the importance of student goal-setting and students' ownership of literacy.

Was the activity in line with students' goals for their own literacy learning?

Did the activity offer students any choices (for example, about the books they could read, the topics they could write about, the projects they could complete, the other students they could work with)?

The next question is related to the point made in chapter 3 that, within constructivist models of instruction, there is still a need for instruction on specific literacy skills. However, as Martha Demientieff's approach shows, the process of skill instruction can at once be both sensitive and highly effective.

Did students receive instruction on needed skills from the teacher?

The question below is related to the point made in chapters 6 and 7 that students of diverse backgrounds need to see connections between school literacy activities and their lives outside of school. The experience-text-relationship approach was given as an example of an appropriate instructional strategy.

Did students have a chance to discuss connections between the activity and their own lives outside of school?

The following question reflects the point made in chapters 6 and 7, that teachers should try to break away from conventional classroom recitation and instead conduct discussion in lessons to promote a lively exchange of ideas with students. Examples were given of adjustments that improved the quality of discussion in classrooms with Native Hawaiian students and in classrooms with Navajo students.

Was the activity conducted in a style of interaction comfortable for the students?

The question below has to do with the idea developed in this chapter, that students' strengths in their home languages are the basis for their learning to read and write in standard English.

Were students encouraged to use strengths in their home languages to help them complete the activity?

Taken together, these questions might form the basis for an analysis of classroom learning situations involving students of diverse backgrounds who are not yet progressing well in learning to read and write.

Perhaps the single most important step teachers can take is to solicit students' advice about how activities might be adjusted to help them learn. Research suggests that even kindergarten students are aware of how they are learning to read and write, what is helpful to them and what is not, and can verbalize these understandings (Mason, Stewart, and Dunning, 1986). Teachers will also learn a great deal through "kidwatching"

(Goodman, 1985) or the close observation of students' language and literacy performance in classroom settings (Wilkinson and Silliman, 1990). Teachers may discover that activities need to be made more interesting, that connections to students' lives are lacking, or that the interactional style used in discussion needs to be adjusted (for example, recall Deanna's frustration at being constantly interrupted during sharing time, as described in chapter 6).

In almost all cases, attempts to adjust classroom learning situations are likely to prove successful, even though it often takes time and several tries to reach a solution. For example, Jacob, a fourth grade student of Native Hawaiian ancestry, was experiencing difficulty during the writers' workshop (Wong-Kam and Au, 1988). He told his teacher, Jo Ann Wong-Kam, that he had many ideas for stories "but they are stuck in my head and cannot come out." Wong-Kam first worked with Jacob in individual writing conferences where she helped him to verbalize his ideas and transcribed what he said. Gradually, she had Jacob write down some of the words himself. In the meantime, Jacob and all of the other students in the class were learning how to conduct peer writing conferences. The learning situation around Jacob was strengthened as he started to turn to his peers, as well as the teacher, for help with putting his ideas down on paper.

Through their willingness to change and strengthen learning situations, especially on the basis of students' ideas, teachers demonstrate their respect for students and their commitment to high standards of literacy achievement. As teachers adjust instruction to meet students' needs and preferences as literacy learners, students will respond to the strengthened learning conditions and perform at higher levels.

Summary

Frequently, schools' use of inappropriate forms of language assessment puts students of diverse backgrounds in a cycle of poor instruction that offers them little chance of reaching high levels of literacy. In the old pattern, schools tend to ignore students' existing language abilities and to value only knowledge of standard American English. This old pattern reflects the power relations in American society and the fact that speakers of standard English are generally members of the dominant group, while speakers of other languages and varieties of English are members of subordinate groups. In the new pattern, teachers seek to build on students' home languages and view proficiency in standard English as a goal rather than a prerequisite for becoming literate. Instruction in both reading and writing is based on the meaningful exchange of ideas with students. Teachers help students of diverse backgrounds become literate in school by acting on the assumption that the source of difficulty is likely to lie in classroom instruction rather than in students' language ability.

Application Activities

1. In most areas of the United States, residents speak a variety of languages. Think about the languages spoken in a community that you know well. Consider both varieties of English and languages other than English. How do speakers of the various languages regard one another?

2. Think about the language history of your own family. What is the language background of your great-grandparents and grandparents? What about the language background of your parents? What experiences, in and out of school, do you think have shaped your own ability to use English and other languages?

Suggested Readings

Barnitz, J.G. (1980). "Black English and Other Dialects: Sociolinguistic Implications for Reading Instruction." *The Reading Teacher*, 33(7), 779-86.

Lee, C.D. (1991). "Big Picture Talkers/Words Walking Without Masters: The Instructional Implications of Ethnic Voices for an Expanded Literacy." *Journal of Negro Education*, 60(3), 291-304.

Wong Fillmore, L. (1986). "Research Currents: Equity or Excellence?" *Language Arts*, 63(5), 474-81.

chapter **9**

Language Differences: Students Who Speak a First Language Other Than English

──────────── CHAPTER PURPOSES ────────────

1. Show how ESL students' strengths in their native language can be used as the basis for furthering literacy in English;

2. Present an overview of research on the issues of bilingualism and literacy development;

3. Discuss instructional activities that appear to promote the literacy learning of ESL students;

4. Outline approaches for involving parents in their children's school literacy development.

From here on, the term ESL (English as a Second Language) students will be used to refer to students of diverse backgrounds who speak a home language other than standard American English.

Additive Versus Subtractive Approaches

In chapter 1 you learned about the difference between **additive** approaches, which seek to incorporate students' own language and culture into school programs, and **subtractive** approaches, which seek to replace students' own language and culture with those of the mainstream. As Cummins (1986) suggests, teachers should take an additive approach, broadening students' abilities in two or more languages. The ability to speak two or more languages gives an individual many advantages, and Americans who can speak a language other than English provide the nation with a valuable resource. Also, as you will learn in this chapter, research supports the conclusion that students can maintain and develop oral fluency and literacy in their native language, while at the same time gaining proficiency in standard American English.

In the past, however, schools often took a subtractive approach. It was commonly believed that, in the education of students who spoke a first language other than standard English, a choice needed to be made between proficiency in standard English and proficiency in the home language. The school's goal was thought to be that of replacing the native language with standard English. This widespread but misguided approach is called subtractive bilingualism.

A subtractive "English only" approach is one of the old patterns that serves to reinforce existing power relations between dominant and subordinate groups in American society and to hinder the school literacy learning of students from diverse backgrounds. As Zentella points out, discussions of language are often really discussions about power:

> It is because language is not the real issue, but a smokescreen for the fact that the U.S. has not resolved the inequality that exists, and finds it convenient to blame linguistic differences. The root of the problem lies in an inability to accept an expanded definition of what it is to be an American today.   (Zentella, 1987, quoted in Cartagena, 1991, p. 24).

Teachers need to be conscious of the ways that power relations tend to condition typical school views of the place and value of the home languages of students of diverse backgrounds. The changing nature of the American population, as described in chapter 1, makes it more important than ever for schools to accept, build upon, and celebrate the diversity in students' languages.

ESL Students in an English Reading Class

The positive value of instructional strategies that build upon ESL students' strengths in language and literacy is highlighted in research by Luis Moll and Stephen Diaz (1985, 1987). Their study took place in a school in California. The school had a bilingual program with the goal of promoting students' academic development in both Spanish and English.

Moll and Diaz studied Spanish-dominant, fourth grade students as they moved between two classrooms. Each day in the first classroom, the students received reading instruction in Spanish, their native language. Then they went to the second classroom, where they received reading instruction in English, their second language.

Here is an example of the kind of instruction Moll and Diaz observed in the English classroom, when they asked the teacher to teach a typical lesson to the lowest reading group:

T (Teacher):	Let's start reading the first page. We are going to meet a lot of new people in this book. (Carla and Sylvia have their hands up.)
D (Delfina):	Can I read first?
T:	(To Delfina only) I'm going to let Sylvia read first. She has her hand up. (Delfina immediately puts her hand up — more like a joke; Sylvia starts reading.)

S (Sylvia):	"You can't guess where we are going, said David."
T:	OK, just a minute, please, Carla. We need you to follow with us. (Carla was not glancing at the book.)
C (Carla):	OK.
T:	Delfina, we need you to follow right along. (To Sylvia) Would you start all over again?
S:	OK, I'll start over again. "You can't guess."
T:	OK, what is this? (Points to a word)
S:	Can't?
T:	Can't. What does that mean? (Pause)
D:	Um. . .
T:	OK, Carla, if I say you can guess or you can't guess.
D:	(With hand raised) Oh! Can't is like no. . .
C:	Don't do that.
T:	Uh, yeah, uh huh. Read the sentence, the whole sentence again and let's see if it says. . .
S:	"You can't guess where we are going, sayd (sic) David Lee."
T:	Good.
S:	"It's going to be a . . ." (Looks at teacher)
C:	Surprise.
T:	Surprise.
S:	"Surprise. I like surprises, sayd (sic) Isabel. You bet, I'll bet you guess where we are all going, sayd (sic) David." (Carla and Delfina raise their hands to read next; teacher selects Delfina.)

(Moll and Diaz, 1985, pp. 132-133)

As you can see, the teacher conducted round-robin reading, having the children take turns reading aloud from the text. Instruction focused on accurate word calling or decoding, not on understanding of the story. The teacher frequently interrupted the student who was reading to work on the definition of an individual word or on pronunciation. In other words, the lesson followed a transmission or skills approach, rather than a constructivist approach to instruction. Research suggests that lessons like this one are typical of those given to ESL students in the elementary grades (Wong Fillmore, 1986).

As discussed in the first chapter, this is also the typical pattern of instruction for the lowest reading group in a class (Allington, 1983), and it is as ineffective with ESL students as it is with students of mainstream backgrounds. As Moll and Diaz point out, because the students were not fluent in English, the process of reading aloud, with constant interruptions by the teacher, was extremely slow and time-consuming. Since most instruction centered on decoding and not on comprehension, the students had little opportunity to experience reading in English as a process of constructing meaning from text.

At times the teacher did attempt to discuss the meaning of the text, although the transcript excerpt does not show this type of interaction. However, when the teacher made these attempts, the students' lack of fluency in spoken English made it difficult for them to say enough to keep the discussion going. Moll and Diaz noticed that comprehension instruction was hampered because the teacher, an English monolingual, could not differentiate between two possibilities:

1. The students understood the story but were unable to verbalize their understanding in English.
2. The students did not understand the story and the little they had to say was an accurate reflection of their limited understanding.

Allowing Students to Use Their Home Language

The researchers decided to determine which of these two possibilities was actually the case. After the end of the lesson described above, Diaz conducted a brief session with the students in Spanish. When he asked comprehension questions similar to those the teacher had asked in English, Diaz made an interesting discovery. The students showed that they had understood much more about the story than they had been able to express in English. In other words, their comprehension was being masked by their limited oral fluency in English.

A particularly striking example of this phenomenon was seen in the case of Sylvia, the student featured in the earlier transcript excerpt. When the English teacher asked about why the others thought the girl was lost, Sylvia's answer was unclear. But when Diaz asked Sylvia almost the same question in Spanish, her extensive and detailed responses clearly showed that she had understood the story.

Diaz also asked Sylvia to read the text aloud in English but to explain it in Spanish. In the process, Sylvia readily produced an accurate and sophisticated translation of the passage. Obviously, Sylvia possessed language and literacy abilities that were not being tapped in the English reading class.

The problems with the English reading situation are better understood if we consider what Moll and Diaz learned when they observed the students in the Spanish reading class. Recall that Sylvia, Delfina, and Carla were all placed in the lowest group for English reading lessons. In contrast, in the Spanish classroom, these three girls were placed in groups at three *different* reading levels: Sylvia was in the high group, Delfina in the middle group, and Carla in the low group.

Although all three were participating in the same reading lessons in the English classroom, they brought very different literacy skills to those lessons. Sylvia, in particular, had considerable resources in Spanish literacy that she could use to comprehend English texts, as shown in her responses to the questions posed by Diaz. However, the structure of reading lessons in the English classroom did not permit Sylvia to use these Spanish-language resources to support her learning to read in English.

How did the situation in the English reading class develop? In the English class, the monolingual teacher used the students' apparent proficiency in spoken English as the basis for reading group placement. She seemed to equate reading ability with the ability to speak English. Thus, Sylvia, Delfina, and Carla ended up in the same group because they all had trouble with decoding and with engaging in English language discussions about the text, as shown in the first transcript excerpt. The teacher apparently did not consider the possibility that being able to read well in Spanish might help students to read well in English, so the girls' Spanish reading ability was not considered. Also, the focus in the lessons seemed to match the students' needs: they were having difficulty with decoding and with verbalizing their thoughts in English, and so the teacher emphasized practice in decoding skills and in oral English.

As suggested in chapter 8, the teacher's lack of regard for students' ability in any language but standard English is an old pattern, a typical reflection of the power relations between dominant and subordinate groups. In this case Spanish reading ability was not given much thought, because Spanish is not the language of power in the United States.

Rearranging Reading Instruction

Moll and Diaz point out that the teacher's approach was misguided, because it did not allow her to build upon the well-developed reading skills possessed by at least two of the students, Sylvia and Delfina. In the English classroom Sylvia and Delfina were limited to reading at a level far below that they had reached in Spanish. This problem was not confined to the three girls. It was common for students reading at the third grade level or above in Spanish to receive English reading instruction at the first grade level.

Using the ideas of Vygotsky (as discussed in chapter 3), Moll and Diaz sought to adjust teacher-student interactions during reading lessons to provide the students with improved opportunities to learn to read in English. They set about to see if they could create conditions in which the low group in the English classroom could work with texts at the fourth grade level.

Here are the first steps Moll and Diaz followed:

1. In English, they read the story aloud to the students in a clear, deliberate manner.
2. In English, they reviewed the plot of the story.
3. In English, they conducted an initial discussion of the story.

They realized, given the students' limited proficiency in English, that they, as the teachers, would have to assume most of the responsibility for the discussion. However, they provided scaffolding through the use of questions (as discussed in chapter 3), so that students would be able to participate to some degree. (In the dialogue below, L is Luis Moll and SD is Stephen Diaz.)

> L: He's explaining, "I'm going to go," and also, "I'm going to bring you some chicken and I'm going to bring you some tortillas. So don't move. Stay right there holding up this big wall. I'm going to get all those things and I'll be right back," he says. "Don't worry, I'll be right back, ah, I'm just going to be gone half an hour." Right? Do you think the fox was serious about returning?
>
> C: No.
>
> S: No.
>
> D: He was lying.
>
> L: He was lying, right.
>
> SD: How long did Señor Coyote stay there?
>
> D: Half an hour.
>
> S: Two hours.
>
> SD: How long? Do you remember how long he stayed there, Carla?
>
> C: No, like. . .
>
> SD: (To Delfina) How long do you think he stayed there?
>
> D: Um, all the night.
>
> L: Right.
>
> SD: That's right.
>
> L: He stayed all night long.
>
> (Moll and Diaz, 1985, pp. 141-42)

As in other examples of scaffolding, the teachers ask questions to elicit the students' ideas and then elaborate upon students' responses. Although the teachers are in control of the discussion, they are continually looking for ways to involve students and to build on their ideas. In this way, students and teachers collaborate to interpret the story.

When the researchers felt the students had at least some understanding of the story, they discussed unfamiliar vocabulary. For homework, they asked the students to reread the story and to make note of any other vocabulary they wanted to learn.

The next day's lesson provided some of the key moments in the study. During this lesson Moll and Diaz gave the students the opportunity to function at the fourth grade level in reading the English text. They continued the instruction of the day before, but now they asked comprehension questions taken from the teacher's guide. These were challenging questions that English-speaking students in the school had difficulty answering.

The students were allowed to use some Spanish in framing their answers. Under these conditions, with little scaffolding, Sylvia provided a summary of the plot in Spanish, showing again that she could understand the stories she read in English. The first question from the guide asked why the Fox began to address the Coyote as "Brother Coyote" instead of as "Mr. Coyote." To answer this question, students had to understand the motives and relationships of the characters in the story. Delfina tried to respond in English, but before the researchers could provide scaffolding in English, she stated her response in Spanish. The researchers elaborated upon Delfina's contribution, and then Sylvia came up with an appropriate answer to the question.

Moll and Diaz found that the students could produce answers comparable to those of their English-speaking peers, when they were allowed to use their native language. The students needed considerable scaffolding to arrive at these answers, but they could deal with a text and questions at the fourth grade level. For example, during a comprehension check made on the third day of instruction, Carla explained that the Fox was probably able to trick the Coyote because the Coyote had overestimated his own intelligence and underestimated that of the Fox. Carla received little help in coming up with this explanation.

The secret to the success of the new pattern of instruction developed by Moll and Diaz was the mobilization of the language and literacy ability the students had developed in Spanish. As this research shows, language and literacy ability in students' first language can have a powerful positive effect on their learning to read in a second language.

Bilingualism and Reading Development

The research conducted by Moll and Diaz raises an important general issue, having to do with the place of native language instruction in the school literacy development of ESL students. In situations where resources are available, should ESL students be taught to read in their native language? And will learning to read in their native language make it more difficult for students eventually to learn to read in English?

These questions are central to discussions of **bilingual education.** Bilingual education is a highly controversial topic, and in practice bilingual instruction may take a variety of forms (Lindholm, 1990). Advocates of bilingual education generally believe that ESL students will be more successful in school if they receive instruction in their native language. Proficiency in the native language serves as the basis for developing students' proficiency in English. The goal of bilingual education is usually to have students develop oral fluency and literacy in both the native language and in English.

Transitional programs represent a different approach to the instruction of ESL students. These programs are usually intended to move ESL students out of native language instruction and into English language instruction. The transition into English is generally made as quickly as possible, and students often do not receive adequate support when the time comes for them to receive instruction exclusively in English-language classrooms (Shannon, 1990). The usual goal of transition programs is to develop students' ability to read, write, and speak in English; proficiency in the native language is not a goal.

In a review of research on the instruction of ESL students, Snow (1990) concludes that ESL students should first learn to read in their native language, instead of being asked to learn to read in a second language they do not know well. She suggests that a high-quality bilingual program is likely to lead to the best outcomes in literacy, in English as well as the native language.

Snow's conclusion is based on research in four areas:

1. Social-cultural identity;
2. Cognitive consequences;
3. Linguistic skills;
4. Academic achievement.

Social-Cultural Identity

Research on social-cultural identity suggests that many ESL students find school a strange and alien environment. Students' feelings that school is a hostile environment increase when policies and practices devalue their language and culture (as mentioned in earlier discussions of students' resistance to school). An example of such an educational policy, common in the not-so-distant past, was forbidding students to speak Spanish in school. When schools do not respect students' cultural values and expectations, they threaten students' sense of cultural identity and self-esteem. On the other hand, when schools offer instruction in students' native language, they signal their recognition of the value of the home language and culture and their concern for students' self-esteem.

Students' self-esteem and confidence are important educational goals in and of themselves. But they are also important to academic success because students with high self-esteem will have the confidence to take on new challenges in literacy learning and in other academic areas.

Cognitive Consequences

Research on the cognitive consequences of bilingualism confirms that children who are bilingual have an advantage over monolingual children in several areas of cognitive functioning. One of these areas, which has particular benefit to literacy learning, is called **metalinguistic awareness**, which involves the ability to analyze the forms of language and to use language in nonliteral ways. It comes into play when we talk about language, make puns, or use figures of speech. Bilingual children have the opportunity to compare and contrast two languages, and so are more likely than monolingual children to develop an abstract understanding of how language works.

Metalinguistic awareness plays an important role in emergent literacy (Snow, 1990). When learning to read and write, children need to learn about phoneme-grapheme correspondence (the relationship between sounds and letters). Metalinguistic awareness is required for children to attend to the sounds within words, rather than to their content or meaning. For example, children can understand that *bear* and *ball* begin with the same sound, or that *Jill* and *hill* rhyme.

Linguistic Skills

Research on linguistic skills reveals that language and literacy instruction in the native language gives students certain advantages that can help them to become literate in English. These advantages come in the form of skills that can be transferred from one language to another. Some language skills, such as vocabulary, may apply to one language but not another. For exameple, knowing the word *rice* in English does not help you to know the Japanese word for *rice*. However, other language skills, such as how to organize ideas in writing, can be useful in any language.

Lanauze and Snow (1989) conducted a study to explore the idea that some skills can be transferred from one language to another. They investigated the writing ability of children with varying degrees of oral proficiency in Spanish and English. They found that the children who were the better writers in Spanish were also the better writers in English. Their Spanish writing ability gave them this edge, whether or not they had a high degree of oral proficiency in English. The researchers concluded that children can transfer certain skills, such as the ability to produce complex descriptions, from one language to another. Children's ability to write in English was enhanced, not diminished, by their ability to write in Spanish.

Academic Achievement

Studies of academic achievement suggest that students who participate in bilingual programs probably achieve at higher levels than comparable students who have not had the benefit of these programs (Willig, 1985). This higher level of achievement, Snow implies, results from the improved opportunities children have for literacy learning. Second-language learners have a better chance to learn to read in the primary grades if instruction is conducted in their native language. Learning to read in the native language gives children an opportunity to learn about the functions of literacy, or the purposes for which people read and write. Learning to read can be a challenging task in any event, and the degree of challenge is increased if children must learn to read in a language they do not yet understand very well.

In short, Snow's review provides convincing evidence of the benefits of native language instruction for ESL students. In addition to offering students the chance to become literate in their native language, bilingual programs can build students' self-esteem and lead to improved literacy learning in English.

It should be added that bilingual programs may be more or less effective, depending on the instructional models followed. For example, it has sometimes been assumed that, because sound-symbol relationships in Spanish are so consistent, beginning reading instruction should emphasize phonics rather than the construction of meaning. However, research suggests that Spanish reading instruction should follow a constructivist rather than a transmission or skills model, and that the process of learning to read in Spanish should *not* be treated as a fundamentally different process from learning to read in English (Barrera, 1983; Freeman, 1988). In the context of both bilingual and monolingual programs, it appears that literacy instruction for ESL students should be based on constructivist models (Rigg, 1991). Using constructivist models, teachers can provide high-quality literacy learning opportunities and put new patterns of instruction in place, whether ESL students are receiving literacy instruction in their native language or in English.

ESL Students in the English Language Classroom

> Teachers may not speak the native languages of their students, but they should encourage students to use their native language abilities to help them deal with English literacy activities.

In practice, it may not be possible to give students the opportunity to learn to read and write in their native language. Teachers and other adults in the school may not speak the students' native language, students may come from a wide variety of native language backgrounds, and/or parents may prefer that their children be instructed in English. In these situations, teachers can still take positive steps to carry out the two guidelines supported by the research:

1. To encourage students to use native language skills to help them learn to read and write in English;
2. To build students' self-esteem by showing respect for students' home language and culture.

Here are examples of how some teachers have applied these guidelines. A student from Thailand, who spoke almost no English, joined a fifth grade classroom. She brought with her a Thai-English dictionary. She and her teacher, who could not speak Thai, communicated in part by looking up words in the dictionary. The teacher helped the student learn to speak English, of course, but she also asked the student to teach her some words in Thai. A related example is reported by Feeley (1983). She describes a 10-year-old Korean girl who made her own dictionary, which contained a mixture of words written in Korean characters and in English.

In a fourth grade classroom there were two girls from Vietnamese families. The first girl, J., had been in the school for several years and was quite fluent in English, while the second girl, D., had come to the school only that year and was much less fluent in English. Every day the teacher had the students meet in small groups to discuss the book they were reading together. J. translated points made in the discussion for D. When D. had something to contribute, J. would let the group know so they would give D. a chance to speak. If necessary, J. would translate D.'s ideas for the group (Raphael, personal communication).

The teachers in these classrooms did not speak the native languages of these students, but they encouraged students to use their native language abilities to help them deal with English literacy activities. They created classroom environments in which students could be accepted into the community of readers and writers.

Benefits of Using Literature with ESL Students

Rigg and Allen (1989) remind us that literacy is part of language development. This means that students should be involved with literacy right from the first, whether or not they can speak English fluently. Rigg and Allen suggest that teachers read literature aloud to ESL students (and to the rest of the class), so that students will become acquainted with the structure of narratives in English and with literary language, including phrases such as "once upon a time." To help students begin to read on their own, teachers will want to find comprehensible materials, such as picture books with illustrations that directly support the text, and stories with predictable patterns and repetitive language. Well-written, high-interest literature provides a better basis for reading instruction than materials written in a simpler but stilted fashion (for suggestions of specific titles, see Routman, 1991). Authentic writing activities (such as dialogue journals, to be discussed later in this chapter and in chapter 10) are also recommended.

Ridley (1990) provides the following example of an ESL student's response to literature. Amin, who is from Iran and a native speaker of Farsi, knows only a few words of English.

Amin, the third grader, goes to the bookshelf where he seems to be looking for something specific; he quickly returns with *Nana Upstairs, Nana Downstairs* by Tomie de Paola (1973). He leafs through the books, which he has already heard during literature-sharing time. He points to the picture of the oldest grandmother and says, "Grandma," and mimes her death, by making a moaning sound and closing his eyes.

"Dead," I respond, offering a word that seems to fit his actions.

"Yes, grandmother dead," he says. "Me grandmother dead."

"I'm sorry," I tell him, while gesturing toward my heart. "Are you . . .," I ask as I mime tears falling down my cheeks. He nods, turns to the page in de Paola's book containing an illustration of Tommy, the little boy in the book, crying over his grandmother's death. "Me grandmother dead," Amin says again as he continues to point to de Paola's book. He pauses. "Picture."

I now understand that he wants to make a picture of his grandmother, and I repeat his thought in expanded form. "Are you going to draw a picture of your grandmother who died?"

"Yes," he answers. "Tears," he continues, remembering the word from a previous conversation. In sharing something important from his life, this student is acquiring new vocabulary in a natural, meaningful way.   (p. 216)

In this example literature provides an ESL student with the opportunity to reflect upon his own experiences. The teacher and student are able to communicate through a mixture of words, facial expressions, and gestures. While the teacher models the use of English vocabulary and grammar for the student, her emphasis is on meaningful communication. The student is encouraged to draw a picture, and the teacher may later assist him in adding writing to his drawing.

Using Dialogue Journals

Leslee Reed uses dialogue journals to improve her sixth grade students' ability to write in English. Kemmy was a Vietnamese student who had recently arrived in the United States. He had not attended school before and knew very little English. The writing in Kemmy's dialogue journal is shown first, followed by his teacher's written reply.

Kemmy:	today we are doing spelling is good and today I am so happy so funny . . . sompob He have New journal and He so happy and I have two journal I am have two . . . Andy He 3 journal.
Teacher:	Andy has his 3rd journal. Sompob has his 4th journal and Kemmy has his 2nd journal. You all are writing in your journal every day. Today we had a spelling bee. Kemmy spelled words for us. It was fun. I am glad Kemmy is spelling.

(Peyton and Reed, 1990, p. 19)

In her writing the teacher repeats some of Kemmy's ideas so he can see how his sentences might be written using conventional English grammar. She shows respect for the message he is trying to communicate, and she responds to his ideas ("I am glad Kemmy is spelling").

Dialogue journals can be used to promote students' native language literacy as well. Robert Bahruth used dialogue journals in his fifth grade class, which included many students who were native speakers of Spanish and from families of migrant workers (Hayes, Bahruth, and Kessler, 1991). One day a student named Patricia wrote:

Can I write you just one time in Spanish in the Journal?

Bahruth wrote back:

If you want you can write to me in Spanish in the journal. I enjoy reading and writing in Spanish, too! (pp. 36-37)

Patricia began writing in Spanish, and Bahruth wrote his replies in Spanish. Patricia, who had gained considerable proficiency in writing in English, now had an excellent opportunity to practice reading and writing in her native language, and to become biliterate.

Principles of Literacy Instruction

Moll (1988) suggests that whether teachers and programs are bilingual or monolingual, the same principles apply in the literacy instruction of ESL students. First, literacy instruction centers on understanding and the communication of meaning. Teachers support students as they carry out meaningful literacy activities, often chosen by the students themselves, involving the full processes of reading and writing. Second, literacy instruction takes place in the context of a rich and challenging curriculum. Content area instruction is included, as it would be for mainstream students, and the curriculum is not watered down (Wong Fillmore, 1986). Third, literacy instruction takes place through a diversity of activities. Examples of such activities include creative dramatics, older students tutoring younger students, reading a book in English but writing an analysis in Spanish, and keeping a journal. Finally, literacy instruction incorporates students' experiences. In this regard the experience-text-relationship (ETR) approach, discussed in chapter 7, is an appropriate strategy.

Daily Experiences for ESL Students

Ridley (1990) presents a list of the daily experiences she provided to students in an ESL program. **Monolingual** refers to students like Amin who know little or no English, and **intermediate level** refers to students with greater knowledge of English. The same variety of activities can also be used by regular classroom teachers.

Monolingual

1. Experiencing language, illustrating, speaking (repeating), reading and writing, rereading (in this order).

2. Reading predictable books: listening, "assisted reading," reading, and repeated reading.

3. Sharing literature: language acquisition and enjoyment of various topics.

4. Writing: the beginnings of using invented spelling (sound-symbol association), selecting topics on their own, and writing predictable books using published, predictable books for ideas.

5. Using creative expressive arts for language acquisition, self-expression, appreciation of each other's cultures.

Intermediate Level

1. Reading process: prereading, reading, and postreading strategies.

2. Selecting topics on their own for writing and for reading, emphasizing verbal exchange of likes, dislikes, perceptions, feelings, etc. among the students, and between the students and the teacher.

3. Exploring themes in literature through speaking, listening, reading, and writing. Extending these into expressive arts: creative dramatics, arts and crafts, reader's theater, musical accompaniment, jazz chants, creative movement, dance, puppetry, movie making using filmstrip and TV boxes with written scripts.

5. Writing process: prewriting; revisions; conferring with peers, teachers, and guests. Writing in a variety of formats for various audiences and a variety of purposes.

6. Reading like a writer: identifying themselves with authors, as authors.

7. Engaging in deep/light, sad/humorous discussions, which become a springboard for more reading and writing activities.

(Ridley, 1990, p. 227)

The activities listed by Ridley are consistent with constructivist, process, and whole language approaches to literacy development. They involve ESL students in authentic literacy activities providing them with opportunities to make choices, to communicate their thoughts, to use reasoning, and to express themselves creatively. For detailed descriptions of the activities recommended by Ridley, see Calkins (1986), Hansen (1987), Routman (1988, 1991), and Weaver (1990).

Parental Involvement

In addition to using constructivist approaches to instruction in the classroom, teachers can strengthen the literacy learning of students of diverse backgrounds by enlisting the help of parents. Considerable research supports the conclusion that parents of ESL students are interested in their children's education and willing to work with the school to support their children's literacy learning (Goldenberg, 1987; Delgado-Gaitan, 1990). Yet teachers often are not aware of parents' interest. One reason may be that parents are unfamiliar with the mainstream culture of the school and feel their limited abilities in English will make it difficult for them to communicate with the teacher (Delgado-Gaitan, 1991). Another reason may be that parents do not know what they can or should be doing to further their children's literacy learning.

What can teachers do to further parents' involvement in their children's literacy learning? First, teachers should try to communicate with parents frequently, especially about the positive steps students are taking in learning to read and write. Communication with parents may be just as important when students are in the upper elementary grades as it is when they are in the primary grades (Snow, Barnes, Chandler, Goodman, and Hemphill, 1991). Class newsletters and brief notes written to parents are an excellent means of highlighting children's accomplishments. In some situations newsletters and notes may be written in the native language. In other situations the teacher may go over the contents of newsletters and notes with students, so they can translate for their parents. Giving communication with parents a positive tone is important, because parents sometimes have had the experience of being contacted by the school only when their children are in trouble.

Most schools have an open house once or twice a year, when parents visit to gain an overview of classroom activities and to look at the work their children have done. Open house offers teachers a chance to make contact with parents and to set up appointments for future meetings.

During an open house or at other times, teachers should try to familiarize parents with the ways that they might become involved in the classroom. For example, some teachers ask parents to help by reading to small groups of children or by listening to children read aloud. Others ask parents to help with the books children are publishing. Still others have parents work with children on projects involving cooking, gardening, and a range of other activities. Parents may also be invited to give presentations, perhaps serving as storytellers or informing students about their culture, occupations, or hobbies. If teachers are from outside the community, they may find parents to be valuable sources of information about the community and children's lives outside of school.

Parent-teacher conferences offer an occasion when teachers can meet at some length with parents about their children's progress. Portfolios of students' work are an excellent means of showing parents what their children are able to do as readers and writers. For example, by comparing writing samples from September and January, parents can see the progress their children have made as writers. Conferences give teachers an excellent opportunity to address parents' concerns and to answer questions about what parents can do to further their children's literacy learning.

Research suggests that parents of diverse backgrounds often make a consistent effort to help their children with homework and are willing to work hard to foster their children's reading and writing (Goldenberg, 1987). Parents may be encouraged to read with their children, to listen to their children read, and to discuss books with their children. These literacy interactions may be more likely to occur if children can bring books home from school, since families may not be able to afford children's books and may live far from a public library.

Teachers should be aware that students of diverse backgrounds may be members of extended families in which they receive help from older sisters and brothers, grandparents, aunts and uncles, and others. Teachers may find it helpful to invite some of these other family members to meetings and conferences, in addition to parents. For example, older sisters and brothers are sometimes in a better position to help children with homework than parents, because they may be more familiar with school procedures, have a greater knowledge of English, and be on more flexible schedules.

Summary

Students of diverse backgrounds often speak a native language other than standard American English. Their school literacy learning is frequently slowed not because of their native language, but because of old, subtractive patterns of instruction that do not allow students to use their existing language skills to promote their learning to read and write in English. Teachers may tend to underestimate ESL students' literacy ability because of a misplaced emphasis on fluency in spoken English. Research suggests that allowing students of diverse backgrounds to use their native language skills leads them to higher levels of literacy achievement, because many literacy skills are readily transferred from the native language to English.

ESL students' chances to attain high levels of English literacy are actually improved, rather than weakened, through native language instruction. ESL students can also become successful readers and writers in monolingual English classrooms, if sound principles of literacy instruction are followed. In both bilingual and monolingual classrooms, literacy instruction should emphasize meaning making rather than skills, challenge students through interesting content, and include a variety of purposeful activities. Parents' involvement in children's literacy learning may be increased if teachers communicate frequently with parents, invite them to participate in the classroom, and encourage them to read with their children.

Application Activities

1. In an elementary school, find out what is done to provide for the literacy learning needs of ESL students. Analyze the school's plan for these students using the ideas presented in this chapter and your own judgment.

2. Imagine that you are a classroom teacher and that a new student has arrived in your class. This student speaks almost no English, and you cannot speak the student's native language. Describe what you would do to help this student become literate in English. Give reasons for the approaches and activities you choose.

Suggested Readings

Mata, S.J., M.B. Trevino and J. Guzman (1992). "Learning Language from Story (in Three Voices): Talking, Reading, and Writing in Bilingual/ESL Classrooms." In J.T. Feeley, D.S. Strickland, and S.B. Wepner, eds., *Process Reading and Writing: A Literature-Based Approach.* New York: Teachers College Press, pp. 217-27.

Reyes, M. de la Luz, and L.A. Molner (1991). "Instructional Strategies for Second-Language Learners in the Content Areas." *Journal of Reading*, 35(2), pp. 96-103.

Rigg, P., and V.G. Allen eds. (1989). *When They Don't All Speak English: Integrating the ESL Student Into the Regular Classroom.* Urbana, IL: National Council of Teachers of English.

chapter 10

Applying the Process Approach to Writing in Multicultural Classrooms

―――――――――― CHAPTER PURPOSES ――――――――――

1. Contrast process with transmission approaches to writing instruction;
2. Give examples of how the process approach to writing can be used in classrooms with students of diverse backgrounds;
3. Present specific instructional activities for fostering students' writing development, including exposing students to good literature, providing them with modeling and skill lessons, and writing in dialogue journals;
4. Present key findings about the English writing development of ESL students;
5. Discuss a philosophy of writing and education centering on students' ownership of projects and connections to the world outside the school.

Process Versus Transmission Approaches to Writing

The process approach to writing follows a constructivist approach to instruction in that it emphasizes students' own experiences and knowledge and the teaching of skills in the meaningful context provided by students' own writing. Process approaches to writing may be contrasted with transmission approaches, in which instruction centers on skills or mechanics such as handwriting, spelling, and grammar, and students' own experiences are not central (Farrell, 1991). In transmission approaches teachers believe that children should begin by writing letters and move gradually to words, sentences, and paragraphs. Most writing instruction centers on the teaching of skills or the forms of writing, and relatively little attention is paid to the messages students might want to communicate or to the functions served by writing. Writing is viewed not as a process but as a set of skills.

While skills are certainly of use to writers, transmission or skills approaches to writing instruction skirt around the central issue of how writers actually go about planning, drafting, shaping, and polishing a piece of writing. Process approaches to writing, in contrast, involve children in actual writing on topics they find personally meaningful. Students are then motivated to revise and edit their writing and to learn the skills they need to make their writing easy for others to read.

Many teachers have used the process approach to writing successfully with students of diverse backgrounds, as well as with students of mainstream backgrounds. For example, Calkins describes how the process approach to writing was implemented in many multicultural classrooms in New York City (1986, 1991). Excellent detailed discussions of the process approach to writing are presented in Graves (1983), Atwell (1987), and Calkins (1986).

Features of the Process Approach

What are the major features of the process approach to writing? One underlying assumption is that students will become good writers if they are allowed to write in much the same way that professional authors write. Another assumption is that teachers need to have the experience of being authors themselves, to write with students and to share their writing with the class and with other adults. Only by experiencing the writing process themselves can teachers fully appreciate the hopes and fears their students have as writers.

In her overview of the process approach to writing, Hansen (1987) highlights five areas: time, choice, response, structure, and community. Under **time**, Hansen emphasizes that students write frequently, usually four or five times a week, and on a regular schedule. Students may spend a long time on a particular piece of writing, perhaps starting a piece, dropping it to work on other pieces, and then returning to the original piece several months later. Students' time and attention is focused on the information in their pieces, rather than on mechanics or skills.

Under the heading of **choice**, Hansen emphasizes that writers write best when they have the opportunity to choose their own topics and can write about what they already know or about what they want to learn.

When discussing **response**, Hansen writes:

> Response rests on Time and Choice. We respond to topics students choose and by responding, we teach. Thus, we teach writing from students' drafts. At first we may doubt our ability to respond, but we learn to respond, initially, to information, and devote a smaller percentage of our attention to mechanics than previously. Also, we respond not only when students have finished their writing but along the way, while they are in the process of working on a draft. We don't spend our time doing something else when our students write. We move among them, teaching. This responsive teaching requires a shift in approach for most of us. (p. 11)

Classrooms with the process approach to writing need to have a high degree of **structure**, according to Hansen. However, structure is not achieved by giving students set assignments or by having them proceed in a linear fashion through a first draft, second draft, and final draft. Rather, structure is achieved by familiarizing students with the options available to them as writers (for example, that they can continue with a piece already started or choose a new one), so that students always know what they can do. At the beginning of the year, teachers in process writing classrooms spend considerable time establishing routines, modeling, conducting mini-lessons, responding to students' writing and teaching them to respond to the writing of others, and otherwise providing structure and organization (Atwell, 1987).

You learned about **community**, the final element stressed by Hansen, in chapter 5. In the classroom community the environment for learning to write is supportive rather than competitive. Students celebrate one another's accomplishments, and all are recognized for the special knowledge and experiences they possess and are willing to share with the class.

Five key areas may be highlighted in the process approach to writing:
Time;
Choice;
Response;
Structure;
Community.

The Writers' Workshop: Classroom Example

Let's look now at how a teacher in a multicultural classroom might apply the process approach through use of a **writers' workshop** (also called a writing workshop; Graves, 1983; Atwell, 1987). This description is a composite of my observations in a number of different classrooms.

The writers' workshop is just beginning in Mrs. Chang's second grade class. Chang follows the process approach to writing and the way she teaches writing has been greatly influenced by the work of Donald Graves and Lucy Calkins. The children in this classroom are from a variety of ethnic groups, but most of them are Native Hawaiians. Most are native speakers of Hawaiian Creole English, and several are native speakers of Asian languages. When the children have gathered on the carpet, Chang reads aloud *The Relatives Came* by Cynthia Rylant (1985). She has the children discuss times when they have gathered together with relatives and suggests that they might like to write about those times, as Cynthia Rylant did.

Then Chang explains that Donna has just finished a draft of a story about walking home in the rain and would like to know whether her draft makes sense. She asks the children to listen carefully to Donna's story. Donna sits in the Author's Chair (Graves and Hansen, 1983), in this case an adult-size rocking chair at the front of the class, and reads her draft aloud. One part of Donna's draft reads:

> Me and Amy was throwing mudballs at each other. I got my clothes dirty and then she got Amy's clothes dirty.

When Donna has finished, the children are invited to make positive comments about her piece. Then Chang asks the class if they have any questions for Donna. Kapuni asks, "Who else was with you?" He says that it sounded like Donna was walking home with someone else besides Amy. "I wondered about that too," Chang adds. Donna explains that she and Amy were alone. Chang asks Donna to look at the middle part of her story, to see if she can figure out why Kapuni thought there was someone else. She reminds the children that, when a classmate asks them for help with a story, they should listen carefully and see if the story makes sense, just as they did with Donna's story.

None of the other children has any questions or suggestions for Donna, so Chang concludes the session by saying, "One thing you can do when you're in a conference is to listen carefully when the author reads her piece. You might be able to spot something confusing, like Kapuni did. That helps the author know how to revise her piece."

Next Chang takes the status of the class. On a sheet listing all of the children's names, she jots down what each child plans to do during the writers' workshop. Donna says that she will be revising her piece, Kapuni says that he will be starting a new piece about playing soccer, and Michael says that he will be doing illustrations for the book he is publishing about visiting his grandmother on Maui. One by one the children are excused to go to their seats, until just three children are left on the carpet. These children all are ready to start a new piece but can't decide what to write about. Chang chats with them for a few minutes until they each have come up with one or two possible topics.

Chang walks around the room to make sure that all of the children have an idea of what they want to do during this time. Many children are drafting and there is low buzz of activity as children chat quietly with one another. Chang sits at a table to meet individually with the children who signed up for conferences with her. Joey has a piece that needs editing, and Chang asks him to circle words he is not certain how to spell and to look for places where periods and capital letters are needed. She asks him to have a friend look over his work before he comes back to see her. Piilani and Debbie have a draft of a Halloween story they wrote together, and they want Chang's advice about how the story should end. As the conferences continue, it seems to Chang that the 45-minute period she schedules every day for the writers' workshop always passes very quickly.

As this example shows, in the process approach to writing students are encouraged to choose the topics they will write about. After students have decided upon a topic, they put their thoughts down in a draft. If they like what they have, they may carry the draft forward to completion. To improve their drafts, students meet with the teacher or peers to receive feedback and advice. After revising and editing their drafts, students may decide to publish their pieces. Publication often takes the form of preparing a book that is first read aloud to classmates and then placed in the classroom library.

Chang and many other teachers working in multicultural classrooms, like the teachers described by Calkins (1986, 1991) and Routman (1991), find the process approach to be a powerful means of developing their students' writing ability. In multicultural classrooms, especially those with ESL students, teachers should make a special effort to

1. Expose students to good literature which can provide them with models and the inspiration for writing;
2. Provide students with daily mini-lessons and modeling of writing skills;
3. Encourage students to participate in storytelling;
4. Involve students in peer response groups.

> In the process approach to writing, students are encouraged to choose the topics they will write about.

In the sections that follow, each of these instructional activities is discussed through the use of classroom examples.

Literature as a Model for Writing

Like Chang, Dawn Harris Martine believes in surrounding her second grade students with good books, and she reads different books aloud to them every day. As a result, her students, almost all of whom are African American, develop an extensive knowledge of books and of the structure and language authors use when they write stories. During the writers' workshop, the children sometimes choose to write stories like those Martine has read to them (you may recall Damien's version of *The Three Little Pigs*, described in chapter 3). Martine has read many folktales and fairy tales to her students, and the influence of these stories is seen in Monica's writing. Monica's fairy tale shows a weaving together of ideas from the literature and her own experience.

> Once upon a time there lived in a far away kingdom a Princess named Esabel. She had long, golden hair, and a dress of sparkling jewels of pure gold. One day the Princess had her favorite dish: chicken, pizza, cake and ice cream. But when she went to the bathroom when she returned her chicken was gone. The next day she asked her mother, "What happened to my chicken last

night?" "The knave stole it." "What! If he did I'll whack his butt so hard he won't sit down for a month." (Center for the Study of Reading, 1990, Viewers' Guide, *The Reading/Writing Connection*, p. 16)

In addition to providing models for writing, literature may be an inspiration for projects unforeseen by the teacher. Allen (1989) describes how a group of three ESL students enjoyed the book *Jumanji* by Chris Van Allsburg (1981) so much that they decided to create a game of their own. Together they planned the game and designed the gameboard, then wrote a set of directions so their classmates could play the game. The directions began:

First you need one dice and you have to choose who is first by every one has to roll a dice who got the highest number get to be first. (p. 61)

After classmates read the directions and ran into difficulty understanding how to play the game, the students revised their writing. In doing so, they showed sensitivity to the needs of their audience. Here are the first sentences of their second draft:

First you need one dice and you have to choose who is first by everyone has to roll a dice. Who got the highest number gets to be first. You need four markers. (p. 60)

In short, reading good literature aloud to students, as well as encouraging students to read literature on their own, is an important part of the process approach to writing in multicultural classrooms. As our examples show, literature provides students with models of good stories and written language and may be the stimulus for different kinds of writing.

Teachers will want to acquaint students with multicultural literature, particularly works by authors who come from a variety of cultural backgrounds, a point to be discussed further in chapter 11. When multicultural literature is featured in the classroom, students of diverse backgrounds can see that authors come from diverse backgrounds, that the experiences of all cultural groups can be the subject of literature, and that experiences similar to their own can be of interest to other readers. Seeing the different worlds depicted in multicultural literature can give students the confidence to write from their own experiences and to share their own unique perspectives.

Modeling and Mini-lessons

Modeling involves demonstrating how something is done, while **mini-lessons** are brief meetings held at the start of the writers' workshop, when the whole class addresses a particular issue that came up in a previous workshop or in the pieces students are writing (Calkins, 1986). The issues vary widely, ranging from the abstract (for example, the difference between revising and recopying, or how to show rather than tell) to the concrete (for example, how to punctuate dialogue) (Atwell, 1987).

In kindergarten, first, and second grade, the teacher can begin the day with a morning message (Crowell, Kawakami, and Wong, 1986). The morning message provides teachers with the opportunity to model writing and to call children's attention to specific skills. For example, here is a morning message lesson in a first grade classroom with many Native Hawaiian students. The teacher, Mrs. Sakamoto, began the lesson by pausing, chalk in hand, and saying, "Now, what do I want to write about today?" She did this to show the children that writers have to think about what they want to say before they start writing.

Sakamoto wrote the following message on the board:

> We will have our pictures taken today. Then we will go to the science circus at the Boys and Girls Club. It will be a busy day.

Several children began reading the message while Sakamoto was writing it. When she had finished writing, the class read the message aloud as she pointed to the words. After the class had discussed the meaning of the message, Sakamoto asked for volunteers to tell her what they noticed about the message. Marie circled the word *day* and the *day* part of *today*, commenting that she saw the same letters in *day* and *today*. Anthony noticed that the word *will* appeared three times.

After Sakamoto complimented the children on their observations, she began a mini-lesson on capitals and periods. She told the children that knowing about capitals and periods would help them edit their stories so they would be easier to read. She reminded the children that she had been helping them make their sentences shorter, so their stories would not consist of one long sentence with many *and*'s.

Sakamoto asked the children how capital letters are used. Several children knew that capital letters come at the beginning of a sentence. Sakamoto reminded them that people's names are written with capital letters, and that the name of a place, such as the Boys and Girls Club, also is written with capital letters. She called on children to look for the capital letters and periods marking the beginning and end of the sentences in the morning message.

Later, during the writers' workshop Sakamoto asked children who were editing their stories to use capital letters and periods at the beginning and end of their sentences. She will continue to call children's attention to these skills until the children learn to use them independently in their own writing.

This lesson shows how a teacher can model and teach writing skills. Sakamoto chose to focus on capitals and periods because she saw from the children's writing that these were skills they could use. She modeled the use of capitals and periods in the message and then taught a mini-lesson on these skills. Asking the children what they had noticed about the message gave her an opportunity to assess the skills they were already applying. In this case, she found that they were noticing identical words and words with similar spellings. In the future, she will watch to see if the children notice capital letters and periods in the message. If they do not, she will continue to review these features of print.

Reyes (1991) advises teachers working with ESL students to spend adequate time on skill instruction and to inform students directly of the what, how, and when of language conventions. In a year-long study of ten Hispanic, bilingual sixth grade students, Reyes noted a lack of improvement in the writing students did in their dialogue journals and literature logs. She attributed this lack of improvement to the brevity of the teacher's skill lessons and to the fact that the teacher did not make it clear to students that they should apply the skills being taught when writing in their journals and logs. Reyes agrees with Delpit's (1988) call for teachers to be direct about their expectations and goals when working with students of diverse backgrounds.

Depending on the needs of the students, teachers may need to extend skill instruction beyond mini-lessons, perhaps using modeling and a somewhat longer lesson format, as shown in the example with Sakamoto. Also, teachers will want to be sure to emphasize the connections between skill instruction and the actual writing students are doing, as Sakamoto did.

Allowing Time for Storytelling

Allowing time for storytelling is an excellent means of helping students of diverse backgrounds to recognize the significant events and feelings they may want to write about. Lucy Calkins (1991) describes the launching of the writers' workshop in a fourth grade classroom at P.S. 148 in New York City. Many of the students in this school are recent immigrants and they speak 18 different languages. Shelley Harwayne, co-director of the Teachers College Writing Project, gathered the students in a large circle. She told the students:

> Today, and often, we're going to share stories, memories, moments. In every family there are stories we tell over and over. These are stories that hold us together as a family; stories of coming to America, of how one child got his name, of the day we found a turtle on the highway, or named our dog, or got stuck in a rainstorm. (p. 28)

Harwayne immediately launched into a story her mother had told her about how, as a young girl in Poland, she had made her own toys. For instance, she turned the small bones from a chicken's neck into jacks, and pieces of brick into checkers.

Soon, students in the circle began to share stories of their own. Jonas described how his sister was just leaving for the church on her wedding day, when a puppy with muddy paws scampered up the train of her bridal gown. Ariel spoke about how an American helicopter pilot had rescued her mother in Vietnam, and that was how she came to be born in America just a few weeks later. Other students, too, shared the family stories they had been told again and again.

Harwayne stopped the group after a time to introduce another possible source of ideas for stories. She said:

> Sometimes the seeds for our stories are not contained in family tales, but in private treasures. I'm thinking of the drawer or shoebox full of stuff that your mother calls junk. In a way she's right, but somehow you can't bring yourself to throw it away, and you're not sure why.   (p. 29)

Harwayne showed the class an old black-and-white photo of a man reading to a child. She told the students that she liked looking at the picture, even though she didn't know the people. One of the boys in the class said he was very attached to a worn-out stuffed animal, a gray bunny that he thought of as his "protector." Marcella told of how she had had to leave a treasured patchwork doll behind when she moved to the United States from Colombia. When she returned to Colombia several summers later, she discovered her grandmother had found the doll and made it new clothes.

The sharing of these memories brought the class together as a community. As the students listened to one another, they shared moments of happiness and moments of sadness. They sensed that they had experiences similar to those of their classmates, and also that there were experiences unique to certain individuals and their families. Calkins suggests that writers need "this sense of fullness, of readiness to write, of responsiveness" (p. 31) before they begin to put their ideas down on paper.

> Prizing the culture of students of diverse backgrounds entails accepting their talk and stories, not just written products, as a vital part of classroom life.

This is not to imply that storytelling is merely a springboard for writing. Storytelling can be valuable in and of itself, as Mikkelsen (1991) suggests. She gives examples from her work with a group of ten fifth graders, eight from working-class African American families and two from working-class European American families. All these students had been described as low-average in achievement, yet Mikkelsen found that they could create detailed and elaborate explanations and stories under a wide variety of circumstances. One of the boys, Cory, was a master storyteller who could captivate an audience for 45 minutes. Mikkelsen argues that prizing the culture of students of diverse backgrounds entails accepting their talk and stories, and not just written products, as a vital part of classroom life.

Findings from Research

Use of a process approach to writing makes sense in terms of research on the English writing development of ESL students. Hudelson (1986) provides a review of this research. Her overall finding is that the English writing development of ESL students parallels the writing development of students who speak English as a first language. Hudelson organizes her review around five major findings.

First, ESL students can begin writing in English before they have complete control over the various systems of the English language, such as its phonology (sounds), grammar, and spelling. Studies of the written products of ESL students indicate that they are applying whatever they know about English at that point in time. When writing in English, some ESL students may apply knowledge of their native language (Edelsky, 1983). As is the case with native speakers of English, ESL children may use drawing as the first means of representing their thoughts on paper. ESL students' writing gradually moves closer to the conventional forms of English, as they gain more knowledge of English and the conventions of writing (such as punctuation). Kemmy's journal entries, discussed in chapter 9, provide an example of this kind of progress.

The practical implication of this finding is that ESL students can be involved in real writing from the very start, before they are fluent in spoken English. Use of a process approach to writing instruction allows students of diverse backgrounds to become involved in authentic writing experiences, and students are encouraged to apply whatever skills they have. In contrast, use of a transmission or skills approach does not give students the opportunity to write in authentic ways from the beginning, because writing is believed to depend on the mastery of English skills which many ESL students do not have yet.

Second, ESL students can do different kinds of writing for different purposes. In common with native speakers of English, ESL students may do expressive writing, to explore their feelings and personal identity; literary writing, to create a work such as a story or poem; and transactional writing, to convey information or a message (three functions of writing discussed by Britton, Burgess, Martin, McLeod, and Rosen, 1975).

The practical implication of this finding is that teachers should involve students of diverse backgrounds in a variety of writing activities. Dialogue journals are an effective method of encouraging ESL students to do expressive writing. As will be discussed in chapter 11, exposing ESL students to children's literature in a variety of genres enhances their ability to do literary writing. Writing in connection with projects for science, social studies, and other content areas promotes their ability to do transactional writing.

Third, ESL students are able to revise their writing in response to the comments made about their work, either by peers or adults. ESL students who are just learning to revise their writing usually make changes only by adding more words or by substituting one word for another; students who are native speakers of English show the same patterns when they are first learning to revise. When ESL students become more proficient as writers, they learn to make revisions by changing sentences and paragraphs and writing several drafts of the same piece. Peers may have as much, if not more, influence than teachers in motivating ESL students to improve their writing. The practical implication of this finding is that teachers will probably want to involve ESL students in peer response groups, as discussed in detail later in this chapter.

Fourth, ESL students' writing development is strongly affected by the teacher's beliefs and the classroom context. Classroom writing instruction reflects teachers' beliefs about writing, and ESL students are quick to understand what their teacher thinks is important. If teachers adopt a process approach to writing, value the expression of students' ideas, and encourage revision, students will try to express complex thoughts in writing, even if they are uncertain about grammar and spelling. Conversely, if teachers take a transmission approach and overemphasize correct grammar and spelling, students will not take risks and will limit their writing to the grammar and spelling they know.

Fifth, ESL students' writing development in English will vary due to the children's own individual strengths and preferences and to their cultural backgrounds. Considerable variability in writing development is expected with ESL students, just as it is expected with students who are native speakers of English. ESL children's writing development will proceed at different rates and follow different paths. As highlighted in earlier chapters, through their experiences in the home and community, children will be familiar with some uses of writing but not others. The language norms of children's homes, whether they speak a first language other than English or a nonmainstream variety of English, may also influence their writing development. Some children will have had more experience with standard English forms, some less.

> If teachers adopt a process approach to writing, value the expression of students' ideas, and encourage revision, students will try to express complex thoughts in writing.

In short, research suggests that ESL students can benefit from a process approach to writing instruction. Process approaches, in contrast to transmission or skills approaches, give students the chance to follow their own individual paths toward becoming capable writers. Process approaches give teachers the flexibility to support students in these different paths, providing skill instruction as the need arises.

Peer Response Groups

Peer response groups can improve the writing of upper-grade ESL students, according to research conducted by Carole Urzua (1987). Two of the students she studied were sixth grade boys, one Cambodian and one Laotian, and the other two were fourth grade girls, both Cambodian. All had been in the United States for at least two years. The purpose of Urzua's study was to determine whether the process approach to writing using peer response groups could be effective with second-language learners.

The students met for the response groups once a week for 45 minutes. They usually arrived with a piece of writing they had started at home. If there was time, the students also wrote during part of the period, and the researchers wrote along with them. The students' writing was discussed before they began drafting and also while a piece was in progress, in order to convey that revision was a necessary and natural part of the writing process.

The revision process was supported through the use of peer response groups, following procedures developed by Elbow (1973) in which each writer reads his or her piece and then hears the responses of others in the group. Urzua describes the use of these procedures with Vuong, one of the sixth graders. Vuong read the first draft of his piece about Outdoor School, a sixth grade camping experience, aloud to the group twice. Here is the beginning of his draft:

> First we got to the river we have to cross the river. On boat and we got to the camp and we pick up our stuff after that and we have to carry our stuff up to the cabin. Then we take our clothes out of the bags and get ready for dinner. After that it was campfire.   (p. 298)

After Vuong's first reading, and again after his second reading, everyone in the group jotted down notes about what they wanted to say to him. Then members of the group, students and researchers alike, took turns reading from their notes. Here are some of the responses given by the other students:

> How was it on the boat when you crossed the river?
> Was it a little boat or a big boat? If it was a little boat, did it take some people and then come back and get some other people?
> He didn't tell us what you do in campfire.   (p. 299)

Vuong made many revisions to his piece to address the concerns shown in his listeners' responses, although he did not address every concern raised. On his own, Vuong added information and clarified and elaborated upon information already in his piece. Here is the start of his second draft:

> When we arrive to outdoor school and all of us cross the river. The water was deep it was green water it has plants in it. When we arrive to the other side we have to wait for peoples to cross the river. And then we walk to cafeteria and get our bags and we to the cabin and take our clothes out of the bag and

put it on my feet. And we went down to eat lunchs after lunchs we have to
sing a song so we can dismiss.   (p. 298)

With previous pieces, Vuong had made few if any revisions. His idea of
revising had been simply to recopy the piece. But this time Vuong revised ·
his piece extensively, showing his respect for the opinions of his audience
and his interest in communicating an important personal experience more
clearly. According to Urzua, Vuong and the other students in this study
improved their writing ability in three ways by developing:

1. A sense of audience;
2. A sense of voice;
3. A sense of power in language.

As implied earlier in the description of Mrs. Chang's class, students
do not automatically know how to respond to another student's writing.
My observations in classrooms in the primary grades suggest that, left to
their own devices, students will often seek help with spelling but seldom
with other writing problems. Students need to be specifically taught to
seek other kinds of help from peers. Some teachers support the process
of peer helping by having the class brainstorm a list of possible issues to
be discussed during a peer writing conference (for example, Does the piece
have a good lead? Is there a part of the piece that doesn't make sense? Is
more information needed? Does the piece have a good ending?). To encourage children to confer with peers about a range of writing issues,
some teachers make it a rule not to look at a student's piece until the
student has held conferences on it with two other students.

Students also need to be taught to respond critically yet constructively
to one another's writing. The students in Urzua's research received this
opportunity because the researchers modeled appropriate responses, and
students also served as models for one another. Some teachers conduct
writing conferences with groups of children, instead of meeting with the
children one at a time, to model for students the process of giving an
author feedback. Teachers can also do this kind of modeling when students
share drafts with the class, as Chang did with Donna.

Dialogue Journals

You were introduced to dialogue journals in chapter 9 through the example
of Leslee Reed, a sixth grade teacher. At that time it was pointed out that
teachers can foster students' literacy development if they focus on the
message students are trying to communicate, rather than on their spelling
and grammar. Improvement in spelling, grammar, and other mechanics
comes as teachers model standard English forms in their own writing, and
as students gain confidence in their writing and further knowledge about
the English language and the conventions of writing.

Reed points out that dialogue journals give students a nonthreatening way of communicating with the teacher (Peyton and Reed, 1990). Having this means of communication may be particularly important to students of diverse backgrounds who have come from other countries, cannot speak English well, do not understand mainstream customs, or are fearful of being ridiculed. Reed writes:

> My own experience with using dialogue journals has convinced me that students who come to the classroom unable to speak English soon find that the journals can be a real source of comfort and satisfaction. Each day my students find messages written specifically for them. They have a sense of personal identity and a personal link with me. They can ask for help in the journal, and no one will laugh at them for asking "dumb questions." The journal is the one area in which the students in my mainstream classroom who come from other countries and are learning English can participate as equals with those who have been in this country all of their lives.   (Peyton and Reed, 1990, pp. 1-2)

Peyton and Reed see dialogue journals as a form of conversation between the teacher and student. This type of conversation is unique because it is entirely private and takes place at regular intervals. Each student has a bound notebook, and the amount of writing and topics covered are up to the individual. Teachers treat students as partners in a conversation and so write back in terms of the issues raised by students, without correcting their writing. However, teachers are modeling the conventions, structures, and vocabulary used when writing in standard English and offering students the opportunity to appropriate these forms in their own writing. Ideally, journal writing takes place every day, and if that is not possible, it needs to occur at least twice a week. Teachers try to respond to each entry students make in their journals.

Here is an example of an exchange between Reed and Michael, a Burmese student who had been in school in the United States for just 10 months.

February 9

Michael: Mrs. Reed you know on this week like the silly week. I don't know what happen on this week. Mrs. Reed what did you mean about the valentines you said we have to bring the valentines. Did we have to made the valentines for ~~people~~ our classroom. I didn't know what are you talking.

Mrs. Reed: No, you don't have to give anyone a Valentine. It is just fun to do. Sometimes we like someone but we do not tell them. We feel funny telling someone you really like them. Giving them a valentine is an easy way of doing it. If you want to give a valentine or 5 valentines — it doesn't matter. You do what you want about that.   (p. 4)

Michael receives an answer to his question about valentines, a question he might have hesitated to address to his classmates. In addition to providing

Michael with many chances to write, the use of dialogue journals encourages his reading development, as he studies Reed's replies.

Peyton and Reed also provide evidence of dramatic improvement in children's writing development through the use of dialogue journals. For example, here are journal entries written by Ruqayya, a fourth grader in Kelly Miller's ESL class, who had just come to the United States from Pakistan:

Sept. 3

I like to fly.
I like school.
I like to play.
I don't lik fish.
I like this day.

May 19

today I was the all most the winner but I just miss the word. So the Sonia was the winner. I'm still very happy that she wan and in the aqua [reading] group their was too winner one was Rofina how was the winner and one was Nhung how was the winner.   (p. 26)

In September Ruqayya stayed with safe, familiar language patterns. But although she was using correct grammar and spelling, she did not develop her ideas about any particular topic. The writing Ruqayya did in May is much more complex. She was able to produce an account of a classroom event and describe her feelings about the event.

In short, the use of dialogue journals lets students communicate in writing privately, without the fear of being embarrassed due to their lack of English writing proficiency. In the safe environment for writing provided by dialogue journals, students become more confident and capable as writers. Improvements are seen both in the complexity of the ideas expressed and in their skills. Of course, dialogue journals do not constitute a complete program of writing instruction, and students' progress will be hastened if they also receive instruction in a writers' workshop, as described earlier.

Connections to the Real World

Considerable research points to the benefits of tying students' writing to their experiences outside of school. In particular, research highlights the value of having students write about their own lives (Calkins, 1991), about the history of their own families and communities (Wigginton, 1989), and about important community issues (Moll and Diaz, 1987). As Barrera (1992) suggests, it is important for teachers in multicultural classrooms to expand the concept of community to include the community outside the school. The *Foxfire* books and magazines — which describe Appalachian culture, traditions, and history and are produced by students at Rabun Gap High School in Georgia — are perhaps the best-known student publications based on ties to the community.

Eliot Wigginton, the high school English teacher who founded the *Foxfire* project, cautions that the *Foxfire* publications are just one possible manifestation of an underlying philosophy (Wigginton, 1989). This philosophy includes the following principles, which you will recognize as being consistent with constructivist approaches to instruction.

The starting point for all work is students' interest (recall the importance of interest in the definition of instruction presented in chapter 3). Students must participate in choosing the project, and then in designing, revising, and evaluating it. In some cases students may not be interested in producing a book or magazine but may prefer to produce a videotape or radio show. Wigginton notes that many imitations of the *Foxfire* magazines failed because it was the teacher's idea to produce a magazine, not the students'. In other words, students' ownership of the project is essential.

> Research highlights the value of having students write about their own lives, about the history of their families and communities, and about important community issues.

Yet for students, the process of deciding upon a project can be a difficult one, and it takes skillful and sensitive teaching to help students find their own direction. Teachers must provide students with guidance without inadvertently making the decision for students or taking away ownership of the project.

Lucy Calkins (1991) gives several examples of writing conferences that nudged students toward projects. Calkins and her colleagues in the Teachers College Writing Project have worked with students and teachers in New York City classrooms on an approach to writing centered on the use of notebooks. Students begin by writing their reflections in notebooks, then go back through their notebook entries to look for themes of importance in their lives. Notebook entries serve as the basis for developing projects.

A seven-year-old named Ilana Goldberg identified the writing she had done about letting her hamster go in the park as the part of her notebook that mattered most to her. Calkins describes her conference with Ilana and the project that eventually resulted. Ilana said that losing her hamster meant she had "no one to come home to." Calkins then asked Ilana if there were other entries in her notebook related to this idea. Ilana was surprised by the question, but once she understood what Calkins meant, she turned to an entry about her grandmother.

Ilana nodded and quietly turned to a particular page. Stroking the page, she said, "This one does, about my grandmother. Because before she died, I had someone." When the workshop ended, Ilana had dedicated a portion of her notebook to this topic. A few days later, after writing more entries on the topic, Ilana moved onto rough-draft paper. Eventually, after peer conferences and share meetings and more conferences with her teacher, Ilana published a book, *Alone in a February Park*, which was about far more than a hamster. In her book, Ilana told the story of losing her grandmother, of coming home each day to only a hamster, and of letting that hamster loose in a cold February park. The final scene had everything to do with a little girl who, like her hamster, feels cold and alone.   (pp. 74-75)

Ilana's example leads us to a second principle in Wigginton's approach, which is that there must be clear connections between the work and the real world outside the classroom. In the case of Ilana, the connection was to her own personal experience, but the connection may also be to the community. Frequently, as in the *Foxfire* project, students will turn to community members as sources of information. The issues explored may include the earth's changing climate, the environment, the homeless, and prejudice. The Latino students studied by Moll and Diaz (1987) explored attitudes about bilingualism. Phyllis Whitin's eighth grade students conducted a family-history project (Whitin, 1990).

Another principle is that, instead of passively receiving information, students are actively involved throughout the work. Students are challenged to move into unfamiliar territory, to go beyond what they already know how to do. (This idea is similar to Vygotsky's notion of the zone of proximal development, discussed in chapter 3.) You saw how Ilana gained an insight about her own life. The students in Moll and Diaz's study designed and conducted interviews, then analyzed and wrote up their results; all of these activities were new to them. Students in Whitin's class experimented with different ways to communicate their family stories through the use of writing techniques such as dialogue and flashbacks, and through art, photography, and videotape.

All work emphasizes the use of peer teaching, collaboration in small groups, and teamwork. Every student is recognized for his or her own unique contribution, as noted in our discussion of classroom communities in chapter 10. For example, Whitin writes:

> The social nature of learning in this project was evident in the students' peer and family relationships. They shared stories and artifacts with each other. One student displays a thirty-year-old checker set; two show videotapes of their interviews; and many others share photographs, news clippings, and yearbooks. As Spencer passes around pictures of his dad as a boy, students exclaim, "He looks just like you!" Spencer beams. He has shared more than a photo; he has shared a part of himself. Spencer's unique identity as a class member is enhanced by his revealing more about his lineage.   (p. 237)

A related principle, mentioned as well in earlier chapters, is that the teacher acts as a team leader and guide, rather than as a lecturer or the repository of all knowledge.

Philosophical principles behind students' writing projects:
  Students' interests are taken into account;
  Clear connections are made between the work and the world out-
    side of the classroom;
  Students are actively involved throughout the work;
  Teachers are team leaders and guides;
  Projects emphasize team work, peer teaching, and collaborating
    in small groups;
  Projects are intended for audiences beyond the teacher.

High academic standards are maintained in students' projects, and students learn skills such as spelling, grammar, and punctuation important in the final editing of any published work. Wigginton expresses the view that writing projects should include instruction on state-mandated skills and content, but go far beyond the narrow perspective typically associated with an emphasis on skills.

Students' work is intended for audiences beyond the teacher. For example, two ninth graders wrote an article for the *Foxfire* magazine about the art of hewing railroad crossties by hand, based on an interview with their grandfather, Dan Crane. In the introduction to their piece, the students stated that the article was a gift to their grandfather "to make his life a little brighter" (Wigginton, 1989, p. 31). Crane had almost every issue of the *Foxfire* magazine and knew many of the people featured in it, but had never been interviewed himself. Similarly, the family history project gave students in Phyllis Whitin's class new ways of connecting with family members. Through their interviews they learned about family stories, and one story often led to others. Parents and grandparents were delighted to see the students' finished scrapbooks and decorated manuscripts.

Even children in the primary grades can develop projects for real audiences. Wigginton (1990) describes how kindergarten students in the Seattle area developed a ten-minute videotape and six books to show younger children what it would be like to enter kindergarten. The tape and books covered topics such as the school bus, recess, and lunch and dealt with the fears the students had had when they first started kindergarten.

In short, writing comes alive for students when they make connections to the real world. These connections may be made when students write about their own lives, when they write about the history of their families and community, when they write about social issues, and when they write for a real audience. As Wigginton points out, the form of the project cannot be set in advance but must grow from the students' own interests.

Summary

A process approach to writing instruction allows students of diverse backgrounds the opportunity to become successful writers through their own individual paths. Process approaches to writing may be contrasted with transmission or skills approaches, which place the emphasis on the forms rather than the functions of writing. The writers' workshop provides teachers with a framework for implementing a process approach, including time for the reading aloud of literature, whole class lessons, and writing conferences. The following writing activities may be of particular value to students of diverse backgrounds: (1) literature to inspire writing; (2) modeling and mini-lessons; (3) storytelling; (4) peer response groups; and (5) dialogue journals. Research on the English writing development of ESL students suggests that these students benefit from a process approach. Finally, a process-oriented philosophy of writing centers on projects based on students' interests and on the making of connections to real-world topics and audiences.

Application Activities

1. Reflect back on your own experiences with learning to write in school. Describe any positive experiences that helped you to become a better writer. Also describe any negative experiences that may have hindered your development as a writer. Analyze your experiences in terms of the ideas presented in this chapter.

2. Observe writing instruction taking place in a classroom, and write up your observations. Was the teacher following the process approach to writing or some other approach? How did the students feel about the writing they were doing? What did you think about the quality of their writing? What long-term effects do you think this approach will have on the students' writing development?

Suggested Readings

Calkins, L.M. (1986). *The Art of Teaching Writing*. Portsmouth, NH: Heinemann.
Harste, J.C., and K.G. Short, with C. Burke and contributing teacher researchers (1988). *Creating Classrooms for Authors: The Reading-Writing Connection*. Portsmouth, NH: Heinemann.
Hudelson, S. (1986). "ESL Children's Writing: What We've Learned, What We're Learning." In P. Rigg and D.S. Enright, eds., *Children and ESL: Integrating Perspectives*. Washington, DC: Teachers of English to Speakers of Other Languages, pp. 23-54.

chapter 11

Multiethnic Literature and the Valuing of Diversity

―――――――― CHAPTER PURPOSES ――――――――

1. Define the terms **multicultural literature** and **multiethnic literature** and outline the benefits of having students read and discuss multiethnic literature;
2. Present an overview of multiethnic literature focusing on African Americans, Asian Americans, Hispanic Americans, and Native Americans;
3. Explain how multiethnic literature can be used to shape students' values and help them to appreciate diversity;
4. Explore issues in the use of multiethnic literature, such as diverse views of history;
5. Examine models for the teaching of multicultural or multiethnic literature.

Defining Multicultural and Multiethnic Literature

Violet Harris (1992) defines **multicultural literature** as literature that focuses on people of color (such as African Americans, Asian Americans, Hispanic Americans, and Native Americans), on religious minorities (such as the Amish or Jewish), on regional cultures (such as the Appalachian and Cajun), on the disabled, and on the aged. The term may also include literature depicting women and girls in roles that do not perpetuate stereotypes. What these groups share is that they all tend to be in a subordinate status with respect to the dominant, mainstream culture.

Consistent with the emphasis of this book, the focus of this chapter is what Harris terms **multiethnic literature**, literature dealing with peoples of diverse backgrounds within the United States, including African Americans, Asian Americans, Hispanic Americans, and Native Americans. As Harris points out, literature about these groups generally lies outside the literary canon (the set of works deemed most important for study by mainstream educators and literary critics), recommended book lists, and the elementary school curriculum. Most valuable for students is multiethnic literature that is *culturally conscious*. As Sims (1982) uses the term, culturally conscious literature is literature that accurately reflects a group's culture, language, history, and values. The characters in the literature are African American, Asian American, Hispanic American, or Native American and the story is presented from the perspective of that particular group. The characters are not presented as stereotypes but as complex human beings. Within the realm of culturally conscious literature, Harris (1992) sees a particular value to books such as *Felita* (Mohr, 1979) or *M.C. Higgins, The Great* (Hamilton, 1974) that give a positive and inspiring view of family relationships. *First Pink Light* (Greenfield, 1991), *Aunt Flossie's Hats (and Crab Cakes Later)* (Howard, 1991), and *The Star Fisher* (Yep, 1991) are other books that project a positive image of families.

Culturally conscious literature accurately reflects a group's culture, language, history, and values.

Literature as a Means of Shaping Students' Values

Multiethnic literature can be used in the classroom to affirm the cultural identity of students of diverse backgrounds, and to develop all students' understanding and appreciation of other cultures. This view of literature is one of the new patterns of instruction that can help to support the school literacy development of students of diverse backgrounds. Schools' emphasis on a literary canon that excludes culturally conscious multiethnic literature is one of the old patterns urgently in need of change.

According to Applebee (1991), throughout the history of the United States there has been a strong belief in the power of literature to shape students' values and direct the path of American society. The *New England Primer*, published about 1686, was used to promote religious beliefs. In the late 18th century, Webster's *Grammatical Institute of the English Language* aimed to develop a common language and sense of being American. The famous *McGuffey's Readers*, first published in 1836, similarly fostered the attitudes believed important to the American way of life.

By the late 19th century there came to be a set body of literature, a literary canon, which most students read in school. The results of surveys published by Tanner in 1907 and by Applebee in 1989 show that, at the high school level, this core literature has remained remarkably similar for over 80 years. It is dominated by traditional British and American works, including *Romeo and Juliet, Macbeth, Huckleberry Finn, Julius Caesar*, and *The Scarlet Letter*. Applebee (1989) reported that only two authors of diverse backgrounds, Lorraine Hansberry and Richard Wright, appeared on the list of the 50 or so authors whose works were most frequently studied. Astonishingly enough, the same books and authors tended to be read even in high schools with a high number of students from diverse backgrounds.

Applebee (1991) suggests that the school literacy achievement of students of diverse backgrounds might be improved if they had the opportunity to read literature they could find more interesting, compelling, and relevant to their own lives. In effect, Applebee states, the present literary canon marginalizes the history, perceptions, and life experiences of students of diverse backgrounds while privileging those of students from mainstream backgrounds. In this sense, the existence of a literary canon excluding culturally conscious multiethnic literature serves to perpetuate the educational inequalities which exist between students from diverse backgrounds and students from mainstream backgrounds.

Benefits of Using Multiethnic Literature

There are many benefits for all students in the reading of multiethnic literature. Such literature presents students with all the cognitive and affective advantages of reading any fine works of literature (Harris, 1992), such as enjoying a good story, gaining insights into the human condition, and acquiring new vocabulary. In addition, there are particular advantages to the use of multiethnic literature as opposed to literature written from a mainstream perspective.

First, when students of diverse backgrounds read literature that highlights the experiences of their own cultural group, they learn to feel pride in their own identity and heritage (Harris, 1992). Students tend to respond more positively to literature when they can identify with the characters and events in the story (Purves and Beach, 1972). Students see that members of their own cultural group can be published authors and that experiences much like their own can inspire the writing of literature. Reading multiethnic literature can affirm students of diverse backgrounds in their cultural identities and provide another source of validation for their experiences and perspectives. For example, in Dawn Harris Martine's second grade classroom in Harlem, students took special pleasure in the rhyme, rhythm, and subject matter of Eloise Greenfield's (1978) poetry (Center for the Study of Reading, 1990). Multiethnic literature may also give students the inspiration and confidence to write from their own unique points of view. For all of these reasons, multiethnic literature may be empowering to students of diverse backgrounds.

Second, all students, whether of mainstream or diverse backgrounds, learn from multiethnic literature about the diversity and complexity of American society and can develop tolerance and appreciation for those of other cultural groups (Walker-Dalhouse, 1992). Certainly, all students can benefit from a recognition that American society is composed of many different cultural groups. Multiethnic literature can help children become aware of the unique qualities of each group, as well as the common experiences shared by many groups (Huck, Hepler, and Hickman, 1987). Students often have stereotypes about other cultural groups, and multiethnic literature may help them gain a more accurate and fair-minded view. For example, *Dragonwings* (1975), *Child of the Owl* (1977), and *The Star Fisher* (1991) by Laurence Yep are engrossing narratives that show the challenges faced by Chinese American young people growing up in different historical eras.

Third, through multiethnic literature all students can gain a more complete and balanced view of the historical forces that have shaped American society and of the contributions of people from different cultural groups. For example, a biography such as *Anthony Burns: The Defeat and Triumph of a Fugitive Slave* by Virginia Hamilton (1988) gives students insights into history from an African American perspective. Multiethnic literature can build students' awareness that traditional mainstream historical accounts have tended to emphasize the achievements of European Americans, men, and the wealthy, and to ignore or denigrate the achievements of people of color, women, the working class, and the poor. All students, those of diverse and mainstream backgrounds alike, need to understand that the history of the United States can be fully and accurately portrayed only through the combined perspectives of different cultural groups.

Finally, students can explore issues of social justice through multiethnic literature. This literature can be used to introduce students to key issues through well-drawn characters, authentic situations, and compelling stories. For example, the Newbery Award winner *Roll of Thunder, Hear My Cry* by Mildred Taylor (1976), the story of an African American family set in the 1930s, can serve as a springboard for discussions of discrimination. Literature can make issues real for students in ways that textbooks cannot.

> Benefits of Using Multiethnic Literature:
>   Students of diverse backgrounds feel pride in their own identity and heritage.
>   Both mainstream students and students of diverse backgrounds learn about diversity and the complexity of American society.
>   All students gain more complete and balanced views of the historical forces that shaped American society.
>   All students can explore issues of social justice.

African American Children's Literature

Harris (1992) discusses authors, characteristics, and themes of multiethnic literature written from a culturally conscious African American, Asian American, Hispanic American, and Native American perspective. She recommends that teachers work primarily with books published since 1970, because these books are less likely to present stereotypes or inaccurate details.

The majority of culturally conscious works of multiethnic children's literature has been written by African American authors. Harris places these authors in three groups. In the late 1960s and 1970s works by a first wave of notable children's authors began to appear. These authors were Lucille Clifton, Eloise Greenfield, Rosa Guy, Virginia Hamilton, Sharon Bell Mathis, Walter Dean Myers, John Steptoe, Mildred Taylor, and Brenda Wilkinson. A second generation of writers whose works were first published in the mid 1970s included Jeanette Caines, Patricia McKissack, Mildred Pitts Walter, and Camille Yarbrough. Authors whose work began appearing in the 1980s were Rita Garcia-Williams, Joyce Hansen, Angela Johnson, Emily Moore, and Joyce Carol Thomas.

Major themes explored by these authors include survival through the love and help of one's family and community, the value of family and cultural traditions, relationships among friends and relatives, factors molding an individual's character, and reactions to ordinary events such as a bedtime story. According to Sims (1982), characteristics of the literature include the use of African American language forms, description of the relationships between the young and the very old, and the portrayal of extended families. All of these characteristics are evident in *The Hundred Penny Box* by Mathis (1975), which tells of young Michael's relationship with his great-great-aunt Dew. Harris (1992) suggests that culturally conscious literature may also deal openly with differences in skin color, incorporate African American names and forms of address, describe African American history and culture, and refer to religion and gospel music.

Asian American Children's Literature

Asian American authors mentioned by Harris include Yoshiko Uchida, Taro Yashima, Paul Yee, Laurence Yep, and Ed Young. Harris cites the work of the Asian American Book Project (1981), which identified characteristics of authentic, culturally conscious Asian American literature. First, these works should deal with Asian American culture itself and not with Asian Americans imitating European American culture. For example, the settings, language, and actions shown should be specific to an actual Asian American group rather than referring to Asian Americans in general. Generalities are inappropriate, since Asian Americans are a diverse group including those of Chinese, Filipino, Hmong, Japanese, Thai, Vietnamese, and other ancestries. For example, Laurence Yep's books depict the experiences of Chinese Americans.

Second, the literature must go beyond common stereotypes of Asian Americans. These works show that Asian Americans have jobs other than working in restaurants and running laundries. Yoshiko Uchida's books, such as *The Best Bad Thing* (1983), show Japanese American adults in many roles, as parents, ministers, farmers, and so on. *El Chino* by Allen Say (1990), the story of a Chinese American who earned fame as a matador in Spain, is an example of a book that shows the varied aspirations and life experiences of Asian Americans.

Third, the literature seeks to correct historical errors and omissions. An example is Paul Yee's (1989) *Tales from Gold Mountain*, a book that celebrates the courage and resourcefulness of the early Chinese settlers. The Asian American Book Project also identified other desirable characteristics, including not perpetuating the myth of Asian Americans as the "model minority," showing women and girls in a variety of roles and avoiding the "China doll" stereotype, and providing realistic visual images of Asian Americans (for example, showing that children typically dress in western clothing).

Hispanic American Children's Literature

Harris (1992) notes that, to date, few books by Hispanic children's authors have been published, and little culturally conscious literature is available. The major authors mentioned by Harris are Pura Belpre, Nicholasa Mohr, Gary Soto, and Piri Thomas.

Some books, such as *Family Pictures* by Carmen Lomas Garza (1990), show the richness of life in Mexican American communities as reflected in unique customs, shared language, and the supportiveness of family and friends. Others, such as *Baseball in April* by Gary Soto (1990), depict the struggles and triumphs of everyday life, as Hispanic young people try out for Little League teams and perform in the school talent show.

Other themes identified by Harris include the struggle to maintain one's cultural identity, the resilience of families, conflicts between family members of different generations, and surviving oppression. These themes are reflected in Nicholasa Mohr's collections of short stories, *In Nueva York* (1988) and *El Bronx Remembered* (1986), which present moving depictions of the lives of Puerto Rican young people, their families, and neighbors

Native American Children's Literature

Harris finds that few culturally conscious works by Native American authors have been published, although other authors have written about Native American subjects, particularly myths and legends. Virgina Driving Hawk Sneve, author of *Jimmy Yellow Hawk* (1972), is a well-known Native American author. Te Ata (1989), a Native American storyteller, presents a traditional Chickasaw tale in *Baby Rattlesnake*, a picture storybook. Others who have written in a sensitive manner about Native American topics include Byrd Baylor, John Bierhorst, Jamake Highwater, and Gerald McDermott.

According to Harris, themes in Native American literature include the passing on of traditional knowledge and history; the mistreatment and injustice experienced by Native Americans; the negative effects of domination by European Americans, which included the denigration of native languages, beliefs, and customs; and the value of relationships with family and friends. Another theme in Native American literature is reverence for nature and all living things, as shown in *Brother Eagle, Sister Sky: A Message from Chief Seattle* (1991).

For further discussion of multicultural and multiethnic children's literature, including many available titles, refer to Harris (1992), Lindgren (1991), Miller-Lachmann (1992), Norton (1991), Rudman (1984), and Tway (1989). Reviews of recently published books may be found in such journals as *Book Links*, *Language Arts*, *The New Advocate*, and *The Reading Teacher*.

Students' Responses to Culturally Conscious Literature

The value for all students of studying culturally conscious literature is demonstrated in research conducted by Linda Spears-Bunton (1990). She studied the responses of poor and working-class African American and European American students to a culturally conscious work of literature, *The House of Dies Drear* by Virginia Hamilton (1968). Spears-Bunton conducted her research in an eleventh grade honors English class taught by a European American teacher. The teacher, Paula Reynolds, had not previously taught any African American literature. Her reasons for participating in the project were that her students had asked her to teach African American literature, she disliked the view of American literature presented in the literature anthology previously used in the course, and, as a matter of professional growth, she wanted to become more knowledgeable about African American literature. Because she was the first in her school to teach African American literature, Reynolds found that she was exposed to challenges from both her colleagues and students. Nevertheless, she wanted to address two issues:

> "What happens to Black kids who never get to read a book written by a Black author, and how do White students feel about the emphasis on Black literature?"   (p. 569)

While Reynolds was committed to having her students read African American literature, she also needed to cover the traditional curriculum. To accomplish both goals, she added works with an African American perspective dealing with the same historical period as the works in the traditional curriculum. For example, while the students were reading *The Scarlet Letter* they also read "The Perils of a Slave Woman's Life" by Harriet Jacobs (1988). Soon Reynolds and her students found that they had to read constantly, in order to cover both the African American literature and the standard works required by the school district and the traditional curriculum. The African American students objected to *The Scarlet Letter* and other traditional works, and cultural conflicts began to emerge. Most of the students seemed to be enjoying the African American literature, and the African American students participated actively in class discussions. However, the European American students generally stayed out of the discussions. Burt, a European American student, disrupted the class one day by popping balloons. The reason he gave Reynolds was that he hated black literature.

Spears-Bunton's interviews with Reynolds' students indicated that Burt's actions were just one reflection of the cultural tensions between the African American and European American students. At the beginning of the school year, Spears-Bunton found that none of the students had previously read any African American literature. Yet their attitudes toward these works already followed along ethnic and cultural lines. The African American students had a sense of peoplehood and expressed the view that African Americans were different from other cultural groups. They felt that the literature was an expression of African Americans' fight for survival. In contrast, the European American students discussed cultural differences in a hesitant and ambivalent fashion and "seemed to distance themselves from the issue of culture." (p. 570) The differences in the students' attitudes can be seen in the following two interview excerpts.

Tasha, an African American student:

I would read about struggle — how long it took to fight for what we have now . . . because this is where our heritage comes from . . . . It'll [African American literature] be different in language and the way people live or the customs they live by . . .

Courtney, a European American student:

I think that slavery and everything — it seems like such an old issue. I think there's no sense in talking about the past. I don't like to be in a position where you have to pick from side to side what you are. We should all be just equal Americans not African Americans . . . they're the same as us. (p. 570)

Tasha and Courtney showed strikingly different attitudes toward the historical struggles of African Americans. Tasha saw a direct relationship between past struggles and the present lives of African Americans. Courtney did not have any personal interest in the past struggles of African Americans and did not recognize any connection between the past and the present, in terms of the relationships between African and European Americans. Her statement that "they're the same as us" seemed to express a wish to avoid or deny issues of diversity.

Despite these mixed attitudes toward African American literature, a dramatic change occurred when Reynolds had the students begin reading *The House of Dies Drear* by Virginia Hamilton (1968). Spears-Bunton describes what happened on the day after students had received their copies of the book:

> One of the students, a vocal, self-proclaimed "White male chauvinist superior being" and erstwhile critic of all literature as "stupid lies," bounced into class and asked [Reynolds] excitedly: "Who was behind the mirror? Was it Mr. Pluto? Who was Mr. Pluto? How did he get into the house?" Another student exclaimed: "I've read more of this already than all of that other one." Before students and teacher could exchange "good mornings" — even before roll could be taken — discussion about the book was initiated and sustained by students for the first half hour of class.   (p. 571)

The students then read silently, totally engrossed in the book, until the end of the period. In the days that followed, students came to class eager to discuss the book and share their interpretations. All finished reading the book before the deadline and received passing grades on the written assignments.

No doubt, students' interest was high in part because *The House of Dies Drear* is a "good story," but it is clear that they were also deeply affected by the book's African American perspective and content. Interviews with Tasha and Courtney illustrate how students' attitudes were changed through the reading of *The House of Dies Drear*. Tasha was a capable student who stated that English and journalism were her favorite subjects and that she wanted to go on to college and law school. Yet when Spears-Bunton questioned her about her reading, Tasha replied, "Unless the spirit hits me, Tasha don't do no reading." Tasha indicated that she read *The Scarlet Letter* as quickly as she could, just to get it over with. Spears-Bunton observed that Tasha put her head down when it was time to participate in discussion or write about the book. As a result, Tasha received poor grades and began to think that she might not be college material after all.

But when Tasha was asked to talk about her reading of *The House of Dies Drear*, she responded eagerly and enthusiastically. Tasha stated that she was enjoying the book and could identify with the main character, Thomas. She said that reading *House* called up vivid images and brought to mind the enjoyable experience of reading aloud to young children, when "you can really get into it, you can put in motion and little voices." Tasha even had an idea for a paper comparing *House* and *The Scarlet Letter*.

> Do you remember those doors? One [in *The Scarlet Letter*] was a prison door; you know, a place for keeping people in like a slave. The other door [in *The House of Dies Drear*] made you free. Do you think Miss P. will let me write a paper about that — about the doors?   (p. 572)

Courtney, too, found herself being drawn into the book. She told the interviewer:

> Oh, I could just see those caves. I can imagine running across that river there
> and getting to that house. I would have explored every one of those caves and
> I would have been so glad to be there and to be safe. . . . You know, maybe
> Black literature should be set aside, special like, so I can see it better for
> myself.   (p. 572)

In contrast to the detached attitude she showed in previous interviews,
Courtney now indicated that she was personally involved in the text. Her
comment that she would like to "see [black literature] better for myself"
seems to reflect her struggle to come to terms with the issues raised by
the book. She identified with Thomas and could visualize herself sharing
his journey. She felt a personal interest in African American literature
and said that she was planning to read the sequel to *House*. Spears-
Bunton observes:

> Her references to African American literary texts changed from comments
> about what "they [teachers] wanted [students] to read and understand" to
> observations on how she felt about her reading. Her references to "them"
> (African Americans) were replaced with "*I* would have run, *I* would have felt
> glad and safe."   (p. 572)

Courtney had never had the opportunity to examine her own attitudes
towards African Americans. Through the reading of *House*, she began to
understand issues of cultural difference that went deeper than appearance
and preferences for different kinds of food or music. As a result of the new
understandings she developed, Courtney began to question her own assumptions and to become critical of friends and family members who
belonged to racist organizations.

This study by Spears-Bunton demonstrates the benefits of having students read culturally conscious multiethnic literature. Reynolds took a
brave step forward when she decided to have her class read African American literature and set the stage for the students to come to grips with the
challenging issues of ethnicity, gender, and social class. Tensions and
negative attitudes had to be confronted. Then, later, as they became im-
mersed in reading *The House of Dies Drear*, students were able to deal
openly and honestly with issues of ethnicity and the relationships between
African and European Americans, both past and present. Students, even
those who had previously performed poorly in class, became committed
to doing well on classroom assignments and tests related to their reading.

Tasha and other African American students had the opportunity to see
the history of African Americans represented in literature, and gained new
insights into the symbolism in both African and European American literature. Courtney and other European American students had the chance to
explore their own attitudes toward African Americans and the historical and
present-day relationships between African and European Americans. In short,
the experiences of Reynolds' class suggest that culturally conscious literature
can lead to improvements in students' attitudes towards the reading of

literature and to new ways of thinking about one's own ethnic group and the relationships among ethnic groups in the United States.

Issues in Using Multiethnic Literature

Like Reynolds, many teachers recognize the potential benefits of using multiethnic literature. Harris (1992) suggests that the decision to use multicultural literature is best made by the individual teacher. Only in this way will teachers develop ownership over the literature and be able to share it with students in a sincere and enthusiastic manner. When the use of multicultural literature is imposed, such as by a district mandate, teachers may feel resentful and unprepared, and as a result, convey to students a negative attitude toward the literature and members of certain ethnic groups.

Teachers who are interested in using multicultural literature will want to become familiar with some of the books suitable for use at their grade level. References with lists of recommended titles were presented earlier in this chapter. Harris (1992) cautions that there are certain popular and critically acclaimed works such as *The Indian in the Cupboard, Sounder,* and *The Cay* which appear to deal with multicultural issues but do not meet the criteria for culturally conscious literature. *The Indian in the Cupboard,* for example, while an imaginative and entertaining story, perpetuates stereotypes about Native Americans (for example, Little Bear's stilted speech).

As you review works of multiethnic literature, you will want to consider the challenging issues they raise and how you will handle these issues in discussions with your students. Culturally conscious children's literature may deal openly with issues of discrimination and acts of violence. For example, in *Roll of Thunder, Hear My Cry* (Taylor, 1976), African Americans are burned and beaten. In *The Star Fisher* (Yep, 1991) Chinese Americans arriving in a small town in West Virginia are called "darn monkeys" by a bystander.

Related to issues of discrimination, culturally conscious literature may present a view of history different from that in typical social studies textbooks (Harris, 1992). For example, in *The Journey: Japanese Americans, Racism, and Renewal,* Sheila Hamanaka (1990) presents her own view of history, including the internment of Japanese Americans during World War II. Teachers may want to do some background reading themselves and allow students to do further reading and research to better understand historical events from diverse perspectives.

Still another issue highlighted by Harris is the use of African American language or other varieties of English in some culturally conscious works. The use of works such as *My Brother Fine with Me* (Clifton, 1975) or *Flossie and the Fox* (McKissack, 1986) may become controversial if teachers and parents do not appreciate and value African American language and other varieties of English. Educators, parents, and members of the community need to understand the dangers of presenting an exclusively monolingual, mainstream view of language and literature, and the benefits of celebrating linguistic diversity through literature.

Models for Teaching Multicultural Literature

> Four approaches to the teaching of multicultural or multiethnic literature are:
> Contributions approach;
> Additive approach;
> Transformative approach;
> Decision-making and social action approach.

Rasinski and Padak (1990) outline four approaches to the teaching of multicultural or multiethnic literature, based on a hierarchy for integrating ethnic and cultural content in the curriculum developed by James Banks (1989). They are the contributions, additive, transformative, and decision-making and social action approaches. They differ in the extent to which they lead to changes in the traditional curriculum and in students' and teachers' commitment to diversity and social justice. The first approach familiarizes students with some multicultural content but does not necessarily lead them to question their existing beliefs, while the fourth encourages students to take action to solve important social problems.

In the **contributions approach** teachers focus on the heroes, holidays, and other components of a particular culture. Lessons typically take place because of a special occasion, such as Cinco de Mayo or Black History Month. Literature is used to introduce children to the contributions of important people or to special customs. For example, students might read a biography of Martin Luther King Jr. The strength of this approach lies in its convenience, since it offers an easy way to present ethnic content without disturbing the existing curriculum. The weakness of this approach is that it gives students only a superficial understanding of their own culture and the cultures of others. As Banks points out, mainstream criteria are used as the basis for selecting the elements of culture to be studied. Because this approach singles out heroes, holidays, and other visible aspects of culture, it may tend to reinforce stereotypes and mistaken beliefs and so hinder deeper understanding. Teachers do not need to avoid teaching students about heroes and holidays, but they should attempt to develop in students a deeper understanding of underlying cultural values and historical circumstances.

In the **additive approach**, concepts and content about other ethnic groups are added to the core curriculum, instead of being treated separately as in the contributions approach. For example, if the core curriculum includes a unit on folktales, *Mufaro's Beautiful Daughters* (Steptoe, 1987) and *Yeh Shen* (Louie, 1982) might be added to this unit, as examples of other versions of the Cinderella tale. The strengths and weaknesses of the additive approach are similar to those of the contributions approach. In both, the basic structure of the curriculum remains unchanged. Diverse cultures are still viewed from a Eurocentric perspective, not on their own terms, and the complex interrelationships between dominant and subordinate groups are not addressed. However, as Rasinski and Padak suggest, these approaches make a contribution by at least exposing students to the literature of diverse groups.

In the **transformation approach**, the goals and structure of the curriculum are changed to promote the study of concepts, events, and issues from the perspectives of subordinate as well as dominant groups. For example, in a unit on the westward movement, students might read literature reflecting the viewpoints of diverse cultural groups. *Spirit of the White Bison* by Beatrice Culleton (1985) describes the slaughter of the buffalo and the depletion of the food supply needed by the Plains Indians. *Tales from Gold Mountain* by Paul Yee (1989) presents spirited tales of the Chinese settlers whose wit and determination enabled them to overcome hardships in the New World. According to Banks, one strength of the transformation approach is that it helps students understand how American society was shaped through the participation of diverse cultural groups. Students gain a broader, more balanced view of American history and of contemporary American life. Another strength is that students of diverse backgrounds see their own cultures recognized and presented in the school's curriculum. If students of diverse backgrounds can feel pride in their own cultures, they are more likely to gain confidence and feel empowered to be responsible for their own learning. A drawback of this approach is that it requires substantial revision of the curriculum. Teachers often need to become acquainted with new content and materials, and in some cases, appropriate multiethnic literature may be difficult to find.

In the **decision-making and social action approach**, students identify important social issues, gather information, clarify their values and assumptions, arrive at decisions, and take action to address the issues. Culturally conscious literature can help students understand and recognize social issues. For example, children in the primary grades may be introduced to the issues in the civil rights movement through *Rosa Parks*, a biography by Eloise Greenfield (1973). Students may discuss their own attitudes towards those of other ethnic groups, what it means to give equal rights to those of all groups, instances of discrimination in their own school or community, and the changes needed to correct the problems.

A strength of the social action approach is that it allows students to sharpen their thinking about social issues. Often, research skills are fostered as well, as students gather data on critical social issues from sources such as newspapers, books, and magazines, and through interviews. Students learn that, by searching for solutions to challenging social problems, they can make a difference. As with the transformation approach, the social action approach requires that teachers move into new ground. A challenge posed by this approach is that it takes considerable teacher planning and effort to organize units. Furthermore, the issues raised may be controversial, and teachers need to be aware of how to handle the sensitivities of students, parents, and other educators. Also, students may find that there is little they can do to address the social issue targeted.

Teachers who adopt the transformation and social action approaches are showing a deep commitment to the literacy learning and citizenship of all students. Through the use of culturally conscious literature, they communicate the idea that diversity is central to the American experience. By having students ponder the issues raised by culturally conscious literature, they enable students to explore social issues in a thoughtful and positive manner. In the social action approach, they help students to understand the responsibility every citizen should feel for the fair treatment and well-being of all groups within the United States.

Literature and Democratic Values

> In discussions of multiethnic literature, teachers guide students not only to interpret the text but also to reflect upon the ways that they might carry democratic values forward in their own lives.

Multiethnic literature and constructivist models of instruction, which allow students to wrestle with issues and develop a broader perspective, can serve democratic values such as equality of opportunity and social mobility. In *Literature as Exploration*, Louise Rosenblatt (1976) attempted to demonstrate how experiences with literature might be at the very heart of the educational process in a democracy (Pradl, 1991). She described how literature might have the potential to help students value diversity.

> As the student vicariously shares through literature the emotions and aspirations of other human beings, he can gain heightened sensitivity to the needs and problems of others remote from him in temperament, in space, or in social environment; he can develop a greater imaginative capacity to grasp the meaning of abstract laws or political or social theories for actual human lives. Such sensitivity and imagination are part of the indispensable equipment of the citizen of a democracy.   (p. 274)

As discussed throughout this book, teachers in classrooms that are literate communities work to celebrate, promote, and build upon the diversity in students' backgrounds and experiences. In classrooms where diversity is valued and new patterns of instruction are in place, both students of diverse backgrounds and students of mainstream backgrounds are likely to achieve high levels of literacy.

For all students, literacy achievement is a matter of heart and motivation as well as of mind and cognition. Critical literacy, a concept developed in chapter 2, is also a matter of conscience and responsibility, since it involves a perception of the world and transformation of the world through practical action. Having students read and discuss culturally conscious works of literature is one way of developing students' critical literacy, because they have the opportunity to learn about a variety of life experiences and to become aware of issues of social justice. In discussions of multiethnic literature, teachers guide students not only to interpret the text but also to reflect upon the ways that they might carry democratic values forward in their own lives. Teachers with a commitment to the values of democracy and diversity accept the challenge of using new patterns of literacy instruction to help the students who are in their classrooms today. Through their positive actions and those of their students, they also work toward a future when the United States will be a more just and fully democratic society, offering all children a wealth of educational opportunities.

Summary

Multiethnic literature, especially culturally conscious works, can be of special benefit to all students. Through the use of multiethnic literature, students of diverse backgrounds gain pride and confidence from seeing the experiences of their own ethnic group represented in literature, and all students can develop an appreciation for other cultures. African American, Asian American, Hispanic American, and Native American authors have all written culturally conscious works of children's literature, and these books reflect the ways of life, traditions, and values of these cultural groups. The use of multiethnic literature, a new pattern in schools, can foster students' pride in their own culture and understanding of other cultures. It contrasts with the familiar old pattern of having students read works from a Eurocentric literary canon that rarely includes works by authors of diverse backgrounds. Research suggests that reading multiethnic literature can broaden the attitudes and literary insights of students of mainstream backgrounds, as well as of students of diverse backgrounds. Multiethnic literature may deal with controversial issues such as discrimination, and teachers will want to think about how they will handle these issues with students and parents. The work of Banks points to four approaches to the teaching of multicultural or multiethnic literature. The last two, the transformation and social action approaches, have the advantages of leading to a restructuring of the traditional curriculum and to a questioning of assumptions. Literature, especially culturally conscious literature, appears to have great value in bringing critical social issues to life for students and in promoting their understanding of democratic values.

Application Activities

1. Read a work of multiethnic children's literature. Discuss the features that appear to make this a culturally conscious work of literature, including the events and issues indicative of the diverse, nonmainstream perspective taken by the author.

2. Reflect back to the books that you read when you were in elementary, junior high, and high school. Did you read and discuss any multiethnic literature in class? If so, how did you and your classmates respond? How did your responses compare to those of Ms. Reynolds' students? If you did not read any multiethnic literature, why do you think this was so? What were the possible effects of an absence of multiethnic literature on you and your classmates?

Suggested Readings

Harris, V.J. (1992). "Multiethnic Children's Literature." In K.D. Wood and A. Moss, eds., *Exploring Literature in the Classroom: Content and Methods*. Norwood, MA: Christopher-Gordon, pp. 169-201.

Lindgren, M.V., ed. (1991). *The Multicolored Mirror: Cultural Substance in Literature for Children and Young Adults*. Fort Atkinson, WI: Highsmith.

Norton, D.E. (1991). "Multicultural Literature." In *Through The Eyes of a Child — An Introduction to Children's Literature*, 3rd ed. New York: MacMillan, pp. 83-126.

Walker-Dalhouse, D. (1992). "Using African-American Literature to Increase Ethnic Understanding." *The Reading Teacher*, 45(6), pp. 416-22.

References

Allen, V.G. (1989). "Literature as a Support to Language Acquisition." In P. Rigg and V.G. Allen, eds. *When they don't all speak English.* Urbana, IL: National Council of Teachers of English, pp. 55-64.

Allington, R.L. (1983). "The Reading Instruction Provided Readers of Differing Abilities." *Elementary School Journal,* 83(5), pp. 548-59.

Allington, R.L. (1991). "Children Who Find Learning to Read Difficult: School Responses to Diversity." In E.H. Hiebert, ed. *Literacy for a Diverse Society: Perspectives, Practices, and Policies.* New York: Teachers College Press, pp. 237-52.

Anderson, A.B., W.H. Teale, and E. Estrada (1980). "Low-Income Children's Preschool Literacy Experiences." *The Quarterly Newsletter of the Laboratory of Comparative Human Cognition,* 2(3), pp. 59-65.

Anderson, R.C., and P.D. Pearson (1984). "A Schema-Theoretic View of Basic Processes in Reading Comprehension." In P.D. Pearson, ed. *Handbook of Reading Research.* New York: Longman.

Anderson, R.C., E. Hiebert, J. Scott, and I. Wilkinson (1985). *Becoming a Nation of Readers: The Report of the Commission on Reading.* Washington, D.C.: National Institute of Education.

Anderson, R.C., P.T. Wilson, and L.G. Fielding (1988). "Growth in Reading and How Children Spend Their Time Outside of School." *Reading Research Quarterly,* 23(3), pp. 285-303.

Applebee, A.N. (1989). *A Study of Book-Length Works Taught in High School English Courses,* Report No. 1.2. Albany, NY: Center for the Learning and Teaching of Literature.

Applebee, A.N. (1991). "Literature: Whose Heritage?" In E.H. Hiebert, ed. *Literacy for a Diverse Society: Perspectives, Practices, and Policies.* New York: Teachers College Press, pp. 228-36.

Applebee, A.N., J.A. Langer, and I.V.S. Mullis (1988). *Who Reads Best: Factors Related to Reading Achievement in Grades 3, 7, and 11.* Princeton, NJ: National Assessment of Educational Progress, Educational Testing Service.

Ascher, C. (1990). *Testing Students in Urban Schools: Current Problems and New Directions.* Urban Diversity Series No. 100. New York: ERIC Clearinghouse on Urban Education, Teachers College, Columbia University.

Asian American Book Project (1981). "How Children's Books Distort the Asian American Image." *Interracial Books for Children Bulletin,* 7(2 and 3), pp. 3-33.

Atwell, N. (1987). *In the Middle: Writing, Reading, and Learning with Adolescents.* Portsmouth, NH: Boynton/Cook.

Au, K.H. (1979). "Using the Experience-Text-Relationship Method with Minority Children." *Reading Teacher,* 32(6), pp. 677-79.

Au, K.H. (1980). "Participation Structures in a Reading Lesson with Hawaiian Children: Analysis of a Culturally Appropriate Instructional Event." *Anthropology and Education Quarterly,* 11(2), pp. 91-115.

Au, K.H. (1992). "Constructing the Theme of a Story." *Language Arts,* 69(2), pp. 106-11.

Au, K.H., and A.J. Kawakami (1985). "Research Currents: Talk Story and Learning to Read." *Language Arts,* 62(4), pp. 406-11.

Au, K.H., and A.J. Kawakami (1986). "Influence of the Social Organization of Instruction on Children's Text Comprehension Ability: A Vygotskian Perspective." In T.E. Raphael, ed. *The Contexts of School Based Literacy.* New York: Random House, pp. 63-77.

Au, K.H., and A.J. Kawakami (1991). Culture and Ownership: Schooling of Minority Students. *Childhood Education,* 67(5), pp. 280-84.

Au, K.H., and J.M. Mason (1981). "Social Organizational Factors in Learning to Read: The Balance of Rights Hypothesis." *Reading Research Quarterly,* 17(1), pp. 115-52.

Au, K.H., and J.M. Mason (1983). "Cultural Congruence in Classroom Participation

Structures: Achieving a Balance of Rights." *Discourse Processes,* 6(2), pp. 145-67.

Au, K.H., J.A. Scheu, and A.J. Kawakami (1990). Assessment of Students' Ownership of Literacy. *The Reading Teacher,* 44(2), pp. 154-56.

Bacmeister, R. (1964). "Magic in a Glass Jar." In W.K. Durr, J.M. LePere, and R.H. Brown, *Windchimes.* Boston: Houghton Mifflin, pp. 68-77.

Banks, J.A. (1988). *Multiethnic Education: Theory and Practice,* 2nd ed. Boston: Allyn and Bacon.

Banks, J.A. (1989). "Integrating the Curriculum with Ethnic Content: Approaches and Guidelines." In J.A. Banks and C.A.M. Banks, eds. *Multicultural Education: Issues and Perspectives.* Boston: Allyn and Bacon, pp. 189-207.

Barnhardt, C. (1982). "Tuning-In to Athabaskan Teachers and Athabaskan Students." In R. Barnhardt, ed. *Cross-Cultural Issues in Alaskan Education,* Vol. 2. Fairbanks, AK: Center for Cross-Cultural studies.

Barr, R. (1989). "The Social Organization of Literacy Instruction." In S. McCormick and J. Zutell, eds. *Cognitive and Social Perspectives for Literacy Research and Instruction,* Thirty-eighth Yearbook of the National Reading Conference. Chicago, IL: National Reading Conference, pp. 19-33.

Barrera, R.B. (1983). "Bilingual Reading in the Primary Grades: Some Questions about Questionable Views and Practices." In T.H. Escobedo, ed. *Early Childhood Bilingual Education: A Hispanic Perspective.* New York: Teachers College Press.

Barrera, R.B. (1992, in press). "The Cultural Gap in Literature-Based Literacy Instruction." *Education and Urban Society.*

Bennett, A.T., and P. Pedraza (1984). "Discourse, Consciousness, and Literacy in a Puerto Rican Neighborhood." In C. Kramarae, M. Schulz, and W.M. O'Barr, eds. *Language and Power.* Beverly Hills, CA: Sage, pp. 243-59.

Bickerton, D. (1981). *The Roots of Language.* Ann Arbor, MI: Karoma.

Bird, L.B., ed. (1989). *Becoming a Whole Language School: The Fair Oaks Story.* Katonah, NY: Richard C. Owen.

Blackburn, E. (1984). "Common Ground: Developing Relationships Between Reading and Writing." *Language Arts,* 61, pp. 367-75.

Bloom, B.S. (1976). *Human Characteristics and School Learning.* New York: McGraw-Hill.

Britton, J., T. Burgess, N. Martin, A. McLeod, and H. Rosen (1975). *The Development of Writing Abilities.* London: Macmillan.

Brown, M.W. (1949). *The Important Book.* New York: Harper and Brothers.

Brown, R.G. (1991). *Schools of Thought.* San Francisco: Jossey-Bass.

Cairney, T., and S. Langbien (1989). "Building Communities of Readers and Writers." *The Reading Teacher,* 42(8), pp. 560-67.

Calkins, L.M. (1986). *The Art of Teaching Writing.* Portsmouth, NH: Heinemann.

Calkins, L.M. (1991). *Living Between the Lines.* Portsmouth, NH: Heinemann.

Carroll, J. (1963). "A Model for School Learning." *Teachers College Record,* 64, pp. 723-33.

Cartagena, J. (1991). "English Only in the 1980s: A Product of Myth, Phobias, and Bias." In S. Benesch, ed. *ESL in America: Myths and Possibilities.* Portsmouth, NH: Boynton/Cook, pp. 11-26.

Cazden, C.B. (1988). *Classroom Discourse: The Language of Teaching and Learning.* Portsmouth, NH: Heinemann.

Cazden, C.B., R. Carrasco, A.A. Maldonado-Guzman, and F. Erickson (1980). "The Contribution of Ethnographic Research to Bicultural Bilingual Education." In J. Alatis, ed. *Current Issues in Bilingual Education.* Georgetown University Round Table on Language and Linguistics. Washington, DC: Georgetown University Press.

Center for the Study of Reading (1990). Teaching Reading: Strategies from Successful Classrooms. Six-part videotape series. Urbana-Champaign, IL: University of Illinois.

Chief Seattle (1991). *Brother Eagle, Sister Sky: A Message from Chief Seattle.* Illustrated by S. Jeffers. New York: Dial.

Clay, M. (1975). *What Did I Write? Beginning Writing Behavior.* Portsmouth, NH: Heinemann.

Clay, M.M. (1985). *The Early Detection of Reading Difficulties.* 3rd ed. Auckland, New Zealand: Heinemann.

Clifton, L. (1975). *My Brother Fine with Me.* New York: Holt, Rinehart and Winston.

Collins, A., J.S. Brown, and J.M. Larkin (1980). "Inference in Text Understanding." In R.J. Spiro, B.C. Bruce, and W.F. Brewer, eds. *Theoretical Issues in Reading Comprehension.* Hillsdale, NJ: Erlbaum.

Crafton, L.K. (1991). *Whole Language: Getting Started . . . Moving Forward.* Katonah, NY: Richard C. Owen.

Crowell, D.C., A.J. Kawakami, and J.L. Wong (1986). "Emerging Literacy: Reading-

Writing Experiences in a Kindergarten Classroom." *Reading Teacher*, 40(2), pp. 144-49.

Culleton, B. (1985). *Spirit of the White Bison.* Illustrated by R. Kakaygeesick. Winnipeg, Manitoba: Pemmican.

Cummins, J. (1984). *Bilingualism and Special Education: Issues in Assessment and Pedagogy.* Clevedon, England: Multilingual Matters.

Cummins, J. (1986). "Empowering Minority Students: A Framework for Intervention." *Harvard Educational Review*, 56(1), pp. 18-36.

Cunningham, P.M., D.P. Hall, and M. Defee, M. (1991). "Non-Ability-Grouped Multilevel Instruction: A Year in a First-Grade Class." *The Reading Teacher*, 44(8), pp. 566-71.

D'Amato, J. (1986). *"We Cool, Tha's Why:" A Study of Personhood and Place in a Class of Hawaiian Second Graders.* Unpublished doctoral dissertation, University of Hawaii.

D'Amato, J. (1988). " 'Acting:' Hawaiian Children's Resistance to Teachers." *Elementary School Journal*, 88(5), pp. 529-44.

D'Amato, J. (1987). "The Belly of the Beast: On Cultural Differences, Castelike Status, and the Politics of School. *Anthropology and Education Quarterly*, 18(4), pp. 357-61.

de Paola, T. (1973). *Nana Upstairs, Nana Downstairs.* New York: Penguin Books.

Delain, M.T., P.D. Pearson, and R.C. Anderson (1985). "Reading Comprehension and Creativity in Black Language Use: You Stand to Gain by Playing the Sounding Game!" *American Educational Research Journal*, 22(2), pp. 155-73.

Delgado-Gaitan, C. (1989). "Classroom Literacy Activity for Spanish-Speaking Students." *Linguistics and Education*, 1, pp. 285-97.

Delgado-Gaitan, C. (1990). *Literacy for Empowerment: The Role of Parents in Children's Education.* Bristol, PA: Falmer Press.

Delgado-Gaitan, C., and H. T. Trueba (1991). *Crossing Cultural Borders: Education for Immigrant Families in America.* London: Falmer Press.

Delpit, L.D. (1988). "The Silenced Dialogue: Power and Pedagogy in Educating Other People's Children." *Harvard Educational Review*, 58, pp. 280-98.

Delpit, L.D. (1986). "Skills and Other Dilemmas of a Progressive Black Educator. *Harvard Educational Review*, 56(4), pp. 379-85.

Edelsky, C. (1983). "Writing in a Bilingual Program: The Relation of L1 and L2 Texts." *TESOL Quarterly*, 16, pp. 211-29.

Edelsky, C., K. Draper, and K. Smith (1983). "Hookin' 'Em in at the Start of School in a 'Whole Language' Classroom." *Anthropology and Education Quarterly*, 14(4), pp. 257-81.

Elbow, P. (1973). *Writing Without Teachers.* New York: Oxford University Press.

Erickson, F. (1984). "School Literacy, Reasoning, and Civility: An Anthropologist's Perspective." *Review of Educational Research*, 54(4), pp. 525-46.

Erickson, F. (1987). "Transformation and School Success: The Politics and Culture of Educational Attainment." *Anthropology and Education Quarterly*, 18(4), pp. 335-56.

Erickson, F., and G. Mohatt (1982). "Cultural Organization of Participation Structures in Two Classrooms of Indian students." In G.B. Spindler, ed. *Doing the Ethnography of Schooling: Educational Anthropology in Action.* New York: Holt, Rinehart and Winston, pp. 132-74.

Erickson, F., and J. Shultz (1977). "When is a Context? Some Issues and Methods in the Analysis of Social Competence." *Quarterly Newsletter of the Institute for Comparative Human Development*, 1(2), pp. 5-10.

Erickson, F., and J. Shultz (1982). *The Counselor as Gatekeeper: Social Interaction in Interviews.* New York: Academic Press.

Fairchild, H.H., and S. Edwards-Evans (1990). "African American Dialects and Schooling: A Review." In A.M. Padilla, H.H. Fairchild, and C.M. Valadez, eds. *Bilingual Education: Issues and Strategies.* Newbury Park, CA: Sage, pp. 75-86.

Farrell, E.J. (1991). "Instructional Models for English Language Arts, K-12." In J. Flood, J.M. Jensen, D. Lapp, and J.R. Squire, eds. *Handbook of Research on Teaching the English Language Arts*, New York: Macmillan, pp. 63-84.

Fasold, R.W. (1972). *Tense Marking in Black English: A Linguistic and Social Analysis.* Washington, DC: Center for Applied Linguistics.

Feeley, J.T. (1983). "Help For the Reading Teacher: Dealing With the Limited English Proficiency (LEP) Child in the Elementary Classroom." *The Reading Teacher*, 36(4), pp. 650-55.

Ferdman, B.M. (1991). "Becoming Literate in a Multiethnic Society." In E.M. Jennings and A.C. Purves, eds. *Literate Systems and Individual Lives: Perspectives on Literacy and Schooling.* Albany, NY:

State University of New York Press, pp. 95-115.

Figueroa, R.A. (1989). "Psychological Testing of Linguistic-Minority Students: Knowledge Gaps and Regulations." *Exceptional Children*, 56(2), pp. 145-52.

Figueroa, R.A. (1990). "Assessment of Linguistic Minority Group Children." In C.R. Reynolds and R.W. Kamphaus, eds. *Handbook of Psychological and Educational Assessment of Children: Intelligence and Achievement*. New York: Guilford Press, pp. 671-96.

Fingeret, A. (1983). "Social Network: A New Perspective on Independence and Illiterate Adults." *Adult Education Quarterly*, 33(3), pp. 133-46.

Flournoy, V. (1985). *The Patchwork Quilt*. New York: Dial Books for Young Readers.

Fordham, S. (1991). "Peer-Proofing Academic Competition Among Black Adolescents: 'Acting White' Black American Style." In C.E. Sleeter, ed. *Empowerment Through Multicultural Education*, Albany: State University of New York Press, pp. 69-93.

Fordham, S., and J.U. Ogbu (1986). "Black Students' School Success: Coping With the Burden of Acting White." *Urban Review*, 18(3), pp. 176-206.

Freeman, Y.S. (1988). *The Contemporary Spanish Basal Reader*. Occasional paper no. 18. Tucson, AZ: Program in Language and Literacy, College of Education, University of Arizona.

Freire, P. (1985). "Reading the World and Reading the Word: An Interview with Paulo Freire." *Language Arts*, 62(1), pp. 15-21.

Gallimore, R., J.W. Boggs, and C. Jordan (1974). *Culture, Behavior and Education: A Study of Hawaiian-Americans*. Beverly Hills, CA: Sage.

Garza, C.L. (1990). *Family Pictures*. San Francisco: Children's Book Press.

Gavelek, J.R. (1986). "The Social Contexts of Literacy and Schooling: A Developmental Perspective." In T.E. Raphael, ed. *The Contexts of School-Based Literacy*. New York: Random House, pp. 3-26.

Gersten, R., and T. Keating (1987). "Long-Term Benefits from Direct Instruction." *Educational Leadership*, 44(6), pp. 28-31.

Gersten, R., and J. Woodward (1985). "A Case for Structured Immersion." *Educational Leadership*, 43(1), pp. 75-79.

Gilmore, P. (1983). "Spelling 'Mississippi': Recontextualizing a literacy-related speech event." *Anthropology & Education Quarterly*, 14(4), pp. 235-55.

Giroux, H.A. (1987). "Critical Literacy and Student Experience: Donald Graves' Approach to Literacy." *Language Arts*, 64(2), pp. 175-81.

Giroux, H.A. (1988). "Literacy and the Pedagogy of Voice and Political Empowerment." *Educational Theory*, 38, pp. 61-75.

Goldenberg, C. (1987). "Low-Income Hispanic Parents' Contributions to Their First-Grade Children's Word-Recognition Skills." *Anthropology & Education Quarterly*, 18(3), pp. 149-79.

Gollnick, D.M., and P.C. Chinn (1990). *Multicultural Education in a Pluralistic Society*. 3rd ed. Columbus, OH: Merrill.

Goodman, K. (1986). *What's Whole in Whole Language?* Portsmouth, NH: Heinemann.

Goodman, Y.M. (1985). "Kidwatching: Observing Children in the Classroom." In A. Jagger and M.T. Smith-Burke, eds. *Observing the Language Learner*, Newark, DE: International Reading Association, pp. 9-18.

Graves, D. (1983). *Writing: Teachers and Children at Work*. Exeter, NH: Heinemann.

Graves, D., and J. Hansen (1983). "The Author's Chair." *Language Arts*, 60(2), pp. 176-83.

Greenfield, E. (1973). *Rosa Parks*. Illustrated by E. Marlow. New York: Crowell.

Greenfield, E. (1978). *Honey, I Love*. New York: Harper Trophy.

Greenfield, E. (1991). *First Pink Light*. Illustrated by J.S. Gilchrist. New York: Black Butterfly Children's Books.

Gumperz, J. (1976). "Language, Communication, and Public Negotiation." In P. Sanday, ed. *Anthropology and the Public Interest*. New York: Academic Press.

Guthrie, J.T., and V. Greaney (1990). "Literacy Acts." In R. Barr, M.L. Kamil, P.B. Mosenthal, and P.D. Pearson, eds. *Handbook of Reading Research*, Vol. II. New York: Longman, pp. 68-96.

Haberman, M. (1990). "The Rationale for Training Adults as Teachers." In C.E. Sleeter, ed. *Empowerment through Multicultural Education*. Albany: State University of New York Press, pp. 275-86.

Hamanaka, S. (1990). *The Journey: Japanese Americans, Racism, and Renewal*. New York: Orchard.

Hamilton, V. (1968). *The House of Dies Drear*. Illustrated by E. Keith. New York: Macmillan.

Hamilton, V. (1974). *M.C. Higgins, the Great*. New York: Macmillan.

Hamilton, V. (1988). *Anthony Burns: The Defeat and Triumph of a Fugitive Slave*. New York: Knopf.

Hansen, J. (1987). *When Writers Read.* Portsmouth, NH: Heinemann.

Harris, V.J. (1992). "Multiethnic Children's Literature." In K.D. Wood and A. Moss, eds. *Exploring Literature in the Classroom: Content and Methods.* Norwood, MA: Christopher-Gordon, pp. 169-201.

Harste, J.C., and K.G. Short, with C. Burke, and contributing teacher researchers (1988). *Creating Classrooms for Authors: The Reading-Writing Connnection.* Portsmouth, NH: Heinemann.

Hayes, C.W., R. Bahruth, and C. Kessler (1991). *Literacy Con Cariño.* Portsmouth, NH: Heinemann.

Heath, S.B. (1982). "Questioning at Home and at School: A Comparative Study." In G. Spindler, ed. *Doing the Ethnography of Schooling: Educational Anthropology in Action.* New York: Holt, Rinehart and Winston, pp. 102-31.

Heath, S.B. (1983). *Ways with Words: Language, Life, and Work in Communities and Classrooms.* Cambridge, MA: Cambridge University Press.

Herman, P.A., and C.R. Weaver (1988). "Contextual Strategies for Learning Word Meanings: Middle Grade Students Look In and Look Around." Paper presented at the Annual Meeting of the National Reading Conference, Tucson, AZ.

Hernandez, H. (1989). *Multicultural Education: A Teacher's Guide to Content and Process.* Columbus, OH: Merrill.

Holdaway, D. (1979). *The Foundations of Literacy.* Sydney, Australia: Ashton Scholastic (distributed in the United States by Heinemann).

Howard, E.F. (1991). *Aunt Flossie's Hats (and Crab Cakes Later).* Illustrated by J. Ransome. New York: Clarion.

Huck, C., S. Hepler, and J. Hickman (1987). *Children's Literature in the Reading Program.* 4th ed. New York: Holt, Rinehart and Winston.

Hudelson, S. (1986). "ESL Children's Writing: What We've Learned, What We're Learning." In P. Rigg and D.S. Enright, eds. *Children and ESL: Integrating Perspectives.* Washington, DC: Teachers of English to Speakers of Other Languages, pp. 23-54.

Hymes, D. (1974). *Foundations in Sociolinguistics: An Ethnographic Approach.* Philadelphia: University of Pennsylvania Press.

Jacob, E., and C. Jordan (1987). "Explaining the School Performance of Minority Students," Theme Issue. *Anthropology and Education Quarterly*, 18(4).

Jacob, E., and P.R. Sanday (1976). "Dropping Out: A Strategy for Coping with Cultural Pluralism." In P.R. Sanday, ed. *Anthropology and the Public Interest: Fieldwork and Theory*, New York: Academic Press, pp. 95-110.

Jacobs, H. (1988). "The Perils of a Slave Woman's Life From Incidents in the Life of a Slave Girl." In M.H. Washington, ed. *Invented Lives: Narratives of Black Women, 1860-1960.* New York: Anchor Books, pp. 16-69.

Jordan, C. (1985). "Translating Culture: From Ethnographic Information to Educational Program." *Anthropology and Education Quarterly*, 16, pp. 105-23.

Labov, W. (1972). *Language in the Inner City: Studies in the Black English Vernacular.* Philadelphia: University of Pennsylvania Press.

Labov, W., and C. Robins (1969). "A Note on the Relation of Reading Failure to Peer-Group Status in Urban Ghettos." In J.S. DeStefano, ed. *Language, Society, and Education: A Profile of Black English.* Worthington, OH: Charles A. Jones, pp. 312-23.

Lanauze, M., and C. Snow (1989). "The Relation between First- and Second-Language Writing Skills: Evidence from Puerto Rican Elementary School Children in the Mainland." *Linguistics and Education*, 1(4), pp. 323-38.

Lee, C.D. (1991). "Big Picture Talkers/Words Walking Without Masters: The Instructional Implications of Ethnic Voices for an Expanded Literacy." *Journal of Negro Education*, 60(3), pp. 291-304.

Lindfors, J.W. (1989). "The Classroom: A Good Environment for Language Learneeing." In P. Rigg and V.G. Allen, eds. (1989). *When They Don't All Speak English: Integrating the ESL Student into the Regular Classroom.* Urbana, IL: National Council of Teachers of English, pp. 39-54.

Lindgren, M.V., ed. (1991). *The Multicolored Mirror: Cultural Substance in Literature for Children and Young Adults.* Fort Atkinson, WI: Highsmith.

Lindholm, K.J. (1990). "Bilingual Immersion Education: Criteria for Program Development." In A.M. Padilla, H.H. Fairchild, and C.M. Valadez, eds. *Bilingual Education: Issues and Strategies.* Newbury Park, CA: Sage, pp. 91-105.

Lipka, J. (1991). "Toward a Culturally Based Pedagogy: A Case Study of One Yup'ik Eskimo Teacher." *Anthropology and Education Quarterly*, 22(3), pp. 203-23.

Louie, A. (1982). *Yeh Shen: A Cinderella Story from China.* Illustrated by E. Young. New York: Philomel.

Malcolm, I.G. (1989). "Invisible Culture in the Classroom: Minority Pupils and the Principle of Adaptation." In O. Garcia and R. Otheguy, eds. *English Across Cultures, Cultures Across English: A Reader in Cross-Cultural Communication.* Berlin: Mouton De Gruyter, pp. 116-36.

Martinez, M., and M.F. Nash (1990). "Bookalogues: Talking About Children's Literature." *Language Arts*, 67(6), pp. 599-606.

Martinez, M.G., and N.L. Roser (1991). "Children's Responses to Literature." In J. Flood, J.M. Jensen, D. Lapp, and J.R. Squire, eds. *Handbook of Research on Teaching the English Language Arts.* New York: Macmillan, pp. 643-54.

Mason, J., J. Stewart, and D. Dunning (1986). "What Kindergarten Children Know about Reading." In T.E. Raphael, ed. *The Contexts of School-Based Literacy.* New York: Random House, pp. 97-114.

Mathis, S.B. (1975). *The Hundred Penny Box.* Illustrated by L. and D. Dillon. New York: Viking.

McCarty, T.L., R.H. Lynch, S. Wallace, and Benally, A. (1991). "Classroom Inquiry and Navajo Learning Styles: A Call for Reassessment." *Anthropology & Education Quarterly*, 22(1), pp. 42-59.

McCollum, P. (1989). "Turn-Allocation in Lessons with North American and Puerto Rican Students: A Comparative Study." *Anthropology and Education Quarterly*, 20(2), pp. 133-58.

McDermott, R.P., and K. Gospodinoff (1981). "Social Contexts for Ethnic Borders and School Failure." In H.T. Trueba, G.P. Guthrie, and K.H. Au, eds. *Culture and the Bilingual Classroom: Studies in Classroom Ethnography.* Rowley, MA: Newbury House, pp. 212-30.

McKissack, P. (1986). *Flossie and the Fox.* Illustrated by R. Isadora. New York: Dial.

McLaren, P. (1989). *Life in Schools: An Introduction to Critical Pedagogy in the Foundations of Education.* New York: Longman.

Mehan, H. (1979). *Learning Lessons.* Cambridge, MA: Harvard University Press.

Mehan, H., A. Hertweck, and J.L. Meihls (1986). *Handicapping the Handicapped: Decision Making in Students' Educational Careers.* Stanford, CA: Stanford University Press.

Mezynski, K. (1983). "Issues Concerning the Acquisition of Knowledge: Effects of Vocabulary Training on Reading Comprehension." *Review of Educational Research*, 53, pp. 253-79.

Michaels, S. (1981). " 'Sharing Time': Children's Narrative Styles and Differential Access to Literacy." *Language in Society*, 10(3), pp. 423-42.

Michaels, S. (1986). "Narrative Presentations: An Oral Preparation for Literacy." In J. Cook-Gumperz, ed. *The Social Construction of Literacy.* Cambridge, MA: Cambridge University Press, pp. 94-116.

Michaels, S., and C.B. Cazden (1986). "Teacher/Child Collaboration as Oral Preparation for Literacy." In B.B. Schieffelin, *The Acquisition of Literacy: Ethnographic Perspectives.* Norwood, NJ: Ablex, pp. 132-53.

Mikkelsen, N. (1990). "Toward Greater Equity in Literacy Education: Storymaking and Non-Mainstream Students." *Language Arts*, 67(6), pp. 556-66.

Miles, M. (1971). "Annie and the Old One." In W.K. Durr, J.M. LePere, and R.H. Brown, eds. *Passports.* Houghton Mifflin Reading Program, 1976. Boston: Houghton Mifflin.

Miller-Lachmann, L. (1992). *Our Family, Our Friends, Our World: An Annotated Guide to Significant Multicultural Books for Children and Teenagers.* New Providence, NJ: R.R. Bowker.

Mills, H., and J.A. Clyde, eds. (1990). *Portraits of Whole Language Classrooms: Learning for All Ages.* Portsmouth, NH: Heinemann.

Mohr, N. (1979). *Felita.* New York: Dial.

Mohr, N. (1986). *El Bronx Remembered.* Houston: Arte Publico.

Mohr, N. (1988). *In Nueva York.* Houston: Arte Publico.

Moll, L.C. (1988). "Some Key Issues in Teaching Latino Students." *Language Arts*, 65(5), pp. 465-72.

Moll, L.C., and R. Diaz (1987). "Teaching Writing as Communication: The Use of Ethnographic Findings in Classroom Practice." In D. Bloome, ed. *Literacy and Schooling.* Norwood, NJ: Ablex, pp. 193-221.

Moll, L.C., and S. Diaz (1985). "Ethnographic Pedagogy: Promoting Effective Bilingual Instruction." In E. Garcia and R.V. Padilla, eds. *Advances in Bilingual Education Research.* Tucson, AZ: University of Arizona Press, pp. 127-49.

Moll, L.C., and S. Diaz (1987). "Change as the Goal of Educational Research." *Anthropology & Education Quarterly*, 18(4), pp. 300-11.

Norton, D.E. (1991). "Multicultural Literature." In *Through the Eyes of a Child — An Introduction to Children's Literature*, 3rd ed. New York: Macmillan, pp. 83-126.

Ogbu, J.U. (1981). "School Ethnography: A

Multilevel Approach." *Anthropology & Education Quarterly*, 12(1), pp. 3-29.

Ogbu, J.U. (1987). "Variability in Minority School Performance: A Problem in Search of an Explanation." *Anthropology & Education Quarterly*, 18(4), pp. 312-34.

Pallas, A.M., G. Natriello, and E.L. McDill (1989). "Changing Nature of the Disadvantaged Population: Current Dimensions and Future Trends." *Educational Researcher*, 18(5), pp. 16-22.

Pearson, P.D., and M.C. Gallagher (1983). "The Instruction of Reading Comprehension." *Contemporary Educational Psychology*, 8, pp. 317-44.

Pearson, P.D., and R. Tierney (1984). "On Becoming a Thoughtful Reader: Learning to Read Like a Writer." In A. Purves and O. Niles, eds. *Becoming Readers in a Complex Society*. Chicago: National Society for the Study of Education.

Pease-Alvarez, L. (1991). "Oral Contexts for Literacy Development in a Mexican Immigrant Community." *The Quarterly Newsletter of the Laboratory of Comparative Human Cognition*, 13(1), pp. 9-13.

Peyton, J.K., and L. Reed (1990). *Dialogue Journal Writing With Nonnative English Speakers: A Handbook for Teachers*. Alexandria, VA: Teachers of English to Speakers of Other Languages.

Phelan, P., A.L. Davidson, and H.T. Cao (1991). "Students' Multiple Worlds: Negotiating the Boundaries of Family, Peer, and School Cultures." *Anthropology & Education Quarterly*, 22(3), pp. 224-50.

Philips, S. (1972). "Participant Structures and Communicative Competence: Warm Springs Children in Community and Classroom." In C. Cazden, V. John, and D. Hymes, eds. *Functions of Language in the Classroom*. New York: Teachers College Press.

Philips, S.U. (1983). *The Invisible Culture: Communication in Classroom and Community on the Warm Springs Indian Reservation*. New York: Longman.

Philips, S.U. (1985). "Indian Children in Anglo Classrooms." In N. Wolfson and J. Manes, eds. *Language of Inequality*. Berlin: Mouton, pp. 311-23.

Piestrup, A.M. (1973). *Black Dialect Interference and Accommodation of Reading Instruction in First Grade*. Monographs of the Language-Behavior Research Laboratory, No. 4. Berkeley: University of California.

Pradl, G.M. (1991). "Reading Literature in a Democracy: The Challenge of Louise Rosenblatt." In J. Clifford, ed. *The Experience of Reading: Louise Rosenblatt and Reader-Response Theory*. Portsmouth, NH: Boynton/Cook, pp. 23-46.

Purves, A.C., and R. Beach (1972). *Literature and the Reader*. Urbana, IL: National Council of Teachers of English.

Rasinski, T.V., and N.V. Padak (1990). "Multicultural Learning Through Children's Literature." *Language Arts*, 67(6), pp. 576-80.

Reyes, M. de la Luz. (1991). "A Process Approach to Literacy Instruction for Spanish-Speaking Students: In Search of a Best Fit." In E.H. Hiebert, ed. *Literacy for a Diverse Society: Perspectives, Practices, and Policies*. New York: Teachers College Press, pp. 157-71.

Reynolds, R.E., M.A. Taylor, M.S. Steffensen, L.L. Shirey, and R.C. Anderson (1982). "Cultural Schemata and Reading Comprehension." *Reading Research Quarterly*, 17, pp. 353-66.

Ridley, L. (1990). "Whole Language in the ESL Classroom." In H. Mills and J.A. Clyde, eds. *Portraits of Whole Language Classrooms: Learning for All Ages*. Portsmouth, NH: Heinemann, pp. 213-28.

Rigg, P. (1991). "Whole Language in TESOL." *TESOL Quarterly*, 25(3), pp. 521-42.

Rigg, P., and V.G. Allen, eds. (1989). *When They Don't All Speak English: Integrating the ESL Student into the Regular Classroom*. Urbana, IL: National Council of Teachers of English.

Rosenblatt, L. (1976). *Literature as Exploration*. 4th. ed. New York: The Modern Language Association of America.

Rosenblatt, L. (1978). *The Reader, the Text, the Poem: The Transactional Theory of the Literary Work*. Carbondale, IL: Southern Illinois University Press.

Routman, R. (1988). *Transitions: From Literature to Literacy*. Portsmouth, NH: Heinemann.

Routman, R. (1991). *Invitations: Changing as Teachers and Learners K-12*. Portsmouth, NH: Heinemann.

Rudman, M.K. (1984). *Children's Literature: An Issues Approach*. 2nd ed. New York: Longman.

Rylant, C. (1985). *The Relatives Came*. New York: Bradbury.

Sato, C.J. (1989). "A Nonstandard Approach to Standard English." *TESOL Quarterly*, 23(2), pp. 259-82.

Say, A. (1990). *El Chino*. Boston: Houghton Mifflin.

Shannon, P. (1989). *Broken Promises: Reading Instruction in Twentieth Century America*. New York: Bergin and Garvey.

Shannon, S.M. (1990). "Transition from Bilingual Programs to All-English Programs: Issues About and Beyond Language." *Linguistics and Education*, 2, pp. 323-43.

Shepard, L.A. (1991). "Negative Policies for Dealing with Diversity: When Does Assessment and Diagnosis Turn into Sorting and Segregating?" In E.H. Hiebert, ed. *Literacy for a Diverse Society: Perspectives, Practices, and Policies.* New York: Teachers College Press, pp. 279-98.

Shepard, L.A., M.L. Smith, and C.P. Vojir (1983). "Characteristics of Pupils Identified as Learning Disabled." *American Educational Research Journal*, 20(3), pp. 309-31.

Siddle, E.V. (1986). *A Critical Assessment of the Natural Process to Teaching Writing.* Unpublished qualifying paper, Harvard University.

Sims, R. (1982). *Shadow and Substance.* Urbana, IL: National Council of Teachers of English.

Sinclair, J.M., and R.M. Coulthard (1975). *Towards an Analysis of Discourse: The English Used by Teachers and Pupils.* London: Oxford University Press.

Siu-Runyan, Y. (1991). "Holistic Assessment in Intermediate Classes: Techniques for Informing Our Teaching." In B. Harp, ed. *Assessment and Evaluation in Whole Language Programs.* Norwood, MA: Christopher-Gordon, pp. 109-36.

Smith, M.L. (1991). "Put to the Test: The Effects of External Testing on Teachers." *Educational Researcher*, 20(5), pp. 8-11.

Smitherman, G. (1977). *Talkin' and Testifyin': The Language of Black America.* Boston: Houghton Mifflin. (Reprint, Detroit: Wayne University Press, 1986).

Smitherman, G. (1984). "Black Language as Power." In C. Kramarae, M. Shultz, and W.M. O'Barr, eds. *Language and Power.* Beverly Hills, CA: Sage, pp. 101-15.

Sneve, V.D.H. (1972). *Jimmy Yellow Hawk.* New York: Holiday House.

Snow, C.E. (1990). "Rationales for Native Language Instruction: Evidence from Research." In A.M. Padilla, H.H. Fairchild, and C.M. Valadez, *Bilingual Education: Issues and Strategies.* Newbury Park, CA: Sage, pp. 60-74.

Snow, C.E. (1983). "Literacy and Language: Relationships During the Preschool Years." *Harvard Educational Review*, 53, pp. 165-89.

Snow, C.E., W.S. Barnes, J. Chandler, I.F. Goodman, and L. Hemphill (1991). *Unfulfilled Expectations: Home and School Influences on Literacy.* Cambridge, MA: Harvard University Press.

Soto, G. (1990). *Baseball in April.* Orlando, FL: Harcourt Brace Jovanovich.

Spears-Bunton, L.A. (1990). "Welcome to My House: African American and European American Students' Responses to Virginia Hamilton's *House of Dies Drear.*" *Journal of Negro Education*, 59(4), pp. 566-76.

Spindler, G., and L. Spindler (1990). *The American Cultural Dialogue and Its Transmission.* London: Falmer Press.

Steffensen, M.S., C. Joag-dev, and R.C. Anderson (1979). "A Cross-Cultural Perspective on Reading Comprehension." *Reading Research Quarterly*, 15(1), pp. 10-29.

Steptoe, J. (1987). *Mufaro's Beautiful Daughters.* New York: Lothrop, Lee & Shepard.

Sulzby, E. (1991). "The Development of the Young Child and the Emergence of Literacy." In J. Flood, J.M. Jensen, D. Lapp, and J.R. Squire, eds. *Handbook of Research on Teaching the English Language Arts*, New York: Macmillan, pp. 273-85.

Tanner, G.W. (1907). "Report of the Committee Appointed by the English Conference to Inquire into the Teaching of English in the High Schools of the Middle West." *School Review*, 15, pp. 37-45.

Taylor, D. (1983). *Family Literacy: Young Children Learning to Read and Write.* Portsmouth, NH: Heinemann.

Taylor, D. (1991). *Learning Denied.* Portsmouth, NH: Heinemann.

Taylor, D., and C. Dorsey-Gaines (1988). *Growing Up Literate: Learning from Inner-City Families.* Portsmouth, NH: Heinemann.

Taylor, M. (1976). *Roll of Thunder, Hear My Cry.* New York: Dial.

Te Ata (1989). *Baby Rattlesnake.* Illustrated by V. Reisberg. Adapted by L. Moroney. San Francisco: Children's Book Press.

Teale, W.H. (1986). "Home Background and Young Children's Literacy Development." In W.H. Teale and E. Sulzby, eds. *Emergent Literacy: Writing and Reading.* Norwood, NJ: Ablex, pp. 173-206.

Teale, W.H. (1987). *Emergent Literacy: Reading and Writing Development in Early Childhood.* In J.E. Readence and R.S. Baldwin, eds. *Research in Literacy: Merging Perspectives.* Thirty-sixth yearbook of the National Reading Conference. Rochester, NY: National Reading Conference, pp. 45-74.

Trueba, H.T. (1984). "The Forms, Functions, and Values of Literacy: Reading for Survival in a Barrio as a Student." *NABE Journal*, 9(1), pp. 21-40.

Trueba, H. (1990). "Mainstream and Minority Cultures: A Chicano Perspective." In G. Spindler and L. Spindler, *The American Cultural Dialogue and Its Transmission*. London: Falmer Press, pp. 122-43.

Trueba, H.T. (1991). "Comments on Foley's "Reconsidering Anthropological Explanations. . ." *Anthropology & Education Quarterly*, 22(1), pp. 87-94.

Tway, E. (1989). "Dimensions of Multicultural Literature for Children." In M.K. Rudman, ed. *Children's Literature: Resource for the Classroom*. Norwood, MA: Christopher-Gordon.

Uchida, Y. (1983). *The Best Bad Thing*. New York: Atheneum.

Urzua, C. (1987). " 'You Stopped Too Soon': Second Language Children Composing and Revising." *TESOL Quarterly*, 2(2), pp. 279-304.

Van Allsburg, C. (1981). *Jumanji*. Boston: Houghton Mifflin.

Vogt, L.A., C. Jordan, and R.G. Tharp (1987). "Explaining School Failure, Producing School Success: Two Cases." *Anthropology & Education Quarterly*, 18(4), pp. 276-86.

Vygotsky, L.S. (1978). *Mind in Society*. M. Cole et al., eds. Cambridge, MA: Harvard University Press.

Vygotsky, L.S. (1981). "The Genesis of Higher Mental Functions." In J.V. Wertsch, eds. *The Concept of Activity in Soviet Psychology*." Armonk, NY: Sharpe.

Walker-Dalhouse, D. (1992). "Using African-American Literature to Increase Ethnic Understanding." *The Reading Teacher*, 45(6), pp. 416-22.

Watson, K.A. (1975). "Transferable Communication Routines: Strategies and Group Identity in Two Speech Events." *Language in Society*, 4, pp. 53-72.

Watson-Gegeo, K.A, and S.T. Boggs (1977). "From Verbal Play to Talk Story: The Role of Routine in Speech Events Among Hawaiian Children." In S. Ervin-Trip and C. Mitchell-Kernan, eds. *Child Discourse*. New York: Academic Press.

Weaver, C. (1990). *Understanding Whole Language: Principles and Practices*. Portsmouth, NH: Heinemann.

Wells, G. (1986). *The Meaning Makers: Children Learning Language and Using Language to Learn*. Portsmouth, NH: Heinemann.

Wheat, T., M. Lindberg, and M. Nauman (1977). "An Exploratory Investigation of Newspaper Readability." *Illinois Reading Council Journal*, 5, 4-7.

Whitin, P.E. (1990). "Language Learning through Family History." In H. Mills and J.A. Clyde, eds. *Portraits of Whole Language Classrooms: Learning for All Ages*. Portsmouth, NH: Heinemann, pp. 229-41.

Wigginton, E. (1989). "Foxfire Grows Up." *Harvard Educational Review*, 59(1), pp. 24-49.

Wigginton, E. (1991). "Culture Begins at Home." *Educational Leadership*, 49(4), pp. 60-64.

Wilkinson, L.C., and E.R. Silliman (1990). "Sociolinguistic Analysis: Nonformal Assessment of Children's Language and Literacy Skills." *Linguistics and Education*, 2, pp. 109-25.

Williams, M.D. (1990). "The Afro-American in the Cultural Dialogue of the United States." In G. Spindler and L. Spindler, *The American Cultural Dialogue and Its Transmission*. London: Falmer Press, pp. 144-62.

Willig, A. (1985). "A Metaanalysis of Selected Studies on the Effectiveness of Bilingual Education." *Review of Educational Research*, 55(3), pp. 269-317.

Winograd, P., and S.G. Paris (1988). "A Cognitive and Motivational Agenda for Reading Instruction." *Educational Leadership*, 46(4), pp. 30-36.

Wixson, K.K., C.W. Peters, E.M. Weber, and E.D. Roeber (1987). "New Directions in Statewide Reading Assessment," *The Reading Teacher*, 40(8), pp. 749-54.

Wolcott, H.F. (1991). "Propiospect and the Acquisition of Culture." *Anthropology & Education Quarterly*, 22(3), pp. 251-73.

Wong Fillmore, L. (1986). "Research Currents: Equity or Excellence?" *Language Arts*, 63(5), pp. 474-81.

Wong-Kam, J., and K.H. Au (1988). "Improving a Fourth Grader's Reading and Writing: Three Principles." *Reading Teacher*, 41(8), pp. 768-72.

Yee, P. (1989). *Tales from Gold Mountain: Stories of Chinese in the New World*. Illustrated by S. Ng. New York: Macmillan.

Yep, L. (1975). *Dragonwings*. New York: Harper and Row.

Yep, L. (1977). *Child of the Owl*. New York: Harper and Row.

Yep, L. (1991). *The Star Fisher*. New York: Morrow.

Credits

Index